Hostel by the Sea
Living, Loving, & Working in an American Hostel

Luanne M. Lusic

Hostel by the Sea

Copyright © 2012 Luanne M. Lusic
All rights reserved.

ISBN-13: 978-1475254815
ISBN-10: 1475254814

Luanne Lusic

Disclaimer: This memoir is based on actual events, characters, and hostel and hotel properties. However, the names of all characters, and the names of the hostel and hotel properties have been changed to protect identities. In addition, most of the cities, states, and countries of residence for the characters have also been changed. The hostel that was the setting for this book is no longer in existence.

Longing for Sunshine

Damp, heavy, sodden mist
    permeates the air.

A dismal, gloomy veil obscures the earth
    and leads to such despair.

Tree limbs laden shake fervently
    to rid this melancholy woe.

Such desolation envelops me
    which weighs heavy on my soul.

Earth and spirit yearn longingly
    to escape this deep, dark dungeon.

A ray of burning light is sought
    to crack this shell of darkness.

Hearts implore the god of Ra
    to hasten to the rescue.

Oh, bright, beautiful, searing light
    release my soul from darkness.

To bathe in a sea of glorious rays
    is all that is desired.

Luanne M. Lusic

Luanne Lusic

Ad Majorem Dei Gloriam

To my lovely daughters
 Laura, Rachel, & Elizabeth

Who are manifestations of
 God's purest expression of love

Hostel by the Sea

Cover photographs and design
by Luanne M. Lusic.

Table of Contents

Chapter 1: Non-Traditional Student 9
Chapter 2: First Impressions 14
Chapter 3: Disillusionment 34
Chapter 4: More Than Just Friends 60
Chapter 5: Emotional Disconnect 84
Chapter 6: A New Job 104
Chapter 7: Let's Be Friends 121
Chapter 8: Lovers 147
Chapter 9: Making A Home 192
Chapter 10: Rifts 218
Chapter 11: Confinement 250
Chapter 12: Alternate Reality 275
Chapter 13: Glad Tidings! 292
Chapter 14: A New Year 319
Chapter 15: Purgatory 333
Chapter 16: New Beginnings 373

Hostel by the Sea

Chapter 1

Nontraditional Student

Life is about experiences. That is my philosophy of life and I have conducted the latter part of my adult life accordingly. True to my philosophy, I have not amassed great wealth or accumulated much in the way of material things. The possession of material things can be fleeting, but rich and rewarding experiences will be a part of you throughout life. My life experiences have shaped me, molded me, and made me into the person I am today; the material things have come and gone.

I have moved quite often over the years, and there came a time, when I began to view furniture as a ball and chain around my ankles. I finally got tired of dragging it around with me and, little by little, I started to shed my belongings until I pared them down to what I absolutely needed to function in society. Without possessions, I found that I could move about freely with nothing to tie me down to one place; a feeling that I found appealing.

While sitting at my desk in my university apartment, I found myself contemplating another major move in my life. I had decided to leave graduate school after one semester and return to Fort Lauderdale, Florida. Money was tight and I needed an inexpensive place to stay until I found employment. I had recently read an article about hostels that prompted me to look for one in the Fort Lauderdale area.

Hostel by the Sea

A hostel is much like a hotel except that there are shared living quarters. Similar to college dormitories, the dorm rooms are furnished with bunk beds that usually accommodate a number of guests in a male, female, or coed dorm. The shared common areas usually consist of one or more kitchens, dining areas, and TV lounges where guests can mingle and interact.

Although well traveled, I had never stayed in a hostel before. From my trips abroad, I knew that they were common in Europe. Many hostels that I had read about were youth hostels; an inexpensive place for university students to stay while backpacking their way across Europe.

This wasn't my first move to Fort Lauderdale. A few years earlier after completing my bachelor's degree at the age of forty-eight, I felt like a dusty, old book that had been on a shelf for too long. I was ready for a change. I had had enough of northeast Ohio's long, frigid, snowy winters; I was longing for someplace warm and sunny. I flew to Fort Lauderdale on a one-way ticket. I didn't know anyone there, but I was attracted by the city's public transportation system, cultural diversity, and warm climate; everything I was looking for in a place to live. The down side was that housing was very expensive and the cost of living high. I wasn't too worried about that since I was only one person and didn't take up much space. I felt fairly sure I could find a place I could afford. At least I was willing to take a chance; things have a way of working themselves out.

Back then after packing up my belongings and putting them in storage, I turned in the key to my apartment that I had rented for three years on the edge of campus. Then with great pleasure, I drove my old clunker with a failing transmission to the junk yard. As I handed over my car keys to the junk yard owner, a sudden realization crept over me that I no longer had any keys; none, no apartment key and no car key. It seemed strange having a key chain without any keys on it. We don't realize how much keys are a part of our life until we don't have any. I didn't feel upset that I didn't have any keys, just a subtle realization that I was officially homeless. Somehow that didn't really matter to me; I really had nothing to lose.

More importantly a key to my hotel room was waiting for me in Fort Lauderdale, but there was another type of key that I yearned for: an intangible key to adventure and challenge, which was more important to me than any key that I could hold in my hand. So, off I went, keyless and with airline ticket in hand, and a heart filled with hope and anticipation.

It all seemed so easy looking back on it. I took a chance and made my way as I went along. I can't say there weren't times when I wasn't terrified I might run out of money before I started working, or that I wouldn't find a job or an affordable place to live. But my biggest fear was that if I failed, I would have to go back to Ohio and live with my daughter or mother; I didn't relish the thought that at middle age this might be a possibility. Despite my fears of failure, it was one of the times when I felt most alive.

After working as a reservations supervisor in a hotel in Fort Lauderdale for a little over a year, I felt compelled to return to Kent State University in Kent, Ohio, to pursue a graduate degree in Rehabilitation Counseling. Although I enjoyed working at the hotel, I didn't find it rewarding to be stuck behind a desk all day on the phone with very little interpersonal contact. I wanted to help people, especially people with disabilities. I had worked in an adult workshop for the developmentally disabled for a number of years and found the experience very rewarding; something which I found lacking in my present position. I was convinced that I was making the right choice, so I packed up my bags and headed back to cold and snowy northeast Ohio, oblivious to the possibility that I was searching to fill a void in my life.

Although I did well in my classes, I quickly discovered that I did not like learning about diseases - physical or psychological. I became so distressed that I began to have anxiety attacks, and I ended up on medication and in therapy. After six months of this, I decided that this was not for me. Sometimes you don't know what something is like until you try it, and it doesn't always work out the way you think it might.

Although I'm always eager for an adventure, my second move to Fort Lauderdale the summer of 2008 was filled with trepidation. The price of gas had skyrocketed to over four dollars a gallon, and the economy appeared to be ready to take a major dive.

I was also concerned about my family. Following my heart had put a strain on my family relationships, especially with my mother whose approval was still important to me, despite being middle-aged. I think, in part, that she worried about me being alone in a big city without knowing anyone, and felt that as a single woman, I would be safer living near my family. I come from a large family, all of whom have stayed in the same area that we grew up in. To my mother's dismay, I was the first one to stray outside our hometown. Despite our differences, she has always been there for me.

I have three daughters: Laura and Rachel who were both married and in their late twenties by this time, and my youngest daughter, Elizabeth, was a sophomore at Kent State University. My children were understanding of my adventurous inclinations or at least they were tolerant of them. They understood that my worldview encompassed more than just my hometown. I had tried my best to be a conventional mother, but after a number of failed relationships, my life took a different turn. I felt like such a failure that I was not able to be in a lasting, healthy relationship with a man and provide a stable home environment, so I struck out on my own. I knew my children loved me and wanted the best for me, as I did for them. But the truth of the matter was that from the first time I had set foot outside the realm of life as I had known it before I traveled abroad, my life had irrevocably changed. I could never go back to being the person I was before. And with that life changing event came a sense of joy from self-discovery and fulfillment, but also a regret of the sacrifices that would be made in spending time away from my family.

Squinting my eyes, I leaned slightly forward towards the

computer screen and peered curiously at the pictures posted on the *Hostel by the Sea* web site. Foremost on my mind, was determining if I would fit in. Here I was, a middle-aged graduate student, thinking about staying in a youth hostel. Would I ever grow up? One of the pictures on the online gallery for the hostel showed a group of guests in the courtyard sitting around a picnic table. I studied their faces intently. I noticed that one of them appeared to be middle-aged. That was all I needed to see to convince myself that I had found a place to stay. I quickly made a reservation for a week's stay.

While at the university, I had bought another car so I decided that this time I would drive to Fort Lauderdale. I finished the semester, sold my furniture, and six weeks later, I loaded up the remainder of my belongings into my car and checked out of my university apartment. Once again, I found myself heading south to sunny Florida.

Chapter 2

First Impressions

Arriving in Fort Lauderdale, I marveled at the palms trees swaying gently in the sun. I had been gone for six months and it felt like I had never left; everything was exactly as it had been before. I was familiar with the area that the hostel was located in since it was only a few miles north of the apartment I had rented the previous year. As I drove down the palm tree lined boulevard, I rolled down my window to bask in the warmth of the sun and breathed a sigh of relief. The warm sun effectively melted away any lingering cares of the past six months and Ohio became a distant memory. I was back where I belonged.

I pulled into the hostel parking lot and got out of the car to stretch my legs, while taking in the sights around me. The hostel was a small, white, two-story building, probably built sometime in the 1950's. It appeared well-kept, and I was satisfied that I had made a good choice for my initial accommodations. The hostel was located steps away from the ocean on a narrow strip of land located between the ocean and the intercoastal waterway. I couldn't believe my luck.

Many of the surrounding buildings dwarfed the tiny hostel. A towering condo building across the street from the hostel blocked any possible view of the ocean. The condo was somewhat of an eyesore with its pink exterior and boxy design that hermetically sealed off its residents from the outside world. I pictured its residents sitting smugly in air conditioned rooms, catching an occasional glimpse of the ocean through airtight windows or sliding glass doors like geese gawking through the bars of a cage; somehow it all seemed so aloof and sterile, a high perch from which to view Mother Nature. I had always preferred the small, quaint and cozy properties with rooms wrapped around lush, open courtyards filled with palm trees and tropical plants – just like the hostel.

When I had made my reservation, Patrice Valdez, the hostel manager, had warned me that the hostel was closed between the hours of 4:00 p.m. and 6:00 p.m. Glancing at my watch, I realized it was already a few minutes before four o'clock. I walked over to the gate of a white, wooden fence that obscured any further view of the hostel. The gate had a combination lock, and I stood quietly for a moment, deciding what to do. Out of the corner of my eye, I noticed a door bell and reached over to press the button. Instantly, a musical melody of bells filled the courtyard of the hostel, rising up to greet me from between the boards of the gated fence. A man promptly responded to the musical summons and opened the gate to let me in. He was only slightly taller than me, with jet black hair and dark eyes. He appeared to be middle-aged and was friendly with a quick smile. He spoke with a heavy Hispanic accent, introducing himself as Carlos. As he led me to a small office, I asked him if he was the owner. With a slight chuckle and a flash of amusement in his eyes, he told me that he was the maintenance man. I should have known better than to believe him. It was Patrice's day off and he was filling in for her.

Carlos checked me in and went over the rules of the hostel with me verbally. The rules seemed reasonable enough: smoking was permitted in the outdoor areas only; beer and wine were allowed on premise, but no hard liquor or drugs; no profanity, arguing, or fighting were tolerated; guests were responsible for washing their dishes and cleaning up the kitchen after use; all food and drinks should be marked with guest's name and room number before putting them in the refrigerators; and guests were not allowed in other guests' rooms. In some ways, the rules were much more lax compared to other hostels that I had read about. Some hostels required a passport and a return airline ticket at check-in and had a maximum stay of two weeks. Others had lock out times during the day, only permitting guests on site during the evening and overnight hours as strictly a place to sleep. I was glad this hostel was much more accommodating to its guests.

 I smiled at Carlos while assuring him that I understood the rules and that he wouldn't have any problems with me. He handed me a set of well-worn sheets and a bath towel. He reached inside a red, plastic cup, and after fishing around for a few moments, he produced a key to room #3. As he held it out for me to take, I smiled to myself at the thought of my new adventure. I couldn't wait to see what my room looked like.

 We stepped out into the courtyard, and Carlos gave me a brief overview on the layout of the hostel. He pointed out the two kitchens and TV lounges in each corner on the first floor and the corresponding second floor kitchen and computer room that was situated directly above them. The hostel had eight dorm rooms with four, six, or eight beds to a room on both the first and second floors. There were separate dorm rooms for males and females, although at times, some rooms were coed. Three private rooms on the first floor completed the property.

 The courtyard had a tropical look to it, but was not overly lush. There were a few palm trees, tropical bushes with tiny colorful flowers, and a cluster of aloe vera plants. What really caught my eye was the enormous cactus plant that spread out across half the width of the back side of the courtyard with a few of its thick, green, prickly arms reaching up past the second floor railing. A round, concrete table and accompanying concrete benches with inlaid colorful tiles, a rather worn wooden picnic table, and propane barbecue grill completed the outdoor furnishings. It was an inviting area, and I hugged myself at the thought of sitting there in the sun to read or just hang out.

So far, it was all I had imagined, and more. Carlos motioned me towards a door nestled under a small overhang. I made my way in his direction, gleefully performing an inner pirouette that ended when both my feet landed squarely in front of the door to room #3. I hoped this would be my lucky number. I had no idea how long I would be here or where it would lead. All that mattered, at this time, was that I had a place to stay. I opened the door and cautiously peered inside.

The room was spacious, but sparsely furnished. Two sets of double beds stood side by side with enough space to walk between them. A large picture window with the blinds drawn was on the opposite wall at the head of the bunk beds. To the right was a large open area with a tall set of metal lockers and plenty of space to stack luggage or backpacks. In the corner, to my right, was a closet with the door wide open, revealing a few distorted, metal hangers. The left wall had a wide set of built in shelves that ran along the wall, leading to the bathroom. The bathroom door stood ajar, revealing a small bathroom with shower, sink, and commode.

Quickly surveying the beds, I noticed the bare mattress on the upper left bunk bed. The three remaining beds were obviously taken since they were made up with sheets, and there was clothing strewn across them. Carlos motioned to the empty bed and then closed the door behind him. Finally alone, I set about getting settled in my room.

With sheets in hand, I climbed up the ladder to my bed. It had been a long time since I had slept in a bunk bed. Perched on the top bunk, I peered cautiously over the edge of the bed. The safety railing was bolted to the other side of the bed up against the wall. In an effort to move it to the other side of the bed, I shook and yanked at the railing to no avail. I would have to sleep without a railing on the open side of the bed. As I made up my bed, I noticed that the mattress was of good quality. It was thick and firm and in good condition. I stretched my sheets over the mattress and looked longingly at the bottom bunks. I vowed that as soon as one of them became available, I would switch to the lower bunk.

I brought in my suitcases and commandeered the empty closet. No one seemed to be using it, and since I planned to be there for a while, it would be a perfect place to keep my suitcases. I didn't think it would be wise to unload all of my belongings from my car as of yet and settled on unloading the suitcases, which held my clothes and some of my kitchenware for cooking.

After I finished hanging up my clothes, I decided that I needed to figure out what I could store in my locker. Sharing a room with other guests necessitated having a secure place to lock up my purse and other valuables. I walked over to take a look at the single stack of small, metal lockers standing in the corner of the room. It was a tight squeeze, but I managed to fit everything in, including my laptop, and secured it with the combination lock I had brought with me. I gave the lock a good spin and stepped back with an air of satisfaction. For now, everything was in place, and my valuables were secure. It was starting to look like home.

There was no sign of my roommates as of yet. I eagerly changed into my swimwear and headed to the beach. This was a perfect time for a walk along the beach. The clear, turquoise water beckoned to me. My steps quickened as I ran to the edge of the water, stretching my arms out from my sides as though to embrace a long lost friend. The swirling water around my feet had a cooling effect, while the soft ocean breezes caressed my body. The hypnotic rhythm of breaking waves upon the sandy beach left me feeling peaceful and content; it was good to be back.

Returning from my walk along the ocean, I noticed that the other guests were starting to trickle back into the hostel from their daily activities. I was anxious to meet some of the other guests, but that would have to wait until after a shower. I returned to my room and gathered my clothes, towel, and travel bag containing my personal hygiene products and makeup. It would be a chore to have to cart everything in and out of the bathroom every time I needed to take a shower. I would need to come up with a better system. Thinking back to my camping days, I remembered how I had used a plastic tote with various compartments to store my shower supplies. That would be perfect for the hostel. I made a mental note to get one the next day when I went to the store.

Bumping up against the bathroom door, I turned the door knob and started to push it open, when I heard the sound of running water. It took a few seconds before I realized that someone was already in the shower. Oops. I apologized profusely and closed the door behind me, silently admonishing my unseen roommate for not locking the door. I sat down on the window sill to wait my turn.

Sitting there with my chin propped in the palm of my hand as I thoughtfully nibbled on my fingernails, I realized that having roommates was going to take some getting used to. I didn't mind the thought of having roommates, but I had to admit that it had been a number of years since I had shared my room with another person, let alone with three other women. What would this be like? I could tell by the type of clothing strewn about the room that my roommates were younger than me and were probably the ages of my daughters. Would they be up all hours of the night going in and out of the room and making noise? What if they turned on the lights in the middle of the night while I was sleeping? And what about the bathroom? How often was I going to have to wait in line for my turn to go to the bathroom or take a shower? I shook my head in an effort to dislodge the whirling thoughts from my mind, like a tree shedding its leaves in the fall, leaving them to scatter in the wind. No, don't do this, I scolded myself; it will all work out. Remember, think positive and good things will come to you.

The door swung open as a young, exotic girl with long, dark hair and skin, who looked to be in her late teens, stepped out of the bathroom. I introduced myself and her smile lit up the room as she motioned to me that she was done in the bathroom. I asked her name and she replied sheepishly, "Aylin." As she dressed, in broken English, she told me that she was a student from the University of Istanbul in Turkey, and she was working at an amusement park as part of a university work program during her summer break. She had arrived at the hostel three weeks earlier and did not yet have a good grasp on her English language skills. While talking, she stopped often while mentally searching for the right word or phrase that she wanted to say. Often throughout the following weeks, she would pull out her English dictionary to assist her.

I had met my first roommate, and I instantly took a liking to her. Her smile was warm and friendly, and I just knew that we would get along well. She seemed shy and unsure of herself, and I thought perhaps I could help her get adjusted to our culture. She was like a daughter to me, and I knew that I would watch over her.

My other roommates, two university students from Switzerland, came back while I was getting dressed for dinner. After my stilted attempt at communication with Aylin, I was relieved to find out that they had a good command of the English language. I felt so much at ease. My roommates turned out to be considerate, kind, and courteous; it was a privilege and a pleasure to share a room with them. These were the first of a long procession of international students that I was to eventually room with.

I was like the house mother; the older, mature women. But even though I was in the position to fill the motherly role, I never had any reason to be anything but a friend to my young, university roommates. As it turned out, I became something of a personal concierge to them, helping them out with information on public transportation, grocery stores, shopping malls, and tourist attractions. They looked to me for advice and guidance.

What good girls! They went out sightseeing through the day, and then came back to the hostel to make dinner and socialize for awhile before going to bed at a decent time each night. They did not drink or smoke or take drugs. As I would come to find out later, they were the cream of the crop of the international guests who came to stay at the hostel.

It was dinner time, and I hadn't had time to think about food yet. There weren't any stores or restaurants close by, so I decided to make a quick trip to the grocery store a few miles away. Since I had a car, I didn't have to rely on the bus for transportation as did many of the other guests. I decided to do enough shopping to last a few days. Getting back to the hostel, I carted my groceries in and stacked them on the counter of the kitchen next to my room.

As I had been instructed by Carlos, I marked my name on my two bags of groceries with a black, permanent marker along with my room number. As time went on, 'Lu #3' became a sort of inside joke among the guests, as I marked it on more and more of my belongings. For now, it was a way to distinguish my groceries from everyone else's. I tightly tied the tops of the plastic grocery bags into double knots to deter anyone from taking my food. The refrigerator was quite full, but I managed to carve out a spot for my two bags. I was warned by Carlos that food sometimes disappeared from the refrigerators, so it was wise to take precautions. I was somewhat concerned about this, since I had limited funds to live on until I found a job. If someone ate my food, it could cause me undue hardship. I decided all I could do was to keep an eye on it.

After putting away my groceries, I flipped through the cupboards and drawers and found a somewhat adequate array of pots, pans, dishes, and silverware. Aware of the problems with cockroaches in the south, I decided to use my own cookware and dishes that I had stored away in my room. I retrieved a small dish from my room and set about making my salad on the kitchen counter, while I brewed up a pot of tea for my ice tea.

There were a few guests sitting in the lounge area next to the kitchen watching TV. One of the guests, a young Asian man, suggested that I prop open the kitchen door to let in the cool ocean breezes, while I was preparing my dinner. I had closed the door earlier since it blocked my way to the kitchen sink when it was completely open. I did as he suggested and immediately felt the difference in the temperature of the room. The door on the other side of the room facing the ocean was also open, allowing a delicious ocean breeze to pass through unobstructed.

I liked the idea of an open kitchen and lounge area. I had always loved the outdoors and had first encountered open hotel lobbies while traveling to various islands in the Caribbean. This open room concept offered the benefits of civilization with the ambiance of nature. The rooms were not air conditioned, but with the constant ocean breezes, they didn't need to be.

I finished making my salad and went out into the courtyard to sit at the picnic table to eat my dinner. It was late evening, and the sun was getting low in the sky. A stiff ocean breeze stirred the air as I ate my dinner, my hair fluttering in the wind like flags on a ship. I took a deep breath and smiled to myself in smug satisfaction; I did it, I made it back to Fort Lauderdale. How many people get a chance to do this? Better yet, how many people have the courage and audacity to do this? There always seemed to be an element of risk and the possibility of failure hanging over my head.

Wanting to make a list of things to do, I jumped up from the table and headed back to my room to retrieve a writing tablet from my purse, which was securely tucked away in my locker. Reaching for my lock, I suddenly realized I didn't remember the combination. With all of the hustle and bustle of the day, I had forgotten to write it down. I went outside to think about what I should do. As I walked back to my table, a young man at the picnic table motioned for me to join him.

Nathan O'Brady had arrived at the hostel a few months earlier. He was a friendly, gregarious man in his early 30's from Wisconsin, who was working in the receiving department of a large retail store. Decked out in a Hawaiian shirt and shorts, he had a casual air about him. With a beer in one hand and a cigarette in the other, he was looking for someone to talk to. I introduced myself and told him that I had just arrived from Ohio. We traded stories about our drives south, and how we had left family and friends behind in our home states. After talking for awhile, I felt comfortable enough to confide in him about my lock.

"No problem, Lu. I just happen to know how to crack the combination on locks. Where's your room? I can get your locker open in a jiffy," he said as he jumped up from the table.

I led Nathan to my room, desperate to get into my locker while my mind noisily obsessed over the hostel rule of not allowing other guests in my room, especially guests of the opposite sex. Was I going to get in trouble for this? And what about Nathan's claim that he could crack any lock? What if he were to enter my room when I wasn't there and get into my locker? Was this wise, letting a man I didn't really know into my room to gain access to my locker? I shooed away the clamoring thoughts and led Nathan to my locker.

With the intent look of a seasoned safe-cracker, Nathan turned the dial back and forth on the lock as he held it up to his ear in an effort to coax the combination from the unyielding metal lock. I stood by anxiously watching his efforts. After numerous attempts, in an act of exasperation, Nathan turned over the lock in his hand, revealing a piece of paper with the combination on it neatly taped to the back side of the lock.

Completely surprised, I looked over at Nathan and said, "Oh, that's where I put it! Nathan, I'm so sorry. It's been a long day, and my mind is going in too many directions."

Nathan laughed it off, and we walked back outside where we sat back down at the picnic table and were joined by some of the other guests. The night was young, and the conversation flowed freely as guests mixed easily with each other. Some had been there for weeks and others, like myself, had just arrived. It didn't matter; we were all welcomed by the other guests indiscriminately and assimilated into the community.

In time, I would come to know and understand this community intimately. It was an entity consisting of a small core group of long-term guests complemented by a larger flux of transitory guests who stayed for a day or so and sometimes up to a few weeks. Later, I would come to find out that those in the core group had been scrutinized, and after passing inspection, allowed to stay on indefinitely. Those who did not pass inspection were promptly ejected out into the streets. Unbeknownst to me at the time, Nathan was part of the core group which, in time, would also include me. For the time being, I had made my first friend.

My first night at the hostel, I slept well despite having three roommates. We took turns getting ready for bed in the bathroom, so as not to disturb any of our roommates who were already in bed asleep. We crept about silently getting into our beds, the only sound coming from the creaking bed frame when someone had to climb up the ladder to the top bunk. The only thing that disturbed me the first night was the constant noise from the cars driving up and down Ocean Boulevard.

The following day, I stopped by the office to meet Patrice. I had talked to her briefly over the phone when I had made my reservation, and I was looking forward to meeting her. The office opened at 10:00 a.m., and I walked through the door shortly after. I found Carlos at the counter in a conversation with a dark skinned woman, who spoke with a bit of an unusual accent.

Carlos and the woman both stopped talking and looked at me inquiringly, as if they were waiting for me to ask them for something. "Hi! I just wanted to stop in and meet Patrice," I said.

Carlos raised his arm, and in a sweeping motion, he pointed at Patrice. "This is Patrice."

Surprised, I stepped forward and extended my hand. "Patrice, my name is Lu. I'm so glad to finally meet you," I said as I shook her hand.

Patrice wasn't what I expected. Over the phone she had sounded much older, and I imagined her to be of European descent. Although she spoke excellent English, she had an accent that I couldn't quite place; when she spoke, she tended to emphasize and draw out her vowels. Patrice looked to be in her early 40's and had dark skin and long black, wavy hair that she pulled up into a pony tail. She wore a pair of black rimmed glasses and was casually dressed in a long sleeved white blouse, with the sleeves rolled up, and black slacks. Her wide smile revealed a set of very white teeth that stood out against her dark skin. Her manner was warm and friendly. It puzzled me that I couldn't quite place her background, but for some reason I didn't feel comfortable asking her where she was from.

Shaking my hand she replied, "I hope everything is okay with your room."

"Yes, I am all settled in," I responded happily.

Patrice's face took on a serious expression. "You don't mind, then, being with the younger girls? My uncle put you in the wrong room. If I had been here, I would have put you upstairs with Freida. She likes to go to bed early at eight o'clock and doesn't like to room with the younger girls because they are up until late at night."

I briefly entertained what it would be like to share a room with someone my age. "Oh, then it's better that I'm in with the younger girls, because I most certainly don't go to bed at eight o'clock. Anyways, I like the younger girls. They are like my daughters, and I enjoy being around them," I assured her.

Relieved, Patrice responded, "Good. It sounds like things will work out well for you then in #3."

Our conversation wound down and armed with my beach umbrella, lounge chair, and magazines, I headed for the beach where I planned to spend the day napping in the sun. I was exhausted from my long drive to Florida. How good it felt to relax in my lounge chair, listening to the soothing sounds of the ocean, as the stress from my long drive and the last six months of my life ebbed with the flow of the tide. I was officially on vacation for the next four days. I promised myself I was not going to worry about anything, at least for now, and enjoy myself for the time being.

After a relaxing day at the beach, I looked forward to going back to the hostel. Returning to my room, I felt a sense of routine starting to develop and felt comfortable here and at home. As I took a shower and changed my clothes, I thought about how far I had come in just a few days. So far, living in a hostel wasn't so bad. I had adapted quickly to my new surroundings. I had a comfortable bed to sleep in and an adequate place to cook and eat my meals. So far no one had stolen any of my food. And after enduring the isolation I experienced from life on campus as a nontraditional student, I could really appreciate the diversity in ages at the hostel, which offered companionship at all hours of the day and night. I didn't know how long I would be here; it didn't even matter. For now, it was home and that's all that mattered. I was happy to have a roof over my head.

On my way to the kitchen to make my ice tea, a middle-aged man watching TV in the lounge caught my attention. There was something about him that I liked. What struck me at first was that he seemed so laid back. Even though sitting, I could tell from his long legs stretched out in front of him that he was tall, with a somewhat expanding mid-drift and a strong upper body. His tightly coiled salt and pepper hair formed rows of waves across the top of his head. His dark brown eyes were set in a rather handsome face with full lips and skin the color of toasted almonds. He had one of those faces that exuded kindness and approachability. There was a youthfulness about him that belied his age.

I stirred my tea absentmindedly, glancing furtively out of the corner of my eye, wondering who this man was.

Gathering my courage, I finally spoke. "Hi, how was your day?"

Distracted from the TV by my voice, he turned his head slowly in my direction. "Not too bad. I didn't do much today. How was your day?"

He came across as friendly, with an easy manner. I liked

him immediately, and for some reason, I felt drawn to him. I wondered if he felt the same.

"Oh, I spent a great day relaxing at the beach. By the way, my name is Lu; it's really Luanne, but I prefer to be called Lu. I just came here from Ohio. What is your name?"

"Elliot Cruz. I am from Belize in Central America, but I've lived in the United States for many years," he replied casually.

"Oh, I don't think I ever have met someone from Belize before. Isn't that near Mexico?"

"Yes, it is on the eastern side of the Yucatan peninsula; it is just a small country."

"So, do you speak Spanish?" I asked.

"No, actually English is the official language since we used to be a British colony, but we mostly spoke Creole at home."

"That's interesting. I'd love to hear you speak Creole sometime. I enjoy languages," I said as I stirred my pot of tea.

"What is that you're making?" inquired Elliot.

"Ice tea." I grabbed my pitcher and started towards the door to the courtyard. "Well, have a good evening. I'm sure I'll be seeing you around."

As the days went by, I became more acquainted with the long-term guests who were staying at the hostel, while working in the area. These were the guests from various states, including Florida, who had relocated to Fort Lauderdale and needed an inexpensive place to stay until they could afford a permanent place to live. Apartments were expensive in Fort Lauderdale, and the pay scale was not very high. The best scenario was to hook up with someone to share an apartment with, but until then, the hostel was the next best thing. Besides that, you couldn't beat the location. I would later find out how important the long-term guests were in providing the steady income needed to keep the hostel in business.

Another important group of guests during the summer months was the European university students who were on summer break. They were backpacking their way around the

United States. Many of them started in the north in New York City, and then made their way to Florida, where they would visit Fort Lauderdale, Miami, and the Florida Keys. They would then fly off to somewhere in California to tour the west coast. These were students whose parents had money that afforded them the luxury of traveling throughout the country, while staying in youth hostels, as is popular for them to do in Europe. These students got to experience more of America than a lot of the people who are citizens living here.

Most of the long-term guests were older than the European university crowd that was just passing through. There were only a few of us in our 50's, and I noticed that we seemed to seek each other out to talk to, as if drawn together like members of some exclusive club. Freida was one of the members of our unofficial *50's club*, and when we first saw each other, we immediately struck up a conversation. Freida was a petite woman with an air of worldliness about her. She had been staying at the hostel for a few months, and she was in the process of making arrangements to return to Denmark to be near her family. Many years ago, she had been a stewardess for an airline and had traveled all over the world. For the last few years, she had worked the front desk at various hotels in Fort Lauderdale. She struck me as someone who had a hard time staying in one place for very long. I sensed that we were kindred spirits, cut from the same cloth.

The two groups that made up the hostel mixed well. It was gratifying to observe a group of people from different parts of the world sitting together watching TV, cooking dinner in the kitchen, or having a few beers together in the courtyard. Despite the difficulty of conversing with international guests who spoke broken English, everyone seemed to have a good time and a few beers went a long way in overcoming communication barriers. I often cast a gratifying eye over the crowd, musing to myself how people from different backgrounds and cultures, who hadn't known each other a few days earlier, sat talking as if old friends.

The next few days brought more of the same things: sunshine, ocean breezes, and lazy evenings filled with laughter and chatter that drifted through the hostel. Each evening, I found myself looking for Nathan as he returned from work to ask him how his day had gone. Soon we would have a small group of guests gathered around us, swapping tales of our adventures in Fort Lauderdale or recounting our stories of how we came to be here. All of the guests were single and eager for conversation and companionship.

Some guests sat and talked for hours, whereas others would stop by for awhile and then be on their way to the beach or to watch TV. Some of the long-term guests included Nigel, a young man from Australia who was looking for work on a yacht; Dwayne, a middle-aged African-American from Washington, D.C.; and Lyle from Chicago, Illinois, a tall, skinny African-American with shoulder length dread locks who worked as a financial advisor in a nearby city. David, a quiet spoken young man from New Jersey, stopped by to talk after returning from his afternoon shift as a security guard at a condo building.

I also kept tabs on Elliot. I usually found him in the evening, sitting in the lounge watching TV. He was older than most of the residents in the hostel, and although friendly, he seemed to keep to himself. We spoke briefly each evening as I made up my salad and pitcher of ice tea in the kitchen. I came to find out that he was one of Nathan's roommates.

The Fourth of July weekend was fast approaching, and a fireworks display was planned for Saturday night at the beach. I was interested in Elliot and wanted to ask him to go to the fireworks with me, but I didn't want to seem too forward. What if he had a girlfriend or was married? He didn't have a wedding ring on, but that didn't always mean anything.

Friday night came, and our usual group sat around the courtyard discussing plans for the weekend. Nathan was going to make sparkler bombs on Saturday to set off for the Fourth of July. We decided that our group would go to the beach together to watch the fireworks. This was perfect. Now I could ask Elliot

Hostel by the Sea

to go to the fireworks as part of our group, which wouldn't seem awkward or unusual. I just had to wait for a chance to ask him.

The opportunity presented itself later that evening as I walked through the computer room on my way to the outside second floor terrace. As I passed through, I noticed Elliot sitting at the computer. The hostel had one computer with internet access that the guests could take turns using. As I walked by, I greeted Elliot. "Hey, how's it going?"

"Not bad. Just checking my e-mail."

"You know, tomorrow is the Fourth of July, and there are fireworks at the beach tomorrow night. I am going with Nathan and a group from the hostel. Would you like to go with us?" I asked eagerly. I held my breath, as I waited for his reply.

Elliot turned slowly in his chair until he came face to face with me. "Sure, that would be nice."

"Great. I'll meet you downstairs tomorrow night at about nine o'clock. See you then."

Elliot went back to his e-mails, and I did a hop, skip, and a jump as I made my way to sit on the terrace. Elliot didn't know it, but we had a date.

Saturday came, and after returning from my outing to the beach, I found Nathan in the computer room working on his 'sparkler bombs.' I watched as he grabbed a large handful of sparklers and bound them together into a bundle with duct tape. He deftly pulled one sparkler halfway out from the bundle to serve as a fuse. He chattered away enthusiastically, describing the spectacle his sparkler bombs were sure to make. He was like a little boy with a new toy. I left him to his finish his project and went to get ready for the evening. I had been looking forward to this all day.

By now my two Swiss roommates had left and two university students from England replaced them. Aylin and the English roommates were busy getting ready to go to the fireworks, also. The girls chattered away gaily, as they went about getting ready for their big night. They had cooked out on the grill with some of the guys in the hostel and were eager to go the fireworks with them. Friendships and romantic interests were quick to spring up in this type of environment.

Ready for my secret date, I showed up at the appointed time and found that Nathan and my group from the hostel were nowhere to be seen. They had taken off without me! How embarrassing. All I could think of was: What would Elliot think? Maybe he would think that I had planned this all along. It was too late to go looking for them. Elliot came walking down the stairs from his upstairs dorm room to meet me.

"They took off without us! I don't know what happened to Nathan. He was supposed to meet us here." Embarrassed, I looked at Elliot expectantly, waiting for his response.

True to his laid back nature, he calmly said, "That's all right. We'll go over by ourselves."

It was an overcast evening, and as we crossed the busy street, it started to sprinkle. I gazed up at the sky, wishing the clouds away. I didn't want the rain to ruin our evening. I had a date; even if Elliot hadn't asked me out, at least I was finally in the company of a man. For the last seven years I had rarely dated, choosing instead to focus my attention on completing my college education. Men had only brought me heartache, and after the breakup of my third marriage, I had sworn off men. Most of the time when I was busy this didn't seem to bother me, but at other times, especially on Saturday evenings, a loneliness overcame me that I found difficult to bear.

Elliot found a spot on the beach where a string of hotel lounge chairs lined the beach. He pulled two chairs together and carefully covered them with the blanket. He motioned for me to sit down. As I did, what was at first a drizzle of rain started to come down harder.

Shielding my head from the rain with my hand, I jumped up and said, "I'll run back to my car and get the beach umbrella."

Elliot nodded as I took off at a fast pace. There was no time to waste. The fireworks were already underway. Returning with the beach umbrella, I pulled it open and covered our heads.

Elliot was surprised to see me so soon. "That was fast!"

Somewhat surprised at his remark, I gushed, "Oh, I guess at my age I still have some pep left in me!"

In walking over to the beach that evening, I had noticed how his pace was slow and deliberate, unlike my spirited gait. He had the laid back, easy manner typical of the Caribbean people. I, on the other hand, came from the northern United States, where the ability to get things done quickly and efficiently was highly valued. We were two people with very different cultural backgrounds and upbringings. I enjoyed cultural diversity, and it was one of the things that had attracted me to Elliot. A chance to get to know someone personally from another culture intrigued me. I loved that fact that there could be cultural differences between people, yet they were bound by the common bond of humanity.

Shielded from the rain by my large, colorful beach umbrella, Elliot and I sat huddled together with eyes wide in wonderment, watching the festive fireworks bursting high above us over the ocean. I couldn't believe how happy I was. That my life could change so completely in a matter of days astounded me. I had been so unhappy for the last six months, and to have my life turn around so completely seemed utterly impossible to me. I had taken a leap of faith in coming back here, and I definitely wasn't disappointed. If anything, I never felt more alive.

The fireworks ended too soon, and with beach umbrella and blanket tucked under our arms, we trudged back to the hostel. Careful not to overstep my boundaries, I politely thanked Elliot for going to the fireworks with me. He nodded his head and went off to watch TV, while I went to find out what happened to Nathan. I found Nathan hunched over a table with one of his sparkler bombs dismantled in front of him. The bomb had fizzled out when he lit it, and he was attempting to correct the problem. I pointed out to him that he had wrapped the sparklers too tight, and they couldn't burn due to lack of oxygen. "You're right Lu.

Why didn't I think of that?" Nathan grabbed the sparklers and started reworking them into a different configuration. Finally satisfied with his new design, he took off to light it on the side street beside the hostel.

Nathan set the sparkler bomb in the middle of the street and lit it. Watching from the second floor terrace, I giggled as I pranced gleefully back and forth along the railing in eager anticipation. Nathan had a way of bringing out the schoolgirl in me. Despite being middle-aged, I found myself acting like a teenager. I was having the time of my life. It was all so silly, but it was all so much fun. To be so carefree and spontaneous made me feel so alive.

The fuse to the sparkler bomb flickered and hissed as we waited for the expected explosion. A car veered off Ocean Boulevard and turned down the side street heading straight for the sparkler bomb. Nathan waved his arms frantically to warn the car off, but instead it headed straight for the bomb and straddled it between its wheels. I held my breath. The gas tank! But alas, the car continued on its way unscathed and oblivious to the drama that it had just been a part of. The sparkler bomb hissed and sputtered, sending out puffs of smoke as it lay dying in the street.

Nathan kicked the smoking carcass to the side of the street, and with his right foot, stomped firmly on it in an effort to distinguish the last dying embers.

Leaning over the railing, I shouted, "Hey, Nathan! You can always try again next year!"

Chapter 3

Disillusionment

The cloud I had been floating on all through the holiday weekend began to dissipate soon after. The cold, hard reality of my financial situation dictated that I find employment as soon as possible since I only had enough money saved to see me through my first month at the hostel. I was determined to spend a good part of each day looking for work, confidant that I would have a full-time job in a matter of weeks, at the most in a month. After all, the first time I had come to Fort Lauderdale a few years earlier, I had three job offers in three weeks. Jobs had been plentiful, and there weren't enough workers to fill all the available positions.

Armed with my college degree and ample work experience, I had my heart set on a management position. I typed up my resume and made copies, intent on making my rounds to apply at the various hotels and resorts in Fort Lauderdale. Experience taught me that by applying in person I had a better chance of getting hired, especially in the hospitality industry where a neat appearance and a courteous manner went a long way in securing a position. Job hunting was a job in itself, and I set myself up on a schedule determined to be disciplined.

During the week, I went job hunting in the mornings then afterwards returned to the hostel to eat my lunch and look for work on the internet. I set up a little outdoor office outside my room with a round plastic table that Patrice had thoughtfully brought over for me to use so that I would have a place for my laptop computer and job hunting notes.

Guests greeted me as they came and went, sometimes stopping to talk for awhile. When Lola, the maid, came to clean, all I had to do was pick up my feet so that she could sweep or mop underneath my table and chair. I felt so spoiled and lucky to be sitting at my outdoor office, filling out on-line applications, while enjoying the warm ocean breezes in the shaded corner right outside my room. Sometimes, I wore nothing more than my bathing suit and a sheer wrap around skirt.

When three o'clock rolled around, I would wrap up my job hunting for the day. If I wasn't already in my bathing suit, I would change into it and head for the beach. I looked forward to going to the beach after a grueling day of job hunting. It was my reward for putting in a hard day's work. I loved to walk along the water feeling the soft sand underneath my feet, while letting my cares drift away.

One especially hot afternoon, I decided to stop and take a dip in the water. I kicked off my flip-flops and removed my wrap around skirt, folded it, and set it on top of my flip-flops. I tucked my key chain under my wrap around skirt for safe keeping and headed towards the water. It was the middle of summer, and the water was bathwater warm. I was always somewhat wary of swimming in the ocean for fear of sharks, sting rays, or whatever else might be lurking about. The hot sand scorching my feet propelled me towards the expanse of crystal blue sparkling sea. Liquid blue-green swells with frothy crests rushed forward to greet me, clasping my ankles and firmly tugging me towards the sea. Tentatively making my way out into water up to my knees, I noticed that I could see the sandy bottom a few feet below. It was readily apparent that there wasn't anything treacherous in sight. Confidant that I wouldn't have any unpleasant underwater encounters, I plunged into the inviting water and began to pull myself forward with long, lazy strokes. As I swam along, I occasionally encountered bands of cool water which was a welcome respite from the unrelenting heat. After a refreshing dip, I gathered my things and continued walking up the beach.

By the time I returned to the hostel, it was dinner time. I took a quick shower and changed into a pair of jean shorts and a tank top. I found it liberating to dress so lightly after being bundled up in heavy clothing for the first part of the year; the pinnacle of comfort was slipping on a pair of well-worn flip flops. Dressed for dinner, I made my way to the kitchen and found Freida and Elliot sitting in the lounge watching TV.

Freida had told me the day before that she was planning on returning to Denmark the following week. "Freida, did you get your airline ticket yet?" I asked her.

"No, they didn't have the flight that I wanted. I think I'll wait another week and see what happens." Freida got up, stretched lazily, and excused herself to go for a walk on the beach.

Freida did not seem to be in any hurry to go home. She often talked of how much she missed her children and grandchildren and seemed anxious to get back to see them. But as the weeks rolled by, I noticed that she kept setting back her departure date, time after time. I was beginning to wonder if she really intended to leave or was just entertaining the idea.

From experience, I knew that some people just had a travel bug that made it very difficult for them to ever stay in one place for any length of time. I could relate to this very well. I always blamed it on the way the stars were aligned at the time of my birth. For me, it was a blessing and a curse. I loved to travel and live in new places, but there is a constant unsettledness that goes along with this. Since I had moved around so much in recent years, I had few friends and I didn't get to see my family very often. If Freida did return home, I doubted that she would stay there for long. Perhaps it is our destiny to wander the earth seeking out new experiences and meeting new people. It seems to be what we thrive on. Anything else is like a death sentence;

just existing in one place until it is our time to go.

Once Freida left the room, I busied myself around the kitchen preparing my dinner. There were three kitchens in the hostel, and I liked this one the best. It was conveniently located right next to my room. The only drawback to using this kitchen was that the back door led to a small enclosed concrete courtyard where the laundry room, clothes line, trash bins, and bike racks were located. It was not unusual to be in the middle of cooking your dinner and have to step aside to make room for someone pushing their bike through or carrying a bag of laundry.

Since this kitchen was in such a high traffic area and was the most used kitchen, I had the opportunity to talk to most of the guests while cooking my dinner. Sometimes we even shared the stove. One evening, a couple from Australia who were looking for work on yachts cooked their dinner using the two front burners, while Aylin cooked her dinner on the left rear burner, and I used the right rear burner - and Nathan had a pizza crisping in the oven. It wasn't even a full-size stove, but somehow we all managed to get our cooking done and had fun in the process.

There was a sense of community and a camaraderie that we shared as we stood slicing, dicing, mixing, sautéing, and cooking our dinners. We exchanged recipes and admired a well-prepared meal often sharing our dinner with other guests. As we cooked and talked, we exchanged information on how our day went with job hunting or sightseeing. Most importantly, especially for those of us job hunting; we gave each other emotional support. We shared our life stories and our hopes and our dreams for the future.

I didn't mind sharing a kitchen with other people who were strangers; often strangers from another land. That made it all the more intriguing. I adapted easily to being around all types of people in close quarters, while sharing facilities that are usually allotted to one-family dwellings. I suppose most people would find it rather odd to share a kitchen with people they didn't know.

I especially looked forward to seeing Elliot each day. He

usually showed up in the early evening to eat his dinner while watching TV. One evening, I found Elliot sitting alone in front of the TV. As I walked towards the kitchen to make a pitcher of ice tea, I smiled to him as I passed by. He was holding a piece of fried chicken in one hand while he absentmindedly tore off strips of meat, placing them in his mouth as he munched away contentedly, like a big, brown bear happily scooping up paws full of honey from a jar balanced precariously on his expanding midriff.

For once, I had the kitchen all to myself. Quietly, I set about mixing up a batch of ice tea.

Elliot looked over at me, while I stirred my tea. "You really do like your ice tea, don't you?" he said in an effort to strike up a conversation.

"Yes, although I could probably use something stronger after a day of job hunting."

Elliot chuckled, "What kind of work are you looking for?"

"Oh, mostly hospitality. I've done a lot of different things. How about you? What kind of work do you do?"

Elliot pulled himself up a little straighter in his chair. "I'm a movie director and I'm trying to get financing to make a movie from a screenplay that I wrote."

I looked up at Elliot, as I busily stirred my pitcher of ice tea. "So what's your screenplay about?" I asked out of curiosity.

"It's a Christian love story. Maybe you would like to read the screenplay sometime?"

I scooped up a handful of ice cubes from a bag of ice in the freezer, dumped them into a tall glass in my hand, and poured hot tea from my pitcher over the ice cubes. I had never met anyone who had written a screenplay before. "Yes. I would really like that. You say it's a Christian movie, what faith are you?"

"I'm Catholic."

As the significance of this sunk in, an idea was forming in the back of my mind. "So am I. Do you go to St. Peter's Church?" I asked hopefully. "It is just right down the street from here."

"Yes, I do."

This idea, now fully formed, danced about madly in my head seeking a chance to make itself known. "I like to go to nine-thirty mass. Which mass do you go to?"

"The same one," he replied nonchalantly.

And like an arrow from Cupid's bow seeking its mark, the words shot from my mouth, "Would you mind if I tagged along with you to mass on Sunday? It's nice to have someone to go with." I looked at him expectantly, waiting for his response, every fiber of my being on high alert.

"Sure, that would be fine. Perhaps you would like to join me in praying the rosary some evening?"

The bow had expertly hit its mark. "Yes, I would really like that," I said with a smile.

I had almost left my rosary back home, stashed away with some of my belongings in storage, when something stopped me. I had hesitated momentarily with my hand suspended in mid-air, clasping my rosary over the 'to be packed away pile,' when from the depths of my being, I felt a sudden compulsion to take it with me. So not thinking much about it, I packed it away in a suitcase.

My mind drifted back to a conversation I had had with my eldest daughter, Laura, six months earlier. It was Christmas, and I was staying at her house before I moved up to my campus apartment at Kent State University. We were having a few drinks together and talking about our lives. Somehow we got on the subject of our purpose in life.

Laura took a sip from her glass of wine and cocked her head to one side. "Yours is about love," she remarked assuredly. "You don't have that many more chances. For sure, one more chance, maybe a couple more. You are running out of time." She hesitated briefly while she seized on a flash of foresight. "There is someone who's going to come into your life, mom." Then her voice rising to a fevered pitch she exclaimed, "Mom, can't you see him? He's coming! He is from another country, or was born in another country, and is living here."

Hostel by the Sea

Then, she reached over and touched the tip of her index finger to the top of her other hand. Leaving it to rest there momentarily, she announced, "He has darker skin." Scrunching her face in an effort to see the muddled vision more clearly, she continued, "And, I think he is in a . . . hospital."

I sometimes have known in advance about things that would happen to me in my life. It didn't always happen exactly as I thought, but the general notion was usually right. Laura seemed to have this same inclination. This was the first she ever shared something like this with me. The next day, though, I just chalked it up to a few too many drinks and promptly forgot all about it. The way my luck was with men, I doubted there would ever be another man in my life. Not after surviving three failed marriages and a long-term relationship that produced my youngest daughter.

Clutching my glass of ice tea, I was absolutely beaming as I walked past Elliot on my way outside to sit in the courtyard. Elated that we had a date for church on Sunday, I quickly decided it would be best to wait for a few days before I joined him to pray the rosary. I didn't want to seem too eager.

I spent the evening in the courtyard talking with the other guests. Nathan stopped by to see how my job hunting was going. He was looking for a better job and had recently applied for a delivery truck driver position. Dwayne sat down intent on joining in on the conversation, changing the subject to karaoke night at the local bar. He asked if we were interested in going with a group of guests from the hostel the following night. Nathan quickly jumped at the offer, but I declined. I was a bit older than them and had no interest in hanging out in bars.

There was something odd that I noticed about Dwayne; he didn't seem to work. He never talked about work, or even about looking for work. I had no idea where he got money to pay his rent at the hostel and money for cigarettes and beer. He was content to spend his nights drinking and partying, and then slept in late the next day only to get up and do it all over again. He was always eager to surround himself with people who were out for a good time. Dwayne was a different breed who was content to lull away the day without ever really accomplishing anything. He was just happy to exist; preferably with a buzz on.

Saturday morning I found Elliot talking to some of the guests in his usual spot. I waited for them to clear out. Eager to finalize plans for attending mass together, I approached Elliot.

"What time do you want to leave here for mass tomorrow morning?" I asked.

He thought to himself for a few seconds and then replied, "I like to get there a half an hour earlier to have time to pray before mass."

Masking an inner excitement, I kept an even tone. "That would be fine. How about I meet you in the courtyard at about nine o'clock?"

"Okay. I will see you then."

I was really looking forward to going to mass with Elliot. How nice to finally have someone to share my faith with.

Sunday morning arrived and I woke up early to get ready. My roommates were all fast asleep after staying out late the night before. I tiptoed around the room, gathering all of my things and went into the bathroom to shower. Afterward, wanting to look my best, I took the extra time to put on makeup and style my hair. I put on a long floral skirt, a dress blouse, and a pair of sandals. I dug through my little black velvet bag containing pieces of jewelry and fished out a bracelet and pair of dangling earrings. The finishing touches of jewelry in place, I sprayed on my favorite perfume, White Shoulders, and with my Sunday Missal in hand, I made my way to the courtyard. Elliot was nowhere in sight, so I sat in the chair outside my door to wait for him.

A few minutes later, I heard Elliot making his way down the stairs from his dorm room. He leaned over the staircase and greeted me when he saw me sitting there.

I stood up and started over towards him.

As I walked towards him, I saw he had something in his hand. "Here, this is for you. It is a prayer book."

It was a small book with a blue paperback cover. I took it in my hands and looked at it appreciatively. The front cover had a picture of the sculpture, La Pieta, with the words, "The Pieta Prayer Book" across the top. "Thank you. I will read it before mass. Do you want to drive or do you want me to?"

Taking his keys from his pocket, he said, "I'll drive."

As he drove, Elliot suddenly took his right hand off the steering wheel and extended it towards me. "I don't believe in shaking hands during mass, so I will shake your hand now. Peace be with you," he said.

Taken by surprise, I stared dumbly at his outstretched hand for a few seconds until I realized that he wanted to shake my hand. Extending my right hand towards him, I clasped his hand in mine. "Peace be with you," I mumbled. Our grasp lingered for a few seconds longer. I liked how his hand felt in mine. It was warm and comforting.

He pulled his right hand away and returned it to its place on the steering wheel, as we slowly made our way up the street towards the church. "I believe that we should kneel and pray during that part of the mass because it is consecrated and should be spent in communion with God. Some people get mad at me for not shaking their hands, but I don't care what they think. Others are more understanding," he said with an air of resignation.

I had never heard of anyone refusing to offer the sign of peace. "Well, I guess people should just respect your wishes," I replied.

Inside the church, the air was cool and the familiar scent of burnt incense and candles lingered reverently in the air. I followed Elliot to a pew near the front, where we knelt beside each other, silently immersed in prayer. Every so often during the mass, I glanced slyly over at Elliot's bent form with a sense of awe and disbelief. His reverent manner gave me a sense of peace and the hope that I had finally found someone who would be good for me. I felt that I belonged by his side. True to his word, during the sign of peace, Elliot knelt in prayer with his head bowed low. I watched as the people in the pew in front of us turned around to shake his hand, only to be met by his head bowed reverently in prayer. I leaned towards them with my right hand outstretched. "Peace be with you," I said as I shook each of their hands.

After mass, Elliot continued with his prayers, as I flipped through the blue prayer book he had given me. Finally rising, he motioned for us to go. I followed him out of the church to the car.

Turning to me, he asked, "How about some lunch? I haven't had anything to eat yet."

I was pleasantly surprised. This was quite a treat: church and lunch. We made pleasant chit chat about the weather as we wound our way down a busy boulevard filled with cars going along their way on a lazy Sunday afternoon. As I looked out the car window, everything began to take on a surreal quality. A dazzling sun shone in a deep, blue sky. We sped past strip malls and restaurants interspersed with swaying palm trees. The windows of the passing buildings sparkled in the bright sunshine. Elliot motioned towards a restaurant along the side of the road, "Will this do?"

Looking over at the restaurant, I instantly recognized it as the very one that I had eaten breakfast at before returning to Ohio seven months earlier. Life is funny sometimes. I never would have thought that someday I would be back here with this man taking me out to lunch after church! "Yes, this will be fine," I replied as I smiled to myself.

This was the first time in years that I had been out to eat with a man. As I sat studying the menu, I was acutely aware that this was a big step for me. Although I enjoyed the company of men, I hadn't allowed a man to get too close to me for a very long time. There was safety in distance. I had been hurt too many times in the past by the men in my life. But now, I was willing to take a chance again; maybe even to love again.

The waitress set our plates of eggs, bacon, and hash browns before us, and Elliot reached over the table to clasp my hands for the blessing.

Our prayer completed, Elliot looked up at me. "Our first meal together."

He said it like it would be the first of many, and I hoped it would be. I felt so comfortable with him, as if I had known him for a long time. Conversation flowed easily as we talked about our families.

Taking a sip of coffee, his eyes met mine. "Are you divorced?"

I looked at him with uncertainty, wondering just how much I should tell him. I decided to play it safe. "Yes, I have been for awhile. What about you?"

"No, I have never been married. Tell me about your children."

"I have three daughters. They are all grown and live in Ohio. I also have two young grandchildren. What about you, any children?" I asked.

"My daughter is really my stepdaughter and she is in her mid-thirties. Her mother and I were in a relationship for many years, since she was a young child. I came to love her as if she was my own. And, I also have two grandchildren."

I eyed him warily. He had mentioned having a daughter when I first met him, but he led me to believe that she was his biological daughter. Why didn't he just tell me she was his stepdaughter to begin with? It was just a little thing, but for some reason it did not set well with me. I didn't like it when people stretched the truth, but then I hadn't been completely honest with him about my history of relationships with men.

The subject changed from talking about our children to talk about siblings, parents, and other family members. Elliot's tone began to change when he talked about his family, as if he had been slighted by some perceived wrong. "My family thinks I should do things for them without getting compensation. My nephew wanted my help with producing a film, but he didn't want to pay me much for doing it. He had no idea how much he would have to pay someone else to produce his film."

Now in his later years, Elliot didn't seem to have the same connection to his family that I did. Although I no longer spent much time with my siblings because I was living in a different state, we still had good relations between us and always got along with each other, never fighting or holding grudges. Elliot came from a large family just as I did. His parents were both deceased, but he did have some siblings still living. He spoke lovingly of only one sister, Leslie, with whom he kept in contact with. He seemed to have no use for his other family members. He had a brother who was a doctor, but he no longer spoke to him because, although his brother was financially secure, he had refused to give Elliot financial support for his movie.

I felt a slight discomfort at the tone of his voice and the direction of our conversation. My family always got along with each other, and it bothered me that there seemed to be so much bad blood in his. In an effort to head off any further complaints about his family, I quickly started to talk about my family before he had a chance to say anything further.

"In my family, we help each other out. We each have our specific talents and abilities, and if we see that someone in our family needs help, we do so voluntarily because we know that they would help us out if we needed it."

My comments had the desired effect and Elliot promptly ended his diatribe. A little voice inside of me clamored loudly with objections at what he had said, but another part of me promptly squashed the uprising, preferring instead to focus on the pleasant aspect of having a companion to share a meal with.

He assumed a more amiable manner as he reminisced about what it was like to grow up in Belize City, and I shared stories with him about my family in Ohio. While talking, I found that our experiences while growing up were remarkably alike. We both came from big families, and we were born and raised Catholics. It seems that the antics of siblings and parents are similar regardless of geographical locations and cultures.

As teenagers, we took part in many of the same activities like playing basketball, riding bikes, or just hanging out with friends after school. Although, there was a notable difference in the type of housing that we had lived in: Elliot didn't have indoor plumbing or electricity while he was growing up. He had to use an outhouse, while I had the luxury of an indoor bathroom, even though I had to share it with six other family members. One of his chores was to fill up buckets of water to bring back to his house for cooking, washing dishes, and bathing. And with no electricity, there wasn't a refrigerator to keep food cold in. His mother went to the market each day to buy fresh food.

His mother, like mine, was the one who took him to mass each Sunday and taught him how to pray. His most amusing tale was when, as a young boy, he would reenact the mass. In an effort to look like a priest, he would fashion a robe made of sheets and then go through the motions of saying mass with his sister, Leslie, filling the role of alter server. I laughed in delight at the thought of him devoutly leading the mass of his imaginary congregation.

After thinking back in time for a few moments, I said, "My brother and I used to do the same thing," I said in a wistful tone. "I had forgotten about that."

It was evident that our deep spirituality was rooted in our younger years; a seed firmly planted and nurtured by our mothers.

"You should have been a priest," I said.

"I didn't feel that I was worthy enough."

Wiping up the last bit of egg from his plate with his toast, Elliot changed the subject abruptly. "Do you like to play Bingo?"

"Yes, I do. Actually, I played Bingo a few times on Thursday evenings at St. Peter's the last time I lived here."

"Would you like to go this Thursday?" he asked tentatively.

I didn't have to think twice about his invitation. "Yes, I would like that," I replied.

On our drive back to the hostel, I mulled over my feelings for Elliot. I was drawn to Elliot's strong sense of spirituality, and I felt that with him I could experience spiritual growth. I looked forward to getting to know him better despite the gnawing uneasiness from some of the things he had said about his family at lunch. Because I so much wanted to have someone to share my life with, I was willing to give our budding relationship the benefit of doubt.

The next morning, I got a call from a new hotel located on the intercoastal waterway that had just opened up a few months earlier. Excited at the prospect of getting a job, I returned the call and set up an interview for later that afternoon. I did a few errands and came back to get ready for my interview.

My two English roommates had left the day before, and when I returned to the hostel around noon, I met my new roommates who were both university students from France. Brigette was soft spoken and reserved, in contrast to Nicole, who was outgoing and bubbly. Their looks were as different as their personalities. Brigette was tall and thin with dark brown hair and eyes, while Nicole had blonde hair and blue eyes, with a shorter stature and a Rubenesque figure.

As the weeks wore on, I did away with last names. It just wasn't important. Roommates came and went so fast that I had difficulty remembering first names, let alone last names. There were a few roommates that I never even met. All I ever saw of them on my nightly trek to the bathroom was a fleeting glimpse of a sleeping form wrapped snuggly in a blanket in what had been an empty bunk when I first went to bed. These guests were one-nighters usually checking-in after midnight and leaving early in the morning. The hostel provided safe, comfortable lodging in which to catch a few winks before moving on to their next destination.

Finished with our introductions, the girls went about making their beds. Pointing to the empty bunk bed, they asked me who our fourth roommate was. When I told them about Aylin, Brigette was anxious to meet her since she had spent a few months in Turkey the previous summer. I was amused that

Brigette and Nicole would ask me questions in English, and then after listening to my reply, they would turn to each other and chatter away in their native language. Since I had studied French in college, I would pick up a word or two that I understood, but I never could understand a complete sentence. Some people probably would have considered them rude to speak French in front of me, but I did not mind at all. I relished the experience of being around foreign languages, even if I couldn't understand a word. Exposure to foreign languages was a way of life at the hostel, and it was like music to my ears.

While getting dressed for my interview, my French roommates eagerly pried information from me about what tourist attractions they should see and where they should shop and eat. I was always eager to give guests information, since I knew the area well. They were always so grateful and appreciative of the help that I gave them. Finished making their beds, the girls changed clothes, and after putting on their finishing touches of makeup, they headed excitedly out the door for lunch. I was happy to hear that I was going to have the same roommates for a few weeks. It was interesting having so many different roommates from all over the world, but for once, I just wanted things to settle down a bit and have some time to get to know them better.

Arriving at my interview, I quickly eyed the staff of the hotel as I entered the lobby area. I noticed that most of the staff was young and fashionable, and the lobby of the hotel had a contemporary, sophisticated look to it. I was greeted by the manager who led me to his office. The manager was also a younger man. I answered his questions, but had a subtle sense of unease that I didn't quite fit in. When I left, I knew I would never hear from him. Somehow, I had grown older and out of sync. Although I had a lot of experience and a college degree, that didn't make me in any more of a demand. It didn't really seem to matter at all.

I had spent three-and-a-half years of my life in pursuit of my bachelor's degree in an effort to right a wrong. I had always regretted not finishing college in my younger years. Instead, I ended up getting married and having children. Through the years, I always felt that not having a college degree had held me back from advancement. What really motivated me to complete my degree was my third husband, who had continually put me down because he had a college degree and I did not. Now I had that coveted degree, but was the time, effort, and cost worth what it could bring to me at this stage in my life at middle age? I was beginning to wonder.

Shaking off the unpleasant experience from my hotel interview, I decided to stop at a few of the temporary agencies to pick up some temporary work. I knew from past experience that temporary agencies were always looking for employees, and I felt sure that I would be able to find something through them. My first stop at a local agency did not go well. They had no work. Nothing. The woman behind the counter, a Hispanic woman with dark hair and a slight accent, handed me an application to fill out to keep on file. The sole applicant in the office, I sat alone huddled over the desk, pen in hand, trying my best to print neatly and legibly.

As I wrote, a mournful voice broke the silence of the empty office. "It's all President Bush's fault," she wailed, "because of his policies the economy is in shambles and we don't have any work!"

Did I miss something? Had I been so caught up in my drama from graduate school that I totally missed out on what was going on in the real world? Thinking back, I remembered that one of my college professors who worked with placing disabled clients in community employment had mentioned that business was slow in northeast Ohio. And there was no way to escape all the media coverage on the record number of people going through foreclosure on their homes. I was operating on the premise of a Fort Lauderdale that existed two years earlier when jobs were plentiful. But still, Fort Lauderdale was an upscale city brimming with huge mega yachts and mansions that lined the intercoastal waterway. Money seemed to be plentiful here.

I handed her my application. "I have worked as a secretary, but I've also done some special events."

Something I said sparked an idea and she bent over to retrieve a piece of paper from a tray. "Wait, here is something," she said with excitement in her voice. "It's for a special event at a hotel in Hallandale Beach for only half a day, but it is better than nothing. You need to be there Thursday morning."

"I'll take it!" A half a day's work was better than no work. Finally, I had a job to go to.

She jotted down the directions and handed me a slip of paper with the job number. As I left the office, I decided to check with some other temporary agencies in the area. A few quick phone calls produced no results. The agencies that I called were not even taking applications. I was instructed to fax or e-mail my resume in to them for review, and then, if they thought they could place me, they would 'invite' me to come in to fill out an application. I was stunned. A slow realization began to dawn over me. Things were a lot worse than I had realized. I knew that the economy was slowing down, but I had no idea it was this bad. It was about to get worse.

That evening, I decided to ask Elliot if I could pray the rosary with him. I felt a panic arising within me over my job situation and felt a need for the consoling effect of prayer. Saying the rosary is much like meditating which leaves me with a calm, uplifting feeling. Although, I must admit to an ulterior motive: I wanted to spend more time with Elliot. I left my dorm room in search of Elliot and found him in front of the TV, eating his dinner. I poked my head around the corner of the doorway of the TV room. "Hey, can I say the rosary with you tonight?"

With a look of surprise, Elliot turned towards me. "Yes. That would be beautiful. I will meet you at nine-thirty on the second floor terrace."

As the appointed time approached, I went to my room to look for my rosary. I had tucked it away somewhere when packing, but couldn't quite remember where. What if I couldn't find it? I dug frantically through my suitcases, lifting clothes and peering into zippered compartments, until I finally caught a glimpse of the silver case peeping out between some folds of material. I snatched it out of the suitcase, and holding it up before my eyes, I let out a deep sigh of relief. I tucked my rosary in the pocket of my jean shorts, sprayed on some perfume, then headed up the stairs to the second floor terrace.

I spotted Elliot in the corner of the terrace, pulling two plastic chairs together. I walked over and grabbed a chair to help him.

Elliot pulled a chair around towards him. "Here, we need to be facing east."

"Okay." I had never heard that before. I knew that the Muslims had to face Mecca when they did their daily prayers, but I never heard that Catholics should face east when saying the rosary. I was to eventually find out that there were a lot of things that Elliot knew about being Catholic that I did not.

Looking around, I was surprised that, at this time of night, there weren't any other guests on the upstairs terraces. The guests usually congregated on the outside terraces at night to talk and drink so as not to disturb the guests who were sleeping, but this was also Elliot's favorite place to pray the rosary. On many evenings while sitting in the courtyard, I could see the back of Elliot's head as he sat facing east towards the ocean; a solitary figure absorbed in prayer.

Elliot and I sat quietly beside each other for a few moments inhaling the delicious, sultry, sea breeze. The crown of a lone palm tree kept us company; its flat, green fronds fluttering in the night breeze, like tousled strands of hair. A sliver of an incandescent moon lit up the heavens and a few tufts of clouds flitted across a night sky peppered with twinkling stars. Voices from a group of guests talking softly in the courtyard floated up to the terrace to blend with the incessant sound of the passing traffic on the street below.

Leaning back in our chairs, our legs stretched out in front of us, we admired our surroundings.

Elliot stirred in his chair. "This is beautiful."

"Yes, it is. I could sleep out here all night," I replied.

Leaning sideways in his chair towards me, he reached out and touched my hand where it sat resting on the arm of the chair. "So tell me about yourself," he said. "Are you looking for a husband?"

Taken somewhat aback, I laughed nervously and moved my hand away from his, tucking it under my leg. "Well, not really. I haven't had much luck in the relationship department." For some reason I sensed that Elliot seemed disappointed at my response.

"You have a lot of good qualities. You should get out there and meet someone," he said encouragingly. "I would ask you out myself, but I am in a relationship with a woman from Port St. Lucie. I met her at a prayer group. I don't believe in dating two women at the same time. I can only commit myself to one woman, and if that doesn't work out, then I like to break it off before I begin to date someone else."

I had been all ears at first thinking that he was about to ask me out, but now I sat back in my chair totally deflated. I was confused. Hadn't he just take me out to lunch a few days ago? We had talked about our families, children, and we touched on previous relationships albeit superficially. Why didn't he say something about this woman then? And when did he see this woman? I had been at the hostel for a couple of weeks now, and I had seen him watching TV every evening. Then there was the Saturday night when we went to the fireworks together. I thought perhaps he was just making this up because he wasn't really interested in me.

Elliot continued talking completely oblivious to the turmoil whirling about in my head. "Although, I am thinking about breaking up with her," he said with a hint of frustration. "She wants everything now, and when I try to explain to her that sometimes you have to wait for what you want, she doesn't want to hear it."

My hopes were lifted by this unexpected proclamation. I had never stolen someone else's boyfriend before, but I fully intended to do so now. I had no idea how to go about accomplishing such a feat. I surmised that somehow things would work out in my favor, eventually. After all, I was here at the hostel with him every day, unlike this other woman, who lived a few hours away.

I felt so attracted to this man. I didn't want to meet anyone else - I wanted to be with him. I had received his message loud and clear: he wasn't available. I could have kicked myself for not asking him earlier if he was involved with someone. Since he was always around the hostel, I just took it for granted that he was not in a relationship. I needed some time to think. This was going to be a long rosary.

After our prayers, I felt strangely calm and serene; saying the rosary had its usual meditative effect. Because of what was said between us earlier, I didn't hang around after we finished. I promptly said goodnight and went back to my room. I tossed restlessly in my bed unable to fall asleep with Elliot's words echoing in my head. I held fast to a small glimmer of hope . . . "I have been thinking about breaking up with her."

In the middle of the night, voices intruded on my deep slumber. What was that noise? I flipped over on my back. There was a large window across the room from the foot of our bunk beds. I realized that the noise was coming from a group of male guests, sitting outside the window.

What had started out as an evening of light chit-chat when I had turned in for the night, escalated into an all-nighter as the beers flowed freely; the volume of their voices and laughter increasing with each can of beer consumed. The guys had taken over my little table and chairs that I had set up outside my door for my outside office and turned it into a beer garden. I tossed and turned for about a quarter of an hour before I had had enough. It was 2:30 a.m. and Aylin, Brigette, and Nicole were all sound asleep in their bunks. How could they sleep through such a racket? I crept from my bed and walked to the door and slowly opened it. I peered round the edge of the door at the group sitting at the table. "Hey, guys! We're trying to sleep in here! You are right outside our window, and we can hear everything you are saying. Can you go somewhere else to talk?"

Everyone stopped talking at once and looked over at me absolutely mortified. Gushing with apologies, the guys gathered up their beer, cigarettes, and ashtrays and went to find a more secluded spot where they would not disturb the sleeping guests. I climbed back into bed and drifted off into a fitful slumber. The noise from the traffic on the main road and the guests partying and talking at all hours of the night were getting on my nerves. I made a mental note to move the table and chairs outside my window before I went to bed at night so that guests would not be compelled to sit there at all hours of the night.

The next day I stopped by a hotel to apply for a position as a Catering Manager. Although I never worked as a Catering Manager, I had worked in special events and as a supervisor in a hotel. I felt that with my experience and college education I was qualified for this position. I didn't let it deter me that the hotel posting explicitly stated they were looking for someone with three to five years' experience. Despite the fact that I had only a year and three months' experience in a hotel, I knew that I could do this job. I filled out the application and submitted my resume, hoping for the best. I wasn't too surprised when I received the inevitable 'thank you for applying, but you are not qualified for this position' e-mail.

I was angry. For so many years I had worked at jobs I couldn't advance at because I didn't have a college degree. Now I had a college degree, but not enough experience. I was expected to take an entry level position and work for years to build up my experience. I felt betrayed by the system, tricked into spending a lot of money on an education that didn't seem to be paying off. Had I just wasted over three years of my life for nothing?

Job hunting started to take on a macabre tone, when suddenly the whole financial system was on the verge of a collapse, caused by a mortgage market meltdown. A string of financial institutions and mortgage companies teetered on the edge of insolvency, while the government scrambled to bail them out in order to stabilize the financial system at tax payers' expense. Jobs and credit came to a complete halt. Alarm and panic gripped the nation as we held our collective breath unsure of what might happen next.

I kept pushing myself on. I did manage to pick up another day's work through a temporary service, filling in for a receptionist who had called off sick. Although it didn't seem like much, every penny that I could make counted towards being able to pay my rent at the hostel so that I could stay in Fort Lauderdale. Again, the possibility of failure hung ominously over my head, while I did my best to block the vision of myself having to run back to Ohio with my tail between my legs.

I kept applying at hotels and resorts for any position I felt qualified for and even those that I did not. I applied for a Sales Manager position, a secretarial position, more Catering Manager positions, and finally as a Front Desk agent. I had no real desire to work as a Front Desk agent. They usually were required to work both day and afternoon shifts, switching off between the two through the week. It was one thing to have to work weekends and holidays, but I drew the line at working a swing shift, unless I became desperate enough.

My days settled into a regular routine which started when I arose at eight o'clock each morning, donning a pair of shorts, a tank top, and socks and tennis shoes. After a light breakfast, I headed out for my two mile walk up and down the streets near the hostel. It was summer and it was imperative to walk early in the morning before it got too hot and humid. Even at nine o'clock in the morning when I started my walk, I was already sweating. I tried looking for the routes that offered the most shade from the tall buildings or trees. As I walked, I stopped to admire the tropical flowers and savored their fragrant scents. I took delight in watching a flock of wild parrots screeching loudly as they soared overhead while making their morning rounds across the city. The noise and fumes from the traffic on Ocean Boulevard was unpleasant, so I sought out side streets that offered shade and solitude.

It took a while to get used to all of the concrete that surrounded me. Everything was made out of concrete. Tall condominiums, apartment buildings, and hotels rose to various heights one after another like cement swells in a sea of concrete. The concrete sidewalks and paved roads and parking lots filled in the spaces between the concrete buildings, leaving only small strips of green grass or a few open spaces for bushes or tropical plants. Fort Lauderdale was part of a concrete divide that separated the sea and the intercoastal waterway.

It was rainy season in South Florida, and after a while, I started to notice a pattern with the weather. In the morning when I went for my walk, the sky was blue and cloudless with bright sunshine. The weather would stay like this until early afternoon. I would be working away at my outdoor office when, about one or two o'clock, the rain would start, and I would be forced to move my outdoor office inside to the TV lounge. This daily rain activity sometimes lasted for a few hours or into the early evening, precluding any excursion to the beach.

I felt sorry for the international guests who came to spend time in the sun on the beach and, instead, found themselves holed up in their rooms reading a book. After a while, I started telling the new guests to make sure that they went to the beach in the mornings before lunchtime brought the afternoon rains. Many of the international guests were restless and bored with the inclement weather that persisted every afternoon. I tried suggesting some alternative indoor activities for them to do; Fort Lauderdale had a lot to offer outdoors as well as indoors.

On rainy afternoons after my job hunting was completed for the day, I would set up my lounge chair in front of the sliding glass doors in the computer room on the second floor. One side of the sliding glass door was usually left open, allowing the trade winds to naturally cool the room. Positioning my lounge chair squarely in front of the open door so that I could watch the rain falling on the terrace, I covered it with a towel and placed a pillow at one end. Reclining in the lounge chair with a good book, I would often doze off to the soothing sound of falling rain.

One afternoon as I set up my lounge chair in the computer room, Freida was typing away at the computer. "Did you find a job yet?"

"Not yet. Just a few assignments with temporary agencies. Even they're not hiring anyone."

"You should try the hotel across the street. The hired some of the staff from the hotel that I worked at after it closed down."

Freida seemed genuinely concerned about the progress of my job hunting, and she often gave me names of people in the area to contact for possible jobs. One of the benefits of staying at the hostel was the social networking in addition to the emotional support that we gave to each other. Many of the long-term guests now had jobs, but they were sympathetic and helpful towards me since they went through the same thing themselves not that long ago. The short-term guests would ask about how my day went taking a passing interest, but the long-term guests took an avid interest in my progress or lack of progress in job hunting.

Weekend nights were dedicated to calling family members back home in Ohio. There was a house phone in the computer room where I could use phone cards that made long distance calling more affordable. I could spend hours on the phone. Every weekend I usually called my daughters, mother, and my cousin Genevie, affectionately known as 'Gene'. My conversations with my cousin Gene were especially important to me. Gene is four years younger than me and is not only my cousin, but my closest friend and confidante. A tall, lanky blonde, with a knock out figure for someone her age and a personality to match with a quick wit, and a penchant for deep, philosophical conversations, we could go on for hours and hours talking about life and love. Gene loved my sense of adventure and referred to me affectionately as her 'kooky cousin.' She admired my audacity at being able to move a thousand miles away to a place where I didn't know anyone. She told me more than once, "You have the biggest balls of any woman I know." I went out into the world to see what it was like and called Gene up to tell her about it.

Gene and I shared everything that happened in our lives with each other, and now I looked forward to telling her about this new man that I had met. That evening on the phone, I confided in her. "Gene, maybe this is the man that Laura saw in her vision. But she said she thought he was in a hospital. But think about it; hospital . . . hostel. There is only one syllable difference between them. Maybe Laura got them mixed up."

As usual, Gene's sense of reason prevailed. "Time will tell," she replied. "But are you sure you want to be in a relationship with this man? I don't like some of the things you told me about how he treats his family."

Things came to a head a few days later while I was lying in the sun on the beach. It was Thursday afternoon, and Elliot and I had plans to go to Bingo that evening. A vaguely, unsettled feeling poked and prodded at me about some of the things Elliot had said about his family. I knew from past experience that the way a person treats his family is how he will treat you. This really concerned me. I wanted someone to share my life with that had the same values as I did. I could be generous and loving, and that is what I wanted in a man. There was a gnawing doubt deep inside of me that wouldn't leave me alone.

Arriving back at the hostel, I went out back to sit under the palm tree still in my bathing suit and wrap around. I was supposed to be getting ready to go to Bingo with Elliot. I felt like I wanted to hit, kick, or punch something. I was so angry. Why do I find men like this? I couldn't seem to get a grip on myself. Before long, Elliot stuck his head out the back door, "Ready to go?"

"No, I'm sorry, but I decided not to go. I just didn't have a very good day with job hunting and I'm just not in the mood."

He walked up to my chair and stood looking down at me, playing with his watch band. "Oh, that's okay. We will go another time." He disappeared back into the room, and I could hear his voice as he sat in the TV room with some of the other guests talking. His voice sounded slightly higher than usual and a bit strained. I could tell that he was disappointed.

A little while later, I went up to him and apologized again. I felt bad for standing him up. Nathan came into the room, and I told him how I didn't want to go to Bingo because I was in a bad mood about job hunting.

"Oh, Lu. Don't worry. Something will come along for you," he assured me.

It was all a lie to cover up my true feelings. I didn't want anyone to know that, although I was attracted to Elliot, I was beginning to have serious doubts about the possibility of a relationship with him.

Chapter 4

More Than Just Friends

One evening, I began to notice a change in the way Elliot looked at me. To get to the kitchen, I had to walk through the TV room where guests sat in chairs lined up against the wall to watch the TV on the opposite side of the room. People coming in and out of the room had to walk between the guests and the TV, briefly blocking their view. As I walked past Elliot, I looked over and smiled at him. "Hello," I said warmly.

Elliot spoke as our eyes met. "Hello, you look nice this evening," he replied in an appreciative tone.

What caught my attention, though, wasn't the sound of his voice; it was the look in his eyes. As he held my gaze, his eyes radiated an intense glow that penetrated my being to the depths of my soul. I felt my face turn red. Embarrassed, I turned away from his idolatrous gaze. I never had anyone look at me that way before. When I dared lock eyes with him again, the 'look' was gone; replaced with the friendly, dark brown eyes I had come to know and expect.

Our relationship had settled into somewhat of a routine. We went to church together on Sundays. At least twice a week, I made it a point to pray the rosary with him. Other than that, I saw him in the evenings seated in his usual chair, watching TV and eating his dinner. Some nights I would sit beside him to eat my salad as he watched TV. I didn't really like to watch TV, but it gave me the opportunity to talk to him. I wanted to get to know him better.

One evening as I sat next to him, I noticed he was dressed in a long sleeve shirt. When I thought about it, every time I saw him he was wearing long sleeves. I found that odd since it was so hot and humid this time of year. Everyone else wore tank tops or sleeveless shirts. Some of the men walked around the hostel without any shirts on at all, wearing only a pair of shorts. I never saw Elliot in a pair of shorts. He preferred long pants, usually blue jeans. The only summery aspect of his attire was a pair of flip flops that he wore on his bare feet.

I looked forward to spending my evenings with Elliot, even if we only talked for a few minutes. Sometimes it was the only bright spot in an otherwise dismal day. A constant dark cloud hung over me as my savings dwindled. Money was getting low, and I was not having much luck with job hunting. I was getting worried about money. I had been paying my rent by the week, and after a discussion with Patrice, I found out that it was cheaper to pay by the month. I only had enough money left to pay for a half of month's rent. I crossed my fingers and hoped that something would come through for me soon.

With my money low, I became increasing concerned that something might happen to the wad of cash that I had safely tucked away in my locker. I diligently secured my locker with a combination lock, but the uncertainty of my financial situation spurred my tendency to overreact. The cash in my locker became a source of consternation, and I was eager to get rid of it. I thought perhaps Patrice would take it as a deposit on a month's rent. The idea seemed to calm my fears, and I decided to speak to Patrice about it as soon as I got the chance.

Patrice and I were getting to know each other, little by little. Each day when I saw her, we would exchange pleasantries. She seemed to take an interest in my well-being and often asked me how my job search was going. I felt that I could confide in her.

One morning on my return from my daily walk, I approached Patrice about the deposit on my rent. To my surprise, she adamantly refused to take it. She would only accept the whole amount due to 'bookkeeping procedures.' I fervently explained my situation to her, and she offered to keep my money in her safe until I could come up with the rest of the money to pay the month's rent. I ran back to my room to retrieve the cash from my locker and handed it over to her in a sealed white envelope. I breathed a sigh of relief as I watched her place the envelope in the safe.

Sitting in my car after leaving Patrice's office, I was suddenly racked by waves of apprehension. What had I done? I had just entrusted all the money I had to someone who I didn't even know very well. She could take that money, and I wouldn't have any proof that she was holding it for me. For a few moments, I actually felt sick to my stomach. I squirmed in my car seat, thinking about how I could get it back from her. I thought perhaps I could tell her I changed my mind and decided to keep the money with me after all. That sounded like the sensible thing to do. I was sure she would understand. I started to open the car door when a tiny voice urged me to stop and think about what I was about to do. If I went in there to ask for my money back, my actions would betray a mistrust in her. My car was parked outside the office window, and I could see Patrice moving about the office through the partially opened blinds. I watched her momentarily, and then slammed the car door shut and started the engine. That monumental leap of faith set the stage for everything that was about to happen.

Sunday morning I sat outside at my corner table, waiting for Elliot to meet me for mass. I flipped through my prayer book and read a few passages. Getting restless, I glanced at my watch. It was already quarter past nine. That was odd. Elliot had never been late before. I started to rise from my chair.

A voice boomed out from overhead. "Lu . . . Lu . . . Are you there?"

"Yes," I replied quickly. Getting up, I took a few steps into the courtyard and looked up to see Elliot leaning over the railing dressed in his pajamas; a long sleeved burgundy top that buttoned up the front and matching bottoms.

Looking frazzled, Elliot ran his fingers quickly through his hair in a self-conscious manner. "I . . . I'm sorry," he stammered. "I slept in . . . My alarm didn't go off. Just give me a few minutes, and I'll be right down."

"Okay. We still have time," I assured him. I returned to my table and sat down to wait.

Before long, I heard Elliot making his way down the stairs. He stopped at the bottom to wait for me.

He stood with his hand resting on the railing. "You look nice today," he said.

I got up and walked towards him. "Thank you."

I glanced at his attire. He was dressed in a long sleeved white shirt over which he wore a black T-shirt with a red heart in the middle, bearing the words in white lettering 'I Love New York,' a pair of blue jeans, and black high-top tennis shoes. A baseball cap completed his outfit.

I felt overdressed. I didn't get to go out much, so I always looked forward to dressing up a bit for church usually wearing a skirt, blouse, and heels. It was a once a week opportunity for me to wear some of my dressier clothes, or what I considered my 'church clothes.' I felt somewhat ill at ease in the differences in our attire, but I tried to not let it bother me. I smiled at Elliot reassuringly and led the way to the car with Elliot following closely behind. I wondered if he was looking at my legs.

As we walked to the car after mass, I wondered if we were going out to eat. I kept silent, waiting for Elliot to make the next move.

Elliot unlocked my car door and pulled it open. "Have you ever had Cuban food?"

Pleased at his inquiry, I stopped and looked up at him. "No, I haven't, but I enjoy eating ethnic food."

"Good. I know of a great little Cuban restaurant right down the street. How about some lunch?"

The Cuban restaurant turned out to be a charming little place with a friendly staff made up of the Cuban family who owned and operated the restaurant. I liked it the moment I set foot in the door. The décor was quaint and cozy. The walls were painted with murals depicting scenes of Cuban life amid the backdrop of the Cuban countryside. The waitress led us over to a small table for two, next to the front window. I ordered Shrimp Creole and Elliot ordered fish. Our dinners were served with rice and a side order of black beans and fried plantains. Elliot ordered a Tama, ground corn wrapped in a husk, so that I could try something new. Everything was delicious.

To drink, Elliot ordered a ginger beer. I had never heard of ginger beer and thought it was an alcoholic drink. When he offered me a sip, I was delighted to find that it tasted like ginger ale, only stronger. We had an enchanting lunch that I never wanted to end. I looked around the restaurant as we ate. I liked it here. I wanted this restaurant to be our special place, and I secretly wished that we would come here often.

Full of good food and content from good companionship, we arrived back at the hostel. Elliot pulled into the parking lot and stopped the car with the engine still running. "I have some place to go today," he announced.

Surprised, I looked over at him. "Oh, okay. Well, thanks again for lunch. I'll see you later." I picked up my prayer book and opened the car door. I shut the door and slowly walked to the gate, as he pulled out of the parking lot. I wondered where he was going. Usually on Sundays, he read the paper and then took a nap.

As I walked back to my room, a sudden realization dawned on me: "He must be going to St. Port Lucie to see that woman!" I was disappointed. We had had such a nice time together. Why did it have to end this way? I changed into my bathing suit, gathered up my beach towel and chair, then walked back outside towards the beach. The sun was out in full force, but it didn't seem to be shining as brightly as it had been earlier.

I set up my beach chair near the edge of the ocean. I liked to lie in the sun and listen to the waves. Usually the rhythmic sound of the waves relaxed me and lulled me to sleep. There wouldn't be any sleep for me today. I was too restless and preoccupied.

It was Sunday, so the beach was crowded. I watched a group of young men in their late teens as they tossed a football back and forth between them near the edge of the water. One of men jumped high, and with an outstretched arm, he plucked the ball from midair, then with the ball safely cradled in his arms, he came crashing down on his side in the splashing waves. A radio blared with rock'n roll music as a group of couples sat around talking and drinking beer. A few older couples from nearby hotels and condos were sprawled out on lounge chairs, basking in the sun.

Alone, I looked out over the water. It was mid-afternoon, and the sun was high in the sky. The surface of the sea, like a giant mirror, reflected the sun's brilliant rays in a dazzling display of light. A few boats sped by in the distance. Overhead, the drone from an airplane flying along the beach, pulling a sign through the air advertising a local eatery, momentarily drowned out everything else. The sights and sounds around me seemed far away. I was caught up in my own little world, awash in a sea of emotion.

I was falling in love with Elliot. I thought about him every day from the time I woke up until the time I went to bed at night. I watched for him at the hostel; I knew what time he would leave and what time I could expect him back. I would perk up at the sound of his voice, looking in vain to catch sight of him. Part of every day was spent planning my next move to get to talk to him, despite the fact that I had serious misgivings about getting into a relationship with him because of the situation with his family. As much as I tried to talk myself out of it, it didn't seem to do any good. It was if I knew he might not be good for me, but

Hostel by the Sea

I couldn't stop myself from wanting to be with him.

I needed to do something about this situation. Elliot had no idea that I was attracted to him. I had been friendly with him, and enjoyed going to church and praying the rosary with him, but there was always a respectable distance between us that was common between people who were just friends. My feelings for him were strong, and I wasn't content to just sit back and wait to see if he would ever make the first move. At times like this, I needed another person's input; someone who was outside the situation who could see things more clearly, someone who knew me well and would have my best interests at heart. I needed to talk to my cousin, Gene.

That night I called up my cousin. "Gene, I can't take this any longer. I think I should just tell him how I feel. What do you think?"

Gene listened intently as I filled her in on all the recent developments between Elliot and me. "I think you should level with him," she advised. "He can't read your mind. Besides, maybe this woman is just a good friend. He can't possibly see her very often. He always seems to be at the hostel."

I let out a deep sigh. "You're right. It would be better to just tell him how I feel. Gene, I've never done anything like this before, usually the man has made the first move."

A laugh escaped from the speaker of my cell phone. "Well, it's about time you started."

After talking to Gene, I sat in the courtyard thinking about what I was going to say to Elliot. It was the middle of the evening; guests had finished their dinner, and now sat around drinking and talking. I sat in my chair looking up at the tall cactus plant in the courtyard when I noticed large, white blossoms shaped like megaphones four or five inches long sprouting out of the leathery, green skin of the cactus plant. I hadn't noticed them during the day. Rising from my chair, I went over to inspect the blossoms more closely.

Nicole and Brigette came out of our room on their way out

on a night on the town. "Hey, look at these flowers. Aren't they beautiful?" I exclaimed.

The French girls came over to stand beside me as we admired the flowers. Nicole reached over and touched a petal gently with her finger. "Lu, have you ever been to the Miami Sea Aquarium?" she asked.

"No, but I would like to go sometime."

She absent-mindedly stroked the petal with her finger. "Do you know how much it would cost for someone to drive us there?"

They both now stood facing me expectantly. "No, I don't know. But there might be someone here that would be willing to take you," I suggested. "I can't go, because I can't afford the ticket to get in right now."

"Oh, Lu, merci. We will ask around. Maybe someone will take us as you say." Bidding me good-bye, they made their way to the gate, disappearing into the night.

I decided I must speak with Elliot before we said our rosary together on Wednesday evening. I had rehearsed my speech and was just waiting for the right opportunity to present itself. Finally, on Tuesday evening, I found him alone watching TV.

I looked around quickly to make sure that no one else was around. There wasn't much privacy at the hostel. With shared living quarters, there was usually someone around or, if not, there soon would be. I walked through the door and stopped a few feet from Elliot. "Do you have a few minutes that I could talk to you?" I asked him.

"Sure." Elliot reached over and pulled a chair towards him. "Here, please sit down."

I took a deep breath. "Elliot, there is something that I need to tell you."

He leaned towards me, fully attentive to what I was about to say. I lowered my eyes and stared at the buttons on his shirt; my jaw squared in determination. Quietly, I said, "I'm attracted to you and I'm starting to develop feelings for you."

My voice was shaking, and when I looked down, I noticed that my hands were also shaking. I quickly clasped my hands together and put them in my lap. I hoped he didn't notice.

I glanced up at him to see his reaction. His eyes widened and his mouth dropped open, and before I knew it, I heard him say, "I feel the same way about you."

My mouth was completely dry. I swallowed hard while trying to get back some saliva. I stared back at him, completely taken by surprise. "You do? I've been wanting to tell you how I felt about you."

He looked deeply into my eyes. "I'm glad that you did. But you know that I am already involved with someone else," he said gently, trying not to hurt my feelings.

"Yes, I know," I replied quietly.

He reached over and gently touched my hand. "As I've told you before, we've been having problems, and I've been thinking about breaking up with her. I don't believe in seeing two women at the same time. I can only give myself to one woman at a time."

"I understand." I was trying to talk quietly, but I could hear my voice echoing in the room. I had been so caught up in our conversation that I quickly looked around to make sure no one had come into the room.

He removed his hand from mine and sat back in his chair deep in thought. After a few moments of silence, he said, "Give me some time to deal with this situation, then we can take our relationship to the next level."

I nodded. "Okay," I said as smiled at him.

There was a clamor in the doorway as Nathan entered. "Hey, guys, what's up?"

Caught unawares, we both looked up in surprise, quickly masking any visible traces of emotion, acting as if we had been talking about nothing more innocuous than the weather. Nathan walked over to Elliot and grabbed his hand into a handshake, launching into what sounded like a prolonged conversation.

This was my chance to catch my breath. I quickly got up

and walked over to the kitchen sink. There was a small wall to the right of the sink that formed a small partition between the TV room and kitchen. I stood leaning against it, trying to calm myself down. I was still shaking in disbelief. For the first time in my life, I had taken the initiative to tell someone how I felt about them. I was brought up in a house where you were expected to keep your feelings closely guarded, and as an adult, I had great difficulty in expressing myself emotionally. For me, this was a big step, and I was proud of myself.

Now it was official; Elliot and I were going to be a couple. It was just a matter of time. This was the happiest I had felt in such a long time. I was filled with such happiness that I could hardly contain myself. Everything was going my way. I lived in a beautiful city in sunny Florida across the street from the ocean. I had a new man in my life. There was only one sore spot in my life: I still didn't have a job. But right now, even that didn't bother me.

Finally calmer, I poured myself a glass of ice tea and made my way out of the kitchen, winking at Elliot as he sat engrossed in conversation with Nathan. I needed to go for a walk.

The next morning I was still floating on a cloud as I went about doing my cooking and laundry. I liked to cook my food in the late morning after I finished my walk. I usually ate my big meal of the day at lunch time and then had a small salad for dinner. I didn't like to have to cook my meals up fresh every day, so I cooked enough to last for four or five days. I didn't mind eating the same thing every day. It was food. As long as it was filling and nutritious, that was all that mattered to me.

The kitchen was quiet this time of day. Most of the guests had finished making their breakfast and had left for the day to go sightseeing. The long-term guests went to work early in the morning, returning later around dinner time. Usually I had the hostel to myself from late morning until after lunch. This was the perfect time to cook my dinner. Having the kitchen all to myself enabled me to spread out all my pots and pans, and I had full use of all the burners on the stove and the oven. It was nice not to have to share the cooking facilities for a change.

Lola was my only companion, and I would quickly get out of her way, when she came through to clean the kitchen. She usually put on a Hispanic radio station on the TV while working, and I would sashay around the room keeping time to the music. I liked listening to ethnic music.

One of the things that I liked about traveling and living in new places was the opportunity to try new foods. I did this every chance I could. Once I tried something new, I would start incorporating it into the way that I cooked, creating a sort of hybrid dish that was partly my own way of cooking, plus part of something new. The first time I ate rice with beans, which is popular in the Caribbean, I thought the beans were raisins. Once I tried it, I liked it, and have eaten it that way ever since.

The hostel was becoming more and more like home to me. By now I had acquired a bottom bunk. There seems to be a biological instinct that urges us to make a place to call our own. I did this with my bottom bunk. Although I was issued sheets when I checked-in, I preferred to use my own sheets that I had brought with me. Two of my own pillows and my comforter completed my bed. Since I liked to read at night, I took the small reading lamp that I had brought with me and mounted it with wire to my headboard. I laid a rug that I had made many years ago on the floor beside my bed so that I would have something to stand on in my bare feet. The top of the air conditioner next to my bed made an ideal shelf on which to lay my alarm clock and eye glasses. I put my reading books and writing tablet under my bed within easy reach. I had made a snug and cozy little nest in which to sleep. The only distraction was the movement and creaking from the frame of the bunk beds when my roommate climbed in and out of the top bunk.

While getting dressed one morning, I noticed a salamander sitting on the side of my suitcase near the top. It was just a small salamander about two inches long and was greenish brown in color. At first I thought it was dead, but when I reached for my clothing, I noticed a slight movement. I greeted him with a 'good morning' and told him he was going to have to move. I shooed the salamander away so that I could get into my suitcase.

Since the closet was empty when I first arrived, I kept all of my belongings in there. I had two suitcases with me: a large suitcase in which I kept my outer wear such as shorts, pants, and tops; and a smaller suitcase in which I stored my underclothes. I used these suitcases like they were a chest of drawers. Both of the suitcases were made out of black cloth with zippered closures. When I needed to take something out of one of them, I would pull the suitcase out of the closet, lay it on the floor, and unzip the front closure. After I was done, I would zip it back up, set it in an upright position, and push it up back into the closet. I utilized the few bent hangers that were in the closet, along with the ones that I brought with me, so that I could at least hang up my dress clothes for church and my suit for job interviews.

I was relatively happy with my room and my roommates. There was only one small irritation which surfaced occasionally involving Aylin. My French roommates and I were both on the same schedule: we got up early and went to bed at a decent time. Aylin was a different story. She would go to bed late and sleep until late afternoon. At night, she would be in and out of the room numerous times, opening and shutting her locker where she kept her cosmetics. I would lie in bed with one eye slightly opened, watching her as she sprayed perfume behind each ear and on the inside of each wrist. Then she would hold each wrist up to her nose to take a whiff. Satisfied that she had on enough perfume, she would put the cap back on and set the bottle back into her locker, and disappear back out the door. When she finally came in for the night, she would root through the bags of food that she had stashed at the head of her bed to find a snack before going to sleep. The peacefulness of the room was disrupted by the rhythmic crunching of her food as she chewed.

She also clomped around in a pair of worn out sandals. The

rubber tips had worn off the heels, exposing a piece of metal spike that tapped against the floor as she walked back and forth across the room. I felt sorry for her that she had to wear such worn out sandals. I honestly wished I had the extra money to buy her a new pair. I was always relieved when she finally took off her shoes for the night and finished eating her snack. Finally, there would be a silence punctuated only by the soft breathing of my sleeping roommates.

Aside from my roommates and the regular guests, I continued to talk to Elliot each evening. After our intimate conversation, nothing really changed in the way Elliot and I treated each other. We continued to say the rosary together and to go to church. After awhile, it started to bother me that Elliot never mentioned anything about our conversation or breaking up with his girlfriend. It was if our conversation had never taken place. Something didn't seem right to me. I began to feel uncomfortable with the situation. The more time that I spent with him, the more I wanted for us to begin a romantic relationship. I started to find it difficult to be around him. I also noticed that he hardly touched me. When he did, he would quickly pull his hand away, as if to thwart any display of affection. What was going on here?

I began to wonder if he was just stringing me along. He had a steady relationship with this woman from Port St. Lucie, and then, he had me waiting in the wings. The green-eyed monster, jealousy, started to rear its ugly head. Jealousy can make you do childish things. It can twist your reasoning to justify your claims that you are protecting yourself when in reality you are just punishing the person. My method of punishment was swift and decisive: I decided I wasn't going to pray the rosary any more with Elliot.

It was early Wednesday evening before rosary when I choose to deliver my particular brand of justice. In the TV lounge, which was fast becoming center stage for the unfolding drama of our relationship, I cornered Elliot and informed him that I could no longer pray the rosary with him.

Elliot looked crushed. A look of shock and displeasure contorted his face. "What? Give me a break. I don't understand what saying the rosary has to do with your feelings for me."

I stood with my hands on my hips, looking sternly down at him seated in his usual chair with his long legs stretched out in front of him, his forearms resting on the arms of the chair.

"Look," I hissed. "I just don't think this is a wise thing for me to do. I find that the more time I spend with you, the stronger my feelings become. Maybe we just need to cool this off for a little while until you can take care of the situation with this other woman that you are involved with."

With an air of resignation, he shrugged his shoulders. "I don't agree with you," he said with a sigh, "but I will respect your wishes. Please let me know if you change your mind."

"I told you before that I haven't been in a relationship for a long time. I don't want to get hurt." I promptly turned on my heel and left the room, leaving Elliot alone with his thoughts.

Thank goodness for diversions. Nathan and Nicole had their own melodrama playing out in the courtyard.

Nathan sat at the picnic table in the courtyard with a beer in front of him. Nicole stood nearby with Brigette quietly at her side. Nicole wailed, "But Nathan, you told us that you would take us to the Miami Sea Aquarium!" Her voice was high and strained, and I thought I detected a slight hint of a suppressed sob.

Nathan took a swig of beer, doing his best to keep an upbeat attitude. "Look, girls, you know I would love to take you to Miami, but I am having problems with my car, so I can't take you."

Nicole became more exasperated, her arms flailing about madly as she argued her case. She was not giving up easily. "But it is just your air conditioning. So what if we have to drive there with the windows down. We won't mind."

Nathan shook his head emphatically. "You must be crazy! We can't drive all the way to Miami without air conditioning. It's too hot. I can't do it. Someone else will have to take you."

Sensing I was the next target, I quickly made my exit. I had no intention of driving to Miami either. Patrice had already given the girls alternative ways to get there for a reasonable cost. They were dead set on having their own private chauffer for a minimal cost. It was getting to be late evening, and they planned to leave for the aquarium early the next morning. They would have to complete their travel arrangements soon.

When I went to bed, I could still hear the girls making their rounds through the hostel trying to line up a ride for the morning. I fell asleep wondering if they were going to make it to Miami in the morning. Early before the break of day, I heard them get out of bed to get dressed to leave for Miami. I promptly turned over and fell back asleep, thankful that they were finally leaving on their trip.

It was Saturday, and it was my day off. It was a relief to have a break from job hunting for a few days. I had grocery shopping to do, and I wanted to go to the library to get a few books. It was mid-afternoon by the time I returned to the hostel from running my errands. I deposited my bags of groceries on the kitchen counter while I ran to my room to drop off my books, slipping them under my bed so I would have them handy later that night. I always liked to read before I went to sleep, so I always made sure that I had a ready supply of reading materials handy. Not wasting any time, I ran back to the kitchen. I didn't like leaving my bags unattended for very long for fear that someone might pass by and help themselves. I dug my old bags of groceries out of the refrigerator to repack them. The plastic bags had become torn and tattered from the constant tying and untying of the top of the bag. I placed everything into two new plastic bags and tied a knot at the top as a deterrent to keep anyone from helping themselves to my rations. It might sound petty, but I was on a strict budget and couldn't afford to have my food come up missing. So far, no one had helped themselves to my food. The thought crossed my mind that the type of food that I ate was a deterrent in itself: brown rice and fish were probably not the most tempting fare to late night scavengers after a night of partying.

As I finished packing my groceries, an older woman came walking into the kitchen carrying a cup of coffee. Seniors weren't very common at the hostel, so I was always quick to get to know someone who was more on my end of the age continuum.

Smiling, the woman walked over to the counter. "Looks like you did some grocery shopping."

I picked up my two bags of groceries. "Yes, I just got back. Did you just check-in?"

The woman pulled open the refrigerator door for me. "I just got here this morning. I flew in from New Jersey. I've stayed here before. I usually come here twice a year."

I placed the bags on the bottom shelf while I continued talking over my shoulder. "Oh, so you are a regular here, that's nice. My name is Lu. I've been here for about a month. I'm from Ohio."

"My name is Ceyda. "

I repeated her name unsure that I heard her correctly. "Ceyda . . . that is an unusual name."

She let out a slight chuckle. "Yes, well, blame it on my parents. They named me after someone they met while travelling overseas. I've travelled quite a bit myself and stayed in different hostels. It's a good way to meet other people. I've also lived in Germany for a few years.

As I made room for my groceries in the refrigerator, Ceyda stood near the counter filling me in about her life. She was a petite, full-figured woman with a light complexion. Her round face was devoid of any color except for a slight touch of blush that highlighted her checks, giving her a cherubic look. Her face was framed by blonde, wavy tresses that were parted in the middle and hung down to her shoulders. I studied her closely trying to figure out how old she was. Her hairstyle suited someone much younger. Woman her age usually wore their hair closely cropped like a man's. It was refreshing to find a woman who was probably in her 60's sporting a longer hair style.

I liked Ceyda the moment I met her. She was warm and friendly, and I liked that she was well-traveled, and spoke numerous foreign languages. She talked to me the entire time that I was in the kitchen repacking my groceries. She continued to talk as I poured myself a glass of ice tea. And then, still talking, she followed me as I made my way through the TV room to go outside to have a cigarette.

As I lit my cigarette, she took a step backwards. "Oh, I don't like cigarette smoke."

"Sorry about that, Ceyda. How about I sit over in the corner away from you?" I sat in my chair facing the courtyard.

Ceyda was undeterred by the cigarette smoke. She was now twice the distance from me than she was earlier, but she continued rambling. "Which room are you in? I'm upstairs in #12 with another older woman, but I haven't met her yet. Do you know who she is? What is she like?"

Finishing my cigarette, I got up. "She's very nice. Her name is Freida, but she is leaving in a few days to go back to Denmark. And, my room is right here." I swung around and pointed to my door. "Well, it was nice talking to you Ceyda, but I have some things to take care of. I'll see you later." I left Ceyda standing in the courtyard looking for her next victim.

Later that evening, I spied Elliot sitting in the TV room. I walked in and sat down in the chair beside him. "Hi. What are you watching? It looks like an old black and white movie."

He picked up the remote control reducing the volume as he spoke, "Yes, it's *Casa Blanca*. Have you ever seen it?"

I leaned back in my chair and looked over at him. "No. I don't watch movies much, but I would like to spend some time watching all the old classics some day. I guess we didn't watch much TV, when I was growing up."

"I like to watch movies, especially the classics. I studied film making at a university in New York many years ago. I moved to Los Angeles to do an internship with Sydney Pollack who directed the movie *Absence of Malice* with Paul Newman and

Sally Field. They were all really nice to work with. I even had a few walk-on parts in the movie."

I looked at him in awe. "Wow! That must have been an interesting experience. How long did you live in Los Angeles?"

"For thirteen years. That is where I met my stepdaughter's mother. We lived there and we had planned on getting married, but then my fiancée's mother caused some problems and we broke up."

I nodded as Elliot spoke, eager to learn more about him.

Pleased with my rapt attention, he continued, "I plan to go back to Los Angeles soon to make my own movie. I just need to finish lining up the financing. It's starting to come together. I have already signed a contract with a distributor. Actually, it is a five year contract."

As he reached up to scratch his head, his tone of voice abruptly changed from irritation to impatience. "The deadline is getting kind of close. I only have until the end of March of next year to get started on it. "

I was eager to give him emotional support. "I'm sure something will come through soon. Just keep trying."

Nathan's birthday was approaching, so I decided to talk to some of the other guests to find out if we were going to do something special for him. I had noticed that Nathan spent a lot of time with Stuart, so I decided he would be a good person to talk to about it.

Stuart was very youthful looking for his age. When I first saw him, I thought he was a teenager, but later found out that he was the same age as Nathan who was in his early 30's. Stuart had a slight, wiry build. He wore his head shaved which, from what I could see when he walked around shirtless, matched the rest of his hairless, skinny, pale body. A pair of wire rimmed glasses adorned his boyish face which was also absent of any trace of facial hair. His thin lips formed a wide mouth that framed a set of gapping teeth.

Stuart was the most social person I think that I have ever met.

I would see him talking to guests each night in the courtyard when he wasn't working as a waiter at an upscale restaurant in a nearby mall. The one thing that impressed me most about Stuart was that he could even talk to guests who didn't speak English, or didn't speak it very well. I don't know how he did it. I would see Stuart conversing with guests that I had tried to talk to earlier who struggled to put two words of English together. Later, I would see them sitting in the courtyard at the picnic table, drinking and talking like they were long lost buddies. This applied to males and females, individuals, or couples. Stuart was a friend to all.

Stuart now stood in the doorway to the kitchen intent on making plans for Nathan's birthday party. "Hey, Lu. Are you coming to Nathan's birthday cookout tomorrow evening? We are planning on having some hot dogs and hamburgers on the grill. I know you just like to eat your salad, but come on, you can break your diet for one night. It won't kill you."

I laughed at Stuart's attempt to lure me from my regular evening salad. "I'll be here for Nathan's party. I don't know about the cookout, but we'll see."

I looked up to see Ceyda lugging bags of groceries in through the gate. "Hey, Ceyda. Come here!" I shouted at her.

Ceyda had by now made friends with everyone in the hostel. She loved to stay up all night long talking to all the guests, not going to sleep until the crack of dawn, and then sleeping until mid afternoon. She mixed well with guests of all ages and especially enjoyed hanging around with younger people. She seemed especially fond of Nathan and Stuart.

Ceyda walked over to where Stuart and I stood. "It took forever to get back here on the bus tonight!"

I looked at Ceyda incredulously. "Ceyda, the buses only run once an hour after seven o'clock. You need to go to the store earlier when they run every half hour. No wonder it took so long to get back here. Anyways, we wanted to tell you about Nathan's birthday party tomorrow night. Stuart is planning a cookout."

"I didn't know it was Nathan's birthday tomorrow! I wished I would have known that, I would have gotten him a card when I was at the store. Oh, that's okay. I'll go and get one tomorrow, and then, we can all sign it."

A thought popped into my mind. "What about a cake? I'd bake one, but I don't have any cake pans."

Ceyda set down her bags. "How about I just pick something up from the bakery at the store?" she offered.

That was it. We pretty much had the party planned. We were like a family: joining together to make sure that special occasions such as birthdays were not forgotten, but celebrated together with everyone making a contribution. This was to become an important part of our community as time went by. While Ceyda and Stuart discussed the details, I walked upstairs to the terrace, promising to spread the word to the other guests about the party.

The next afternoon I had the chance to tell Freida about the party. I found her sitting on the terrace with a book in her hand. "Freida, did you hear about Nathan's party tonight?"

"Yes, but I don't think I'll make it. I am busy getting packed to leave. I have something to ask you."

"Yes, what is it?"

She put her book down into her lap. "I'm looking for someone to take me to the Miami airport. I can pay you for gas. Do you think you could take me?"

I looked at Freida, weighing the decision silently in my mind. I really didn't want to drive forty miles to the Miami airport, but I liked Freida. She had been kind and friendly to me and had tried to help me find a job. "Okay, Freida. What time do we need to leave?"

She filled me in on her schedule, and I left her to continue her reading. As I walked away, I thought to myself, "She is really going to do it. She is finally going back home." I couldn't help but wonder: "But for how long?"

That night Nathan's birthday party was a success. It was a beautiful, warm night with a slight ocean breeze; the perfect weather for an outdoor party. Nathan was the life of the party dressed in his Hawaiian shirt, with a beer in one hand, and a cigarette in the other. All of the guests joined in and laughter and chatter filled the courtyard. Surrounded by his new friends, many of whom by now were like family, he was in his element. There was one guest that was conspicuously absent; I didn't see any sign of Elliot.

Ceyda had picked up a few packages of mini-cupcakes. We stuck a candle in one of them and sang 'Happy Birthday.' Ceyda gave Nathan a card that she had bought earlier in the day and had passed around to all the guests in the hostel to sign. It was a musical card that had a drawing of a mug of beer inside; Nathan's favorite beverage.

The next morning, I drove Freida to the airport. I was sad to see her go. I thought of the other people through the years that I had crossed paths with briefly during my travels. It left me feeling a little sad, grieving the loss of our brief encounter. We exchanged e-mail addresses, but I knew I would never hear from her again.

Although I was no longer praying the rosary with Elliot, we continued to talk each evening. I would stop in the TV room to sit with him for a while, or, if I was outside, he would stop by to join me as I sat at my table reading or listening to music. Late evenings, I would look up at the terrace to see the back of his head as he sat in his usual spot praying the rosary. I couldn't help but notice, with a twinge of regret, the empty chair sitting next to him on his right. As much as I would have liked to join him, I kept myself from relenting. I was stubbornly determined that I was doing the right thing by keeping my distance. I consoled myself with the thought that at least we were still going to church together.

I looked forward to Sundays when Elliot and I would go to mass and then out to lunch at our favorite Cuban restaurant. We were beginning to get to know the friendly staff who always treated us in a warm and welcoming manner. I liked that we were beginning to feel at home there. It was nice to get to know people as a couple and have a favorite restaurant, even though we still weren't officially a couple, yet.

Getting ready for church one Sunday morning, my unresolved situation with Elliot weighed heavily on my mind. He still had not followed through with his promise to break up with his girlfriend. I had expected him to break up with her in a timely fashion of a week or two, but for this to drag on for three weeks was disturbing to me. What was going on here? Again thoughts of being strung along toyed with me. I was caught in a state of limbo just biding my time, waiting for something to happen. I didn't like where this was going. After thinking this through, I decided to discuss the matter with Elliot. I would rather face a situation squarely and deal with it, even if the prospect of rejection was painful; it was better than wallowing in uncertainty.

The opportunity presented itself later that day, as we sat comfortably seated at what was now our 'regular' table at the Cuban restaurant. I gazed out the window of the restaurant into the bright sunshine. A cloudless, blue sky formed a backdrop to the assortment of buildings, palm trees, and passing cars that lined the boulevard. Inside the restaurant it was cool and quiet. The restaurant was just opening for lunch and a few other patrons had trickled in for their Sunday meal. I sat rearranging my silverware, waiting for the right time to bring up this touchy subject. Not too long after we had ordered our usual meals, the waitress set hot plates of steaming food in front of us.

Elliot began scooping large heaps of rice and black beans into his mouth. In between bites, he took a swig of his ginger beer. Conversation flowed easily as we talked about the other guests at the hostel, and I told him about my drive to take Freida to the airport. There was a sense of ease between us, as if we had been together for a long time.

Finally, gathering up my courage, I broached the subject. "Elliot, I need to talk to you about something."

He continued scooping up his rice and beans working away at

cleaning up his plate. "Mmm-hmm." Was all he could manage to say while chewing with his mouth full.

I stopped eating and laid my fork down beside my plate. "I was just wondering what is going on with your girlfriend. You haven't said anything more about breaking up with her."

Elliot stopped chewing and swallowed. "Well, I have talked to her a couple of times now about breaking up. But she said she has feelings for me and she wants us to stay together."

I sat speechless. It took a few minutes for what he said to sink in. My mind churned with all kinds of thoughts, as I searched for the right words to express myself. Struggling to maintain my composure, I said, "I can understand that she has feelings for you, but I thought that you were unhappy with your relationship and had decided to break up with her."

Elliot stopped eating and leaned back in his chair. He spoke in a calm and forthright manner. "Well, she is a nice lady and I don't want to hurt her. It's not like she has done anything wrong to make me want to break up with her; it's just that we want different things in life."

I was stunned with disbelief. "I understand that, but do you think it is right for us to be going to church and out to eat together if you are involved with someone else? I know I wouldn't like it if I was in a relationship and I found out that my boyfriend was taking someone else out!"

I was trying desperately to make Elliot see my side in this.

Elliot's manner became agitated as he threw his hands up in the air. "I don't know why you would feel that way. We are *just friends*!"

His words had a sting to them, like a sharp slap in the face. 'Just friends.' We are just friends? What happened to the conversation we had had about wanting to be together as a couple? This didn't make sense to me. It was now evident that he had no intention of breaking up with this other woman. Why should he? He had a perfect situation. He was in a steady relationship with a woman, while he had me on the side. I was seething at the unfairness of it all.

We finished our meal with Elliot making attempts at lighthearted conversation, while I sat lost in my thoughts. I needed time to be alone and think about this. I was stunned by this coup de grâce.

Chapter 5

Emotional Disconnect

After another fruitless morning of job hunting, I returned to the hostel and changed into my bathing suit and then went to the kitchen to heat up my fish, rice, and beans. Sitting in the courtyard under the shade of a palm tree, I had a quiet lunch alone with my thoughts. My job predicament was not the only vexation in my life. There was also the situation with Elliot to contend with. I was angry and bewildered by our previous Sunday's conversation at the restaurant. His comment that we were 'just friends' confused me.

After lunch, I crossed the street to the beach to take a walk. I think best when I'm walking outside in the fresh air, immersed in nature. From all the jumbled thoughts competing for attention in my mind, I knew that this was going to be a long walk. I set up my beach chair facing the ocean, laying my towel carefully over it. Satisfied that all was in good order, I walked to the edge of the water. With an approving eye, I scanned the vast expanse of sea laid out at my feet. I thought how I often greeted the sea as one would greet a lover: with eager anticipation of a passionate embrace, filled with ardent desire.

The cool water splashing against my feet was a welcome contrast to the warm sun on my shoulders. The delicious ocean breezes softened my cares and lifted my spirits. Life never seemed so bad when you had an expanse of ocean to lose your cares in. I dug my toes in the sand, reveling in the damp coolness of the gritty grains.

Thoughts drifted through my mind; the scene from the restaurant replaying countless times in my head. A vision of Elliot's face projecting an air of righteousness loomed larger than life in my mind's eye, chiding me for my unsolicited assault on his intentions, or should I say lack of them. I was furious with him. I felt betrayed by how Elliot was treating me since confiding in him about my feelings. I had dared to bare my soul to this man, and proclaimed my feelings towards him; something I had never done before. I felt foolish. Some things are better left alone, and perhaps, this had been one of those times. I never would have dared to tell a man how I felt about him in my younger years, but now in my middle years, I didn't see anything wrong with it. I was more confident in verbalizing my feelings, and I believed in taking chances. What hurt me the most was that Elliot reciprocated my advances, leading me to believe that we were going to be in a relationship.

If we were 'just friends,' then so be it. But I would not allow him to have his cake and eat it, too. If he wasn't going to break up with his girlfriend, then he wasn't going to have the pleasure of my company. He would soon find out the depths of my indignation at his indiscretion.

My walk completed, I returned to my beach chair to lay out in the sun for the rest of the afternoon. Content that my thoughts were in order and my heart set straight, I soon drifted off into a blissful sleep, lulled by the rhythmic sounds of the sea and the fluttering fronds of palm trees. A few hours later, refreshed, I packed up my belongings and headed back to the hostel. As usual, I spotted Elliot's car in the parking lot. I crossed the street and went straight to my room.

As I opened the door, a naked Nicole squealed in surprise and quickly covered herself with her towel. "Oh, Lu, it is you!" she gasped.

"Sorry, I should have knocked first. I didn't think anyone was here."

Nicole dug through her suitcase in search of clothes. Brigette came out of the bathroom wrapped in a towel, her hair dripping wet from her shower.

Nicole pulled some clothing from her suitcase and started to dress. "Lu, we have to talk to you. We think Aylin is turning off the air conditioner."

Brigette piped in. "Yes, and it is so hot in here! We have to have the air conditioner on."

I looked at both girls. "Yes, you are right. I think it is Aylin. I will speak to her about this. She must not like it cold in here. Perhaps we can adjust the temperature so that it is cool, but not too cold. That should be a good compromise."

The girls nodded their heads in unison. "Oui, oui. That would be good."

I looked over at Aylin's bed and noticed that she only had sheets on her bed. I had sheets and a comforter, which gave me extra warmth if I was cold at night. Perhaps I should ask Patrice if she had a blanket that Aylin could use. I decided I would ask Patrice later that evening. Aylin was gone and probably wouldn't be back until later that night.

After my roommates were done in the bathroom, I went to gather my things to take a shower. By now, I had bought a plastic tote to store all of my bath products in. The tote had various compartments where I kept my shampoo, body wash, razor, toothbrush and toothpaste, contact solution, lotion, and nylon scrub puff. It was a handy way to cart everything to and from the bathroom. I grabbed the towel off the end of my bed where I had hung it to dry and went to take my shower.

It felt good to scrub off the sand and suntan oil from my skin. I took an extra long shower, luxuriating in the fresh, clear water pelting my skin. I felt a sense of relief in my new found freedom from my recent cares. When I stepped out of the shower, I felt like a new person.

Returning my plastic bath tote to the closet, I noticed the salamander sitting on the top of my small suitcase. He seemed to have taken up permanent residence in our room usually sleeping on my small suitcase. I leaned over and looked at him. "Hello again. Well, if you are going to stay with us, then you need a name. I think I'll call you Charlie."

At that, the salamander opened his eyes. Alarmed by the looming figure hovering over him, he scampered off the suitcase to hide out in some dark corner. I grabbed the handle of my suitcase and lifted it up to set out on the floor to open. I needed to get a change of underclothes.

Getting dressed, I remembered I wanted to get a blanket for Aylin. I looked at my watch. It was shortly after six o'clock. Patrice would be back in the office by now, returning from her break. I finished getting dressed, grabbed my keys, and headed to the office.

The door was slightly ajar. I opened the door and stuck my head in. "Patrice, how are you this evening?" I asked.

Patrice looked up from her chair behind the desk. "Good, Lu. What can I do for you this evening?"

I filled Patrice in on the situation with the air conditioner in my room.

She handed me a blanket. "If you have any more problems with the air conditioner, please let me know, and I will take care of it."

Taking the blanket, I replied, "Thanks, Patrice. I appreciate your offer. I will talk to Aylin myself, and hopefully, that will take care of it."

She smiled as I closed the door behind me, and I took the blanket back to my room. I set it on Aylin's bed and went to eat dinner.

I looked forward to evenings at the hostel. It was nice to have people around to talk to at the end of the day. It reminded me of when I was growing up in a household with five children and my parents. There was always someone to talk to and something going on. It was like that here, too. I felt like I was part of a family, even if some of the members changed on a regular basis. I could always count on the long-term guests to be there for me.

While I was sitting at the picnic table in the courtyard, I heard Nathan's laugh echoing through the hostel as he made his way down the stairs from the upstairs kitchen. "Hey, Nathan!" I shouted. "You sound like you are in a good mood tonight!"

Nathan walked over and plopped himself down on the opposite side of the table. "Hey, Lu. Guess what? I got a new job."

"That's great Nathan. Where at?"

"It's with a food distribution company. I will be driving truck. It's better pay and hours than I have now. I just have to go for my drug test."

As Nathan prattled on about his new job, I noticed Aylin walking through the courtyard on her way towards our room. "Nathan, hold on. I need to talk to Aylin about something."

I got up from the picnic table and ran across the courtyard. Turning the knob, I opened the door to find Aylin standing in front of the mirror, brushing her hair.

Aylin had been here for a few months, but her English was not very good. I wondered to myself how I was going to talk to her about this. "Aylin, I need to talk to you about the air conditioner."

Aylin took a few steps away from the mirror and looked at me; her dark eyes filled with a quizzical expression.

I walked over to the air conditioner. "Come here. Look, you need to keep this on." I leaned over and turned the knob. "Set this on 70 degrees." Aylin stood watching me with a disdainful look on her face. I pointed to our roommates' bunk beds. "They said it's too hot in here without the air conditioner on."

Remembering the blanket, I walked over to Aylin's bed and picked up the blanket. In a soft voice I said, "Here, I got this for you, so you won't be cold at night when you are sleeping."

I held the blanket out for Aylin. She reached out and took the blanket and then looked up at me in surprise. "For me?"

With a smile on my face I nodded. "Yes, for you."

Her whole face lit up as she smiled broadly. "Thank you."

I had made a friend.

That week, I made it a point not to spend much time with Elliot. I spoke with him briefly a few evenings as we saw each other in passing. I had decided that it was best to keep my distance from him. I knew the time was drawing near that he would find out exactly how displeased I was with our current situation. Although I was at peace with my decision, I wasn't looking forward to telling him.

Saturday evening, I went to the kitchen for ice cubes for my drink. I acknowledged Elliot with a nod as I walked by him as he sat watching TV.

He watched me with interest as I poured my ice tea. Glass in hand, I started towards the door. Elliot's gaze followed me back across the room. In a presumptuous tone, he said, "I'll see you tomorrow morning for church."

I stopped and turned on my heel to face him. "No, I'm not going to church with you tomorrow."

Elliot's mouth dropped open, his eyes widening in disbelief. "What, what are you saying?"

As I spoke, my voice sounded strained and emotional. "Look, I told you before that I don't feel right about seeing you while you are involved with this other woman. I want someone that I can date. You are already in a relationship."

Elliot sat up bolt right, his face flushed. "I told you that I would break it off with her. It just takes time. I am an artist. I do things differently than other people!"

I looked at him in disbelief. What kind of line was he trying to feed me now? "You told me that she doesn't want to break up with you. I want someone I can be intimate with. I can't even touch you!"

Our verbal sparring completed, like two wounded boxers in a ring, we retreated to our respective corners to attend to our wounds: Elliot by escaping into a TV show, and I by taking off on a long walk. Walking was therapy for me and right then I needed that more than ever. It had hurt me deeply to take this stand with Elliot. I cared for him immensely and wanted more than anything to be in a relationship with him. I found myself enormously attracted to him in part because he was born and raised in another culture. Cultural diversity was important to me. I looked forward to getting to know him and learning about his native culture. I felt a deep sense of regret at losing the prospect of having a relationship with him.

That Elliot didn't smoke or drink was another quality about him that I found particularly attractive. After my history of involvement with men that abused alcohol, he was a refreshing change. I didn't have to deal with the Dr. Jekyll and Mr. Hyde complex that is so common in men that drink. I knew that the Elliot I spoke with in the morning would be the same Elliot I could expect to talk to that night. I had dealt with enough verbal and emotional abuse from men who had too much to drink. It was also appealing to know that I wouldn't play second fiddle to the bottle. Our relationship had a sense of balance that I hadn't experienced in my past relationships.

Also, I felt that we had something that was special. I felt comfortable with him and found it easy to be myself around him. There was an easy manner between us that was reminiscent of couples that had been together for a long period of time. That we shared the same religion gave our relationship a strong foundation on which to practice our faith and experience spiritual growth. We both had commented when we were first getting to know each other that God had brought us together for a purpose. It was hard to believe that it would all end like this.

The next day my French roommates left for France. We took turns taking each other's pictures so that we would have something to remember each other by. I was sad to see them go. They were such nice young ladies and had been good roommates. I felt so lucky to have crossed paths with them.

Aylin and I had the room to ourselves for a few nights. It was a nice change of pace not to have so many people in our room. Because Aylin was on an opposite schedule than me, it was like I had the room all to myself for a change. She was usually gone in the evenings when I was there, and I was gone during the day when she was sleeping. It gave each of us some time to ourselves.

That only lasted a few days. After all, this was a hostel. People came and went at all hours of the day and night. I knew we could not expect to have the room to ourselves for very long. That didn't really concern me. All the roommates that I had had so far had been a delight. I had no reason to expect otherwise.

Our new roommate made her entrance a few days later, and she came in with a bang. Helen was a brash, middle-aged woman from New York City who was moving to Fort Lauderdale permanently. She was staying at the hostel until she could find and job and a place to live just like myself. Helen didn't take long to stir things up in the hostel. She hadn't even been there for a full day before Patrice came knocking at my door as I got ready for dinner.

Patrice came into my room and closed the door. She looked around to see if we were alone. "Lu, I need to speak with you."

I was slightly alarmed by the tone of Patrice's voice. "Yes, what is it?"

Patrice stood with her hands on her hips. "It's about the closet. Helen feels that she should be able to use half of the closet. She wants to hang up some of her clothes."

I was surprised that Helen hadn't said anything to me about this earlier when we first introduced ourselves to each other and stood talking about our moves south. I had all of my belongings stored in the closet. It was a convenient place to store my possessions since I had so much more than the regular guests that were just passing through. All of my other roommates kept everything packed in their suitcases. I felt somewhat irked at the way Helen chose to go about this. Instead of talking to me directly to work this out, she chose to have Patrice exert her authority over me. I felt hurt by Helen's behavior. I prided myself on my ability to get along with other people, even people that did their best to be difficult. I did my best to respond in a nonchalant manner. "Well, that's alright. I don't mind sharing the closet."

Patrice walked over to the wall near the bathroom and pointed to shelving built into the wall. "How about putting some of your things over here?"

A forced smile on my face, I tried to look upbeat. "Yes, that's fine. I'll move my things right now."

Patrice looked at me with a concerned look. "If you have any problems with Helen, please let me know. Maybe I should have put her upstairs with Ceyda."

I watched her as she walked out the door. I had a bad feeling about Helen.

Later that evening Helen came in the room, and I showed her the empty side of the closet. In her brusque New York accent, she responded, "Well, you know, what's fair is fair. We are roommates, so we are supposed to share everything."

I looked her squarely in the eye, with a smile on my face, all the while gritting my teeth. "Helen, really, it's no problem. I'm happy to be able to share the closet with you."

She had a toughness to her that I found abrasive. I had a feeling that she was going to be a difficult roommate, but I was going to do my best to keep a positive attitude. She was the first roommate I had that was about the same age as myself. All of my roommates up until this time had been young university students who were like my daughters. I was like a doting housemother to them, and they had treated me with courtesy and respect. Helen was going to require some getting used to.

That evening I sat on the terrace watching the cars pass by in the street below. This was the very same terrace where Elliot and I had sat praying the rosary. I glanced behind me at the chairs still sitting in the corner of the terrace where we had sat side by side with our rosaries clutched reverently in our hands. Without him in my life, I felt so alone. Despite the glow from the lights shining on the buildings around me, everything seemed cold and forlorn. The clamor from the passing traffic was a blatant reminder of the impersonal nature of a big city. I felt so small and alone.

After all the excitement of moving to Fort Lauderdale, I suddenly found myself thinking about leaving. Everyone that I loved lived up north. In search of a better opportunity, I dared to leave them all behind and strike out on my own. I possessed an inherent quality that thrived on this challenge, but at times the loneliness was unbearable. I found it difficult to start new roots in a new city, especially at middle age. There were a lot of transients in Fort Lauderdale who were tourists from up north or from abroad, creating a variegated melting pot. It was interesting meeting so many different people, but I longed to meet someone to settle down with.

Yearning for companionship I decided to contact Rhoda, an acquaintance and former co-worker from the Fort Lauderdale hotel I used to work at, who was also from Ohio. We had kept in touch by e-mail while I was in graduate school, and we had planned to meet each other for dinner when I returned to Florida. This seemed like a good time to do so. With things on the blitz with Elliot, I thought it wise to get out and circulate. I called Rhoda, and we made plans to meet for dinner on Friday evening at a local seafood restaurant not too far from the hostel. I was excited that I had a dinner date, even if it was with a female friend. At least I had an opportunity to get out and visit for awhile.

Friday afternoon I returned from the beach earlier than usual and set about getting ready for my dinner date with Rhoda. I took extra pains to look my best, styling my hair and applying makeup. I slipped into a pair of Capri pants and a summery top that I accented with a fashionable necklace and dangling earrings. Spraying on my perfume, I couldn't wait until Elliot saw me all dressed up, hoping it would make him wonder where I was going or if I had a date. I thought back to earlier that morning when I had seen Elliot taking out a handful of shirts to his car. It looked like he was on his way to the laundromat. I didn't know it yet, but I was the one in for a big surprise that night, not Elliot.

The seafood restaurant was a few miles north of the hostel right on the ocean. There was a lot of traffic near the restaurant due to all of the shops and bars in the area. I decided to take the bus instead of paying to park my car. Arriving at the restaurant, I caught a glimpse of Rhoda at the bar surrounded by a crowd of people. The restaurant was really busy and Rhoda had saved a seat for me. Rhoda and I ordered dinner and then spent hours catching up on each other. During dinner she scolded me a number of times for moving back to Ohio for graduate school. "No more Ohio! You need to stay here and make a life for yourself!"

We laughed at my folly, and I agreed with her wholeheartedly. I didn't have the heart to tell her that because of financial difficulties I might have to go back.

After dinner, we went outside for a walk along the ocean. It was nice to spend time with a friend. We walked through some of the beach shops near the restaurant and then bade each other goodbye at a decent hour. I needed to catch the last bus for the night back to the hostel which was due to come by at about ten o'clock. I hopped the bus and headed back to the hostel, eager to come waltzing into the hostel after a night out.

I got off the bus and walked the half block to the hostel where I quickly scanned the parking lot for Elliot's car. It was nowhere in sight. That was odd. I hadn't seen his car when I left, but I didn't think too much about it at first, thinking he was out on errands. It was very unusual for him to be out this late at night. I changed into shorts and a tank top and went to sit in the courtyard. Unable to sit still for long, I decided to walk up to the second floor terrace where I leaned over the railing desperately looking for his car. There was still no sign of his car and it was now past eleven o'clock. Finally, I gave up and went to bed.

Sunday morning I got up and went to church. Going to church without Elliot was heart wrenching. We had a favorite pew that we used, and he always sat on my right side. As I walked in the church, I ruefully looked over at the pew where we usually sat, and then walked clear around it to the other side of the church, staying as far away as possible. I couldn't bear to sit near that spot, let along look over at it. The memories were too fresh and it was just too painful. I sat by myself, feeling more alone than ever. I was inconsolable over the void that was created by his absence, which was made all the worse, knowing that I was the cause of it. I kept glancing over to my right side, half expecting him to magically appear. When mass was over, I bolted from the church. In the parking lot, I started my car as tears streamed down my cheeks. Sobbing into handfuls of tissues, I blew my nose and dabbed at my eyes. There would be no lunch together at our favorite restaurant today, or ever, for that matter. I put the car in gear and headed back to the hostel.

There still was no sign of Elliot or his car all day on Sunday. He had now been gone for three days. I came to the conclusion that he left for good. No one said a word about him and I didn't ask. If anyone at the hostel was aware of the attraction between us, nothing was ever said about it. Elliot and I had kept our affection for each other as private as possible. By Sunday, I was convinced that this was for the best. Having to live in close quarters with someone I had feelings for was very difficult, especially after breaking things off with him. The friction between us was palpable, which made for an uncomfortable living arrangement. The hostel wasn't big enough for the both of us; one of us had to go.

I was sure that he had left for good, and I wondered where he had moved to. I thought perhaps he had moved in with his girlfriend. Not having to deal with the situation any longer was a welcome relief. I no longer had to look into rooms or around corners, wondering if I was going to run into him. I could just be myself and not worry about it. I was glad that he had the common sense and decency to bow out.

Later that afternoon, I stood in the courtyard recounting to Ceyda the latest developments in my job hunting. As we spoke, Helen walked out of our room. She looked at Ceyda. "Are you ready?"

Ceyda nodded her head. "Yes, let's go."

I looked at the both of them. They each wore a one piece bathing suit with shorts pulled over the bottom and carried a beach towel in their hands. "Where are you going?" I asked. "To the beach?"

They both laughed in response. Ceyda looked over at me as they walked to the gate. "No, we are going swimming at the Seagull Inn!" she said. "But don't tell anyone!"

I laughed in amusement. "I'm sure no one will even notice. They will just think you are guests there. Have fun!"

And with that, off they went to enjoy a cool dip in the pool of an upscale, oceanfront hotel. Ceyda had been quick to make friends with Helen so that she would have someone to pal around with. I thought that they made a good match; both of them liked to talk a lot, and they both acted in a bold and assertive manner. They would be good company for each other.

A few hours later, when returning from the beach, I stepped off the curb to cross the street when suddenly out of the corner of my eye, I saw a car in the hostel parking lot that looked like Elliot's. I thought to myself that it couldn't be. He had been gone since Friday. That was four days ago! I ran across the street and inconspicuously looked at the car sitting in the parking lot. Then I saw the tell tale sign; hanging from the rear view mirror was a rosary. It was Elliot's car. I couldn't believe it. I had been so relieved that he was gone and now this. How would I ever deal with having to live in such close quarters with someone that I was attracted to? There was no getting away from him. Even if we didn't frequent the same common areas, we would still see each other in passing. Oh, why couldn't he have just stayed away?

Caught up in my internal drama, I didn't notice Patrice leaning out of the half opened office door until I heard her voice. "Lu, come here for a minute!"

I set my beach chair down outside, and walked into the office. "Hi, what's up?"

Patrice stood behind the counter leaning towards me. "I need to talk to you about Aylin."

Surprised, I replied, "What about Aylin?"

A wry smile spread over Patrice's face. "I got a complaint from Helen about her. She said that Aylin is eating in her bed at night and is making noise all hours of the night."

I sighed and shook my head back and forth. "I think Helen is blowing things out of proportion. Aylin does like to stay up late at night and then sleeps in until mid-afternoon, but really, Aylin is very considerate. She tries to keep the noise down."

With a stern voice, she replied, "Well, she shouldn't be eating in bed."

For some reason I found myself defending Aylin. She was a good girl and I felt protective of her. "I think Helen is picking on her. Really, it's not that bad. What does she expect when you're sharing a room with three other people? There's going to be a certain amount of noise from other roommates!"

Patrice nodded her head in agreement. "Yes, but I will still have a talk with her about the food in her bed." Then she quickly changed the subject. "How are you getting along with Helen?"

Nonchalantly, I replied, "Okay. She spends a lot of time with Ceyda, so I don't talk to her much." And I thought to myself, "Which is for the best."

"By the way, how is your job hunting going?"

"Not very well," I replied.

"Would you be interested in a driving job?"

"Sure. What did you have in mind?"

"I am off on Wednesdays when Carlos fills in for me, and I like to go to the casino. Would you be interested in picking up some extra money by driving me there?"

Excited by the prospect of making some money, I replied eagerly, "Sure, just let me know what time you want to leave."

Patrice smiled back, happy to have lined up a personal driver. "Great. You can take me this Wednesday. We will leave here at three o'clock, and then I'll call you when I want you to pick me up. How does that sound?"

"Perfect."

I walked out of the office with a light step, happy at the prospect of making some money to tide me over until I could find a real job. You just never know what might come your way and this was one of those times.

Walking back to my room, my lighthearted feeling quickly evaporated when I suddenly remembered the conversation with Patrice concerning Aylin. I knew that she was going to be hurt and offended by Helen's accusations. And once again, Helen had chosen to go to Patrice first instead of trying to work it out directly with Aylin. Helen's behavior went against the prevailing spirit of community that existed in the hostel, which was an unspoken understanding that you first discussed problems with your roommate before going to a higher authority. Each time Helen did this, she alienated herself from those around her.

Later that night when Aylin came back to the room after Patrice had talked with her, I pointed to Helen's bunk bed. "Some people just aren't very nice, are they?" and I smiled at Aylin.

Aylin smiled back at me and nodded her head. I wanted her to know that I was not the one who had complained, and that I was on her side. Then I whispered, "And don't worry. She won't be here too much longer. She told me she was leaving soon."

Aylin looked visibly relieved.

It would be a relief to see Helen go. She had been nothing but trouble since she arrived. All she did was complain and demand her rights as a roommate. She didn't fit well into group quarters because she didn't possess the give and take qualities that were necessary to make it work. I was relieved one evening earlier in the week when she told me that she would be leaving soon to rent a room from a woman that she did pet sitting for. I was counting the days until she left.

I was exhausted when I climbed into bed that night, so I didn't even bother opening a book to read. It was a relief to just lie in the darkness and try not to think. Helen was already in bed asleep, and Aylin was out somewhere for the night. The room was peaceful and quiet, and I drifted off into a restful sleep, thankful that the day was over.

Loud, obnoxious noises intruded on my peaceful slumber, wrestling me from a deep sleep. I sat up partially resting on my elbow trying to make sense out of the boisterous racket. I listened intently and distinctly heard a few German words. I then realized it was the group of German tourists, a group of young men, who had checked-in the day before. They were obviously partying, acting as if they had the run of the place. Glancing at my clock, I realized it was two-thirty in the morning. As I laid listening to the drunken shenanigans, I debated whether I should get out of bed to ask them to quiet down. I couldn't quite make out where they were sitting at. It wasn't outside my door, but somewhere near enough that their voices carried throughout the hostel. Where was Patrice while all this was going on? Something kept me from going outside to complain, and eventually, I fell back into a fitfull sleep.

The next morning, Aylin's alarm went off at eight o'clock as I laid in bed half asleep, trying to muster up the energy to get out of bed and go for my morning walk. Aylin's bed was right next to mine about three feet away. I watched as she stirred in her sleep, reaching over to shut off her alarm. I was surprised to see her getting up so early. She looked like she was having an even harder time waking up than me. As I watched her, I figured if she got out of bed before I did, then she would get into the bathroom first. The thought of having to wait to get into the bathroom was the push I needed to get myself out of bed and make a dash for it. I wanted to wash up and get dressed to go for my walk. As I came out, Aylin was waiting her turn.

Helen was still asleep in her bunk, so I whispered as quietly as I could, "Go ahead. I'm done. Where are you going so early?"

Aylin scampered across the floor in her bare feet towards the bathroom. "I go to work today."

"Oh, well, have a good day. See you later." With that, I headed out the door on my daily walk.

Aylin was finally starting her job. It seemed like at least a month ago that she told me she was going to start working soon. She was participating in a summer internship program that was offered through the University of Istanbul. From what I could understand from her limited English, she had mentioned something about working at an amusement park operating rides. I was glad to finally see her go to work. It would be good for her to get out and meet some new people. I noticed she spent most of her time at the hostel sleeping. She didn't mix very well with the other guests because of the communication barrier, although, I did see Stuart doing his best to bring her out of her shell. Aylin was an attractive young lady with her long, dark flowing hair, dark eyes, and shy smile. The guys at the hostel were eager to get to know her, but she kept her distance from them. When I first met her, she had told me that she was nineteen years old. I tried to imagine what it must be like to be living in a foreign country at such a tender age, especially when you couldn't even speak the language. I had to admire her courage. She was by herself here, although she kept in touch with another student from her university who was staying in Miami. Still, she didn't know anyone here and had to grapple with the challenges of learning a new language and finding her way around in a new and strange city.

I shut the door quietly so as not to disturb Helen. As I started through the courtyard to go on my walk, I noticed the group of German tourists all lined up outside the office waiting to check-out. They were slumped over their suitcases bleary eyed; serves them right after keeping everyone up half the night, I thought to myself. Most guests were considerate and kept the noise to a minimum at night, but every once in a while, we would get a group of guests that acted like they owned the place and had no consideration for the other guests. They would party all night, leaving empty beer and wine bottles strewn about the property along with dirty dishes piled on the counters and table tops, left for someone else to clean up.

As we had agreed earlier in the week, on Wednesday afternoon I drove Patrice to the casino which was only about a half an hour's drive from the hostel. I pulled up to the entrance to drop off Patrice. Getting out of the car, she reminded me that she would call me later that evening to pick her up.

It was four o'clock when I got back to the hostel. I had just enough time to go for a walk on the beach and to lay out for awhile. Returning from the beach that evening, I finished my dinner and sat outside passing the time until I had to go back and pick up Patrice.

It was dark when I drove back to the casino to pick up Patrice. As the casino came in view, I was dazzled by the splendor of the bright lights that lit up the hotel and casino and the lake in front of it. It looked enticing, and I hoped someday I would get a chance to walk through it, but tonight would not be a good time for that. I would have to come back sometime on my own. I knew Patrice needed to get back to the hostel. Carlos, who was actually her uncle and the owner of the hostel, was filling in for her. Since he lived quite a ways from the hostel, he wanted to leave by ten o'clock to drive home.

Patrice was waiting for me when I pulled up to the front entrance to pick her up. She had a big smile on her face when she got into the car.

"How did you do with the slots?" I asked.

"Great! You wouldn't believe how much luck I had tonight!" Happy with her winnings, Patrice leaned back in her seat relaxed. "I'm hungry after all that excitement. Do you mind going through the drive through on your way back?" she asked.

"No, not at all. Just tell me which one you want to stop at."

On the way back, Patrice motioned to a fast food restaurant, so I pulled in the drive thru to order her food. Patrice held onto her bag of food as we made our way back to the hostel. I could see that she was in a good mood and why shouldn't she be? She had had a good night at the casino, a late night snack in hand, and her own personal driver. Life was good.

And it was about to get better, somewhat, for me. The night was not quite over yet. As I drove winding through traffic, I noticed Patrice looking over at me. "Would you like some other work?" she asked me.

I was surprised at her offer and eager to hear more. "Sure. What kind of work?"

"I need some work done on the upstairs terraces. There is some mold that needs to be scrubbed off the floors and the tracks in the bottom of the sliding glass doors. I'll pay you to do both terraces. What do you think? Do you want the job?"

I liked what I was hearing. "Sure, that would be great. I like doing physical work and working outside. I'll start on it tomorrow. It will probably take me a few days."

"Take as long as you need. It's no hurry. It's something I've been wanting to get done. I may have some other things for you to do, too."

This was working out better than I ever imagined. Now, not only did I have driving jobs, but also some extra jobs around the hostel. I couldn't believe my luck. Patrice seemed to have taken a liking to me and this was a way for us to help each other out.

The rest of the way back to the hostel, I couldn't help but think of the irony in the relationship between Patrice and I. Patrice was a black woman from the Caribbean islands who was now my boss, of sorts. Here I was an educated, white woman picking up odd jobs just to survive on.

The next morning I woke up early. I knew I had to get started on the terraces and doors before it got too hot outside. It didn't take long before the sun became unbearable and the humidity could be suffocating. I happily set about my work for the day. I used buckets of bleach and water and vigorously scrubbed out the mold and mildew the best I could from the middle of the terraces where rain water had collected. I took a screwdriver and scraped the clumps of mold from in between the tracks of the sliding glass doors. I definitely earned my pay with all the scrubbing and scraping that I did. None the less, I took my time and did the best I could.

I completed the job in a few days and Patrice paid me as she had promised. I happily added it to my windfall from my driving job to the casino. I felt blessed to have such luck at getting this extra work. Things were not going well with job hunting and money was getting low. I was beginning to admit to myself that I might have to leave the hostel before long because I could no longer afford to stay here. I even began to think about returning to finish my graduate program despite my difficulties with psychosomatic symptoms. Returning to Ohio would resolve my employment situation and my problems with Elliot. Little did I know what awaited me in a few short days.

Chapter 6

A New Job

They say there is a silver lining in every cloud, and I was about to stumble onto my very own serendipitous silver lining. The storm clouds had been gathering for some time obliterating any hopes of finding gainful employment. The economy was still in a shambles and hiring had come to a complete halt, while businesses were bleeding jobs with a vengeance. I was living day to day without any sure sign of what direction my future would take me.

I stopped going to church, no longer able to bear the thought of going without Elliot. Now when I got up on Sunday mornings, instead of getting ready to go to church, I got dressed and went for my early morning walk. It seemed odd at first not to follow my usual Sunday routine of getting dressed up for church. My heart grieved over not only the loss of going to mass, but also the loss of the spiritual union that I had shared with Elliot. I struggled to erase from my mind all past memories of my Sundays with him.

My roommates were peacefully asleep early Sunday morning as I pulled on a pair of light gray walking shorts and wiggled into a white spandex top. Sitting down on the window sill, I slipped into a pair of tennis shoes and firmly laced them up. While going through my morning routine of washing up and combing my hair, I suddenly stopped and studied my face in the mirror. My darkly tanned face stared back at me with doleful eyes. I blinked back the tears I felt swelling up inside of me, and with grim determination, I set out for my walk.

My usual route took me past the church. I hesitated as I looked up the street, thinking perhaps it would be best to go a different route. Dismissing the idea, I continued on my way. Approaching the church I could see that the nine-thirty mass was in session and the parking lot was full of cars. I quickly glanced over to the tree that Elliot usually parked his car under, half expecting to see his car; it was nowhere to be seen. He had disappeared again for the weekend, leaving on Friday evening as he had done the weekend before. I was certain that he was many miles north in Port St. Lucie.

My paced quickened in an effort to swiftly get past the church. Although it was still morning, already the heat and humidity sapped my strength, and my brisk pace gave way to an easy saunter. Staring straight ahead, I kept my mind busy watching the passing cars as they sped along their way, leaving a trail of noxious fumes that assaulted my nose and mouth. Finally out of sight of the church, I conceded that I would have to find a new route to take on my morning walks. I finished the last remaining stretch of walkway leading back to the hostel. Opening the gate, I breathed a sigh of relief that my walk was finished, and I could now head to the beach. I was eager to escape the anguish from my morning walk to take refuge in the solitude of my seaside sanctuary.

Because it was rainy season, I knew that I needed to get to the beach early before the afternoon rains came. It was already mid-morning. On my way to my room, I saw Patrice stomping through the courtyard in an agitated manner. In place of her usual pleasant expression was a seething scowl. I watched as she forcefully yanked a large bag of garbage from the courtyard trash can, throwing it over her shoulder, then with long, deliberate strides, she headed towards the dumpster in the back of the hostel. It was clear that she was upset about something. I looked around for Lola, but she was nowhere in sight. I shrugged my shoulders and went into my room to change into my bathing suit. Stepping back outside I looked up to see Patrice walking quickly down the steps with another bag of trash in tow from the upstairs kitchen. Her lips were pursed tightly together as if to keep herself from vocalizing her displeasure. Something must have happened with Lola.

Lola worked at the hostel seven days a week. On Sundays she had a light day and only had to clean the kitchens and take out the trash. She was married and had a young daughter about ten years old who she would bring to work with her on occasion. Sundays were family days and I'm sure Lola had more important things to do than cleaning the hostel every Sunday, even if it was just for a few hours. I had never known Lola to miss work, and I was sure things would be back to normal the next day.

Arriving at the beach under a sun that was already scorching hot, I set up my beach chair under the shade of a palm tree. I took a dip in the water to cool off before laying out on my chair to relax. The beach was crowded with weekend visitors. It was mid August and the kids were still out of school. Families came in droves to spend a day at the beach. By one o'clock, ominous, dark clouds started gathering in the sky. I got up quickly and started packing my things together. The last thing I grabbed was my flip flops off of the hot sand. I could run a lot faster in the sand in my bare feet. Just as I got to the street, the rain came down in torrents. I shrieked as the stinging drops of rain battered my skin, and I made a bee line across the street for the hostel. I ran through the gate and the courtyard, going up the steps to the second floor computer room where I set my chair up in its usual rainy day spot in front of the sliding glass door. I stretched out in my lounge chair content to just lay there and listen to the sound of the falling rain.

Monday morning dawned with blue skies and bright sunshine. I looked around the room quickly to see who was still sleeping. Helen now had the bunk next to me where Aylin used to sleep.

Aylin took the bed above Helen's since the air was warmer on the top bunk and Aylin was always cold. Helen's bunk was already made up with the sheets and blanket neatly stretched across the bed. I glanced at the top bunk bed and could see Aylin sound asleep. I figured she must be off from work for the day. I slipped quietly out of bed ready to start my day with a walk on a new route. I planned to walk in the opposite direction of the church, following the sidewalk along the ocean.

I went to the kitchen to grab a quick bite to eat before starting off on my walk when I saw Lola coming out of the kitchen on the other side of the courtyard. I was glad to see that she had come back to work.

I remembered that I wanted to take my camera along on my walk to take some pictures, so I ran back inside my room to retrieve it from my locker. No matter how quiet I tried to be when opening my locker, it never failed to make an annoying screeching noise of metal against metal. I slowly pulled the door open so as not to wake my sleeping roommates and retrieved my camera from the back of my locker. I shut the door as quietly as I could and replaced the lock. With camera in hand, I was looking forward to my morning walk.

As I stepped outside, I was surprised to see Patrice pacing back and forth in front of my doorway. She swung around when she heard the door open.

"Good morning, Patrice!" I said.

Not mincing words, Patrice asked, "Lu, would you like a job?"

And in an instant my life changed.

Taken by surprise, I replied, "What job? What are you talking about?"

"Lola quit. I need someone to clean the hostel. You would need to take out the trash, clean the common areas, and the dorm rooms. Do you want the job?"

Patrice waited for my answer with a look of quiet desperation. I could see that she was in a pinch and didn't have anyone else to turn to for help on such short notice. There was no time to discuss what had happened to Lola.

To me, this unexpected job offer was a blessing. I had never cleaned in a hostel before, but what did that matter? I had done plenty of cleaning at home through the years.

Looking around me, I asked, "Where should I start?"

Patrice pulled a ring full of keys from her pocket. "Here are all the keys to the rooms." She flipped through the keys until she found the one she was looking for. "This one is for the supply closet where all the cleaning supplies are kept. Come here, I'll show you what to use."

I followed her to the supply closet where she unlocked the door and pulled it open. Rummaging through the closet, she pointed out all the cleaning supplies, towels, and rags that I would need. She handed me the large ring of keys that were attached to a large clip. I took hold of the keys and clipped them to the belt on my fanny pack that I always wore around my waist. I usually wore my fanny pack around the hostel; it was easier than lugging a purse around. It made a perfect belt on which to clip my keys.

Patrice handed me a large bottle of bleach cleaner. "The bucket and mop are out back. Just put some of this in the bucket to mop the floors."

After filling up the bucket, I looked around trying to decide what to do first. I noticed that the trash bin was empty in the kitchen. Lola must have started taking out the trash that morning and then something must have happened. I couldn't help but wonder if she got upset at something Patrice had said to her. After all, Lola had missed work the day before.

I decided that I would clean the common areas first, and then do the dorm rooms. I took out all the trash, cleaned up the sinks, and wiped down the counters, microwaves, and stove tops. Then I tackled the sweeping and mopping. Two hours passed before I finally finished the common areas.

My clothes were soaking wet from sweat. The common areas

were all open rooms with no air conditioning. By this time, the midday sun was searing hot and the humidity high enough to cause a drenching sweat while just standing still. I kept drinking gobs of water to replace the water lost from sweating. My face was red and flushed from perspiration. Even my scalp was sweating, causing my hair to stick to the back of my neck and the sides of my face. I leaned over the kitchen sink and splashed some cold water on my face. I was ready to start cleaning the dorm rooms. At least there would be air conditioning in them.

I ran back to the laundry room to get some clean rugs for the rooms. Patrice was in the laundry room loading the washer with an armful of sheets. When I reached into the cupboard, Patrice turned around and looked at the hair plastered to my head with sweat, and then at my clothes soaking wet with perspiration. With some concern, she asked, "Is this too hard for you?"

Worried by the concern in her voice, I felt the need to reassure her. I didn't want her to think I couldn't handle the job.

"Oh, no! I feel fine! I like doing physical work. And besides, working up a sweat is good for me. It's a great work out!" I said as convincingly as possible.

"Okay, if you're sure," she replied somewhat warily. She then turned and pointed to a pile of dirty rags and rugs on the floor. "You need to wash those once a week on Wednesdays. The detergent is here in this cupboard."

"Okay. I just came back to get some clean rugs. I'm just getting started on the rooms."

Patrice glanced at her watch.

"I know that I'm taking longer than Lola," I said apologetically, "but that is to be expected. I'll get faster once I do this for a few days." Not waiting for her reply, I grabbed my rugs and bolted out of the laundry room. I still had a lot of work to do. I had all of the rooms to clean yet. Most of them only needed tidied up, but a few of them needed a complete cleaning since the guests had checked-out.

I made my way to the first dorm room. It was a room like

mine with two sets of bunk beds. Two of the beds had sheets on them, and the other two were stripped. I didn't need to do anything with the beds themselves. Guests at the hostel were responsible for making their own beds, or they could leave them in a rumpled mess if they so desired. My job was to clean the bathroom, and sweep and mop the floor. Not having to deal with making the beds or changing the towels saved a lot of the time. Mopping the floor in some rooms was easier than others. Most guests were fairly neat and didn't have anything on the floor around their beds. Others had bags, clothing, shoes, food, and drinks stacked around and under their beds. I just mopped around their belongings, being careful not to disturb anything.

I finished the dorm rooms on the first floor, and then grabbed my cleaning supplies and hauled them up the steps to the second floor. One by one I worked my way down the row of rooms until I arrived at Elliot's dorm room. I hesitated outside his door. It was midday and I knew he wouldn't be in his room. He usually left early in the morning, and didn't return until late afternoon when he came back to take his nap before dinner. I knocked on the door and shouted "housekeeping!" as I put the key in the lock and turned the door knob to open the door. The room was quiet and dark. Two bunk beds were set up against the wall on the right side of the room. Nigel was asleep in the top bunk nearest the door. He usually never made an appearance until mid-afternoon, preferring to sleep in after staying up late at night. I tiptoed into the room carrying my cleaning supplies and walked across the floor towards the bathroom on the opposite end of the room. As I passed by the bottom of the second bunk bed, I noticed a pair of burgundy pajamas lying neatly folded on the bed. I recognized the pajamas as the ones that Elliot had worn the morning he woke up late for church. I momentarily paused at a bedside table which was strewn with an assortment of papers and books. I recognized a small stack of the blue La Pieta prayer books like the one that Elliot had given me. Beside them was a stack of index cards rubber stamped with a religious website that

Elliot liked to hand out to people. I felt like I was spying on him, so I quickly turned away and went to clean the bathroom. I felt a bit uncomfortable cleaning his room. My worst fear was that he would come back during the day when I was there. I wondered what he would think about my new job. I was relieved when I was finally done with his room. Nigel was still asleep in his bunk as I backed out of the room, shutting the door behind me.

I finished the remaining dorm rooms and lugged all the cleaning supplies back downstairs to put them away. Finally, I was done. I looked at my watch. It was three o'clock. It had taken me almost five hours to clean the hostel. Patrice told me earlier that Lola cleaned it in three hours.

I went to my room and peeled off my sweaty clothes. I was exhausted from all the manual labor. The only exercise I was used to was a two mile morning walk. Physical exercise was important to me and I had exercised often through the years doing aerobics and weights. Now that I was getting older, I preferred to just take walks.

Cleaning the hostel was the best workout I had in a long time and the best part about it was that I got paid for working out. I always thought that it was unfortunate so many of us pay to go to health clubs to work out when we could just as well find jobs that require physical exertion. After working so hard, I was famished. It is surprising how much better food tastes after hours of manual labor. My simple lunch consisting of brown rice, fish, and vegetables tasted like a feast. Even relaxing at the beach afterwards was more enjoyable. I took a dip in the tepid sea water and let the water massage my aching muscles. Walking back to my lounge chair, the sun's rays melted the tension from my body. As I laid back in my lounge chair, a delicious sleepiness crept over me, and I promptly fell asleep in the shade of a palm tree. Even after a nap, that night I fell into a deep, dreamless sleep.

My second day of cleaning went much better. I knew where everything was at, and I started to develop my own system of the best way to go about cleaning the hostel. The only thing Patrice needed to tell me was which rooms needed tidied up and which ones required a complete cleaning after the guests checked-out of the room.

In the morning as I carried the trash down from the second floor, I looked up and saw Lola going into the office. I wondered if she was coming back for her job. I hoped not. I liked doing the cleaning, and until something better came along, at least I had work. I was sure I would find out soon from Patrice what was going on.

In the afternoon as I made my way to the second floor to clean, Ceyda passed by me on her way out. "Lu, you must know what you are doing. You look like you've been doing this for years!"

I laughed at her comment and continued hauling my mop and bucket up the steps. After my cleaning was done for the day, I stopped by the office for my pay. As Patrice handed my pay to me, she said, "Lola wants to come back to her job. I told her to take a few weeks off and then we'll see what happens. I think she just needs to get away from here for awhile."

With a sigh of relief, I nodded in agreement. Patrice had come up with a perfect solution: Lola got two weeks of vacation to give her a break from the place, and I got two weeks' worth of work which I desperately needed. Again, I couldn't believe my luck.

My days took on new purpose as I got up every morning to do the cleaning. I was working seven days a week. I didn't mind working every day since I finished in the early afternoon and had the rest of the day to myself. On Sundays, I had a light day with just cleaning the common areas and the dorm rooms for new arrivals.

My days fell into a routine that I found enjoyable. I loved working at a job where I wasn't sitting behind a desk all day. I spent a good part of my day working outside cleaning the terraces and courtyard. One morning after it had rained overnight, I grabbed a broom to sweep the large puddles of water from the middle of each of the terraces. With long strokes, I swept the water with the broom towards the drainage pipe. Little by little, the puddle got smaller and smaller. I looked up at the bright blue sky; there wasn't a cloud in sight. It was early morning and the air was fresh. I inhaled deeply, filling my lungs with the salty sea air. The birds flitted around happily at the start of a brand new day. For a moment I stopped what I was doing to take it all in. And as I did so, a little voice inside of me began to make itself known. I heard the first whispers from my heart of how nice it would be to work here permanently.

My mind snapped to attention at the sudden realization of what I was feeling. Could this really be possible that I wanted to work here? Being of an analytical nature, I started to scrutinize the idea. I liked living at the hostel. More importantly, I liked working here. But my mind was not convinced. I was a college graduate. Is this what I went back to school for? To be a cleaning lady in a hostel? This was insane. What was I thinking? I kept going back to how I felt: I liked the idea of working on my own and doing physical work. My mind shot back with the rebuttal that I was an intellectual person and this would not be challenging enough for me. As I mechanically went about my cleaning, my heart and my mind continued to do battle; two opposing forces parlaying arguments back and forth. I had not yet learned the true significance of listening to my heart over my head. That would come later.

Meanwhile, I worked hard at my job. I am a perfectionist and I always strive to do more than is expected of me. I soon found out that my efforts didn't go unnoticed. One afternoon as I swept the courtyard sidewalk Patrice walked by and with a big smile on her face she said, "This is just perfect. Everything is soooooo perfect!"

I was happy to have my boss's approval. I liked Patrice and wanted to please her. I worked really hard to do the best job I could. Even the guests noticed how hard I worked. A few days after I started cleaning, Ceyda complimented me on the cleanliness of the microwave oven, pointing out that she didn't think it had ever been cleaned before. And that was how I worked. I did the extra things that made a difference. It took me longer to clean, but I wanted to do a thorough job. It gave me a good feeling inside to know that my efforts were appreciated by Patrice and the guests.

Patrice was so pleased with my work that she asked me if I would be interested in working in the office to fill in for her when she went on vacation. Her girlfriend, Madeline, was coming to visit for two weeks in December, and then Patrice planned to go to Denmark for two months the following summer to visit her. If I decided to go back to graduate school, Patrice even offered to fly me down to Fort Lauderdale during my school breaks to fill in for her. I was definitely interested in doing so. But more importantly, the little voice in my heart was getting louder every day. It was beginning to drown out any objections that my mind would throw its way. I was beginning to admit to myself that I really did want to work here permanently. I just wasn't sure how to tell Patrice since she planned on having Lola come back in a few weeks. I felt a growing sense of urgency to speak to her about this. I just needed to wait until the right time.

I wasn't the only one starting a new job. Nathan finally got a call that he passed his drug test, and he started driving truck for a frozen food company. Nathan had an extremely early schedule. He had to get up to go to work at three o'clock in the morning, and he finished in the early afternoon about the time that I was done with my cleaning.

Now that Nathan had to get up so early, I noticed a change in his schedule. He no longer stayed up late at night drinking beer with the other guys. He would have a few beers after work and retire to bed at nine o'clock at night. Nathan worked mostly through the week with the weekends off. Then he would have time to stay up late and party with Stuart and Dwayne and whoever else happened to be at the hostel.

Ceyda was getting ready to return to New Jersey after a

month's stay. She had enjoyed herself so much that she was already planning to come back for another month over the winter. Since she lived alone, the hostel with its ever present flow of guests was a nice change of pace for her. Ceyda was extremely garrulous and some of the guests were irritated at her constant chatter. The day she left, I imagined her talking nonstop the whole way home. The hostel was a much quieter place without Ceyda. But I must say that I did miss her when she left. When I felt like talking, I always knew that Ceyda would be fair game and we could talk for hours. She never lacked for something to say.

    Aside from cleaning his room, I didn't see much of Elliot at this point. The only time I saw him was in the evenings when he came down to watch TV for a few hours. I would sit outside the TV room at my outdoor desk, reading the paper or surfing the internet. I didn't even care to acknowledge him when he passed by me on his way in the door, preferring to just ignore him instead. Since we couldn't have a relationship, I thought I could just cut him completely out of my life by ignoring him. He continued to leave on the weekends disappearing for two or three days. I assumed he was with his girlfriend and tried not to notice. But even though I wouldn't admit it to myself, I did notice, and each time he left, his absence created a void that tugged at my heart. When he was at the hostel, as much as I tried, I couldn't escape the sound of his voice or the sight of his bulky frame with his slow, deliberate gait as he made his way to and from his room. Still, I did my best to cut him out of my life and out of my thoughts.

    One afternoon, Patrice asked me to pull weeds around the aloe vera plants in the courtyard. On my knees, I was hunched over the plants diligently trying to yank the weeds out by the roots. Engrossed in my work, I suddenly heard footsteps. I glanced up to see Elliot walking right in front of where I was working. I averted his gaze and went back to pulling the weeds with a new found vigor. I hadn't expected to see him this time of day, and I had been taken off guard. From the corner of my eye, I looked at his feet as he passed by. The silence between us was deafening. Words that needed to be spoken were willfully repressed. I took solace in pulling the weeds while trying to console my aching heart with the knowledge that I probably wouldn't be here that much longer anyways.

As much as I wanted to get away from Elliot, I knew that if I did have to leave the hostel, I was really going to miss the guests. I was especially fond of Aylin. We had been roommates for almost two months, and I looked after her like she was my daughter. She was staying at the hostel until October. Now that she was working, she was on a regular schedule getting up early in the mornings and returning in the late afternoons. I noticed a marked improvement with her English once she started working. Gradually as the weeks went by, she was communicating more and more with me and the other guests in the hostel. Stuart, in particular, had taken a liking to Aylin and every chance he got he would tease her about her English until she would break out into a hearty laugh. With Stuart's help, she was coming out of her shell. I began to see the two of them sitting together in the TV room, or out in the courtyard at the picnic table talking and laughing. I think Stuart did more for international relations than most U.S. ambassadors.

Aylin started to talk to me more often, asking questions about the United States. One evening as we sat in our little corner outside our room, she asked me where Los Angeles was located. I ran to my car and dug out a map of the United States and gave it to her. She unfolded the map and I pointed out the state of California and the location of Los Angeles. For a long time afterwards, she sat holding the map in front of her with a studious look on her face. When she tried to give it back to me, I told her to keep it. She smiled back at me with gratitude.

Aylin also started cooking at the hostel. I have no idea what she ate before. She kept bags of snacks by her bed, but I never saw her eat a full meal until one evening when she was deep frying breaded cauliflower. She had the electric burner on high and had walked out of the kitchen for a few minutes. As soon as I entered the room, I smelled something burning, and I could see a smoky haze billowing from the frying pan. I ran over to the stove and set the burner at a lower temperature. Looking at the cauliflower, I could see that the underside was burnt. Minutes later Aylin came back into the kitchen, and I showed her how to adjust the settings for the burner. Grateful for my help, she smiled sweetly at me, and I left her to finish her cooking.

The days flew by at an alarming rate. Each morning it was a joy to get up and work around the hostel, but there was a heaviness in my heart at the thought that my days were numbered. I became more and more preoccupied with my desire to stay and work at the hostel. My heart was winning the battle.

One morning while the air was still cool enough to work outside, I went to pull weeds from along the side of the hostel where I could work in the shade. A few of the rooms on this side of the hostel had back doors that opened up onto a narrow strip of concrete that ran along one side of the hostel. Long ago abandoned flower beds now teeming with prodigious weeds ran along the wall separating the hostel from the property next door. I tugged at the weeds using both hands pulling out large fistfuls of green shoots at a time. My mind drifted as I worked. I didn't want to go back to school. I liked it here and prayed to God that there was some way that I could stay. I knew I had to do something soon about this situation. I finished weeding and gathered up my tools to put them away. I entered the back door of the kitchen as Patrice was pulling a plastic basket overflowing with sheets to the laundry room.

"Good morning, Patrice." I said as I walked by her to the supply closet.

Patrice answered with a stifled yawn. "Good morning." She was not a morning person and had trouble getting started in the mornings.

"Oh, I wanted to talk to you about something," I said. I

finished putting the tools in the closet and walked over to where she stood near the doorway. "You know, I wanted to tell you that if Lola doesn't come back to work here, I would consider taking this job permanently."

A look of surprise flashed across her face as my words sunk in. Then smiling broadly, she replied, "Reeeeally!?"

My spirits were lifted by the unbridled excitement in her voice. Maybe there was hope for me staying here after all.

"Yes, I know you said she was coming back after a few weeks' vacation, but I love working here so much that I wanted you to know that, instead of going back to school, I would consider staying here."

Patrice gave me a thoughtful look. She said, "Let me think about this and get back to you later today." Then she tipped back the laundry basket on its wheels and continued on her way to the laundry.

"Okay." I said with a smile as she went through the back door. I reached into the closet and grabbed the cleaning basket to start on my daily rounds. Walking to the back of the hostel where my bucket and mop were kept, I grinned to myself. She said she would think about it. That meant that I stood a chance. Buoyed with the hopes of working something out with Patrice, I felt a new sense of vigor as I zipped through the hostel going about my daily duties. The sun seemed brighter, the sky bluer, and the air fresher than usual. I could imagine myself doing this every day. I never wanted to leave here.

I couldn't imagine a better place to work. I was footsteps from the ocean and close to shopping and the downtown area. Each day presented the possibility of meeting new guests from some far off land. There was always someone interesting to talk to and it was gratifying to see guests from many different countries sitting around together and conversing as if old friends. I especially enjoyed all the company at the hostel after living a lonely life by myself for so long. I couldn't think of a better place to live. Still, I tried not to get my hopes up too high in case things didn't go the way I wanted them to.

I finished my cleaning and, as usual, changed into my bathing suit to eat my lunch. It was still too early to go to the beach, so I walked down to the corner to get the newspaper. Getting back to the hostel, I went out back and pulled up a chair under the shade of a palm tree. I was caught up in reading when I looked up to see Patrice coming out of the back door towards me. I lowered the newspaper and laid it in my lap. I wondered if she was coming to talk to me about the job.

She walked over to where I sat and stopped in front of my chair with a serious look on her face. She propped one of her feet up on a short brick wall in front of her and leaned over, resting an elbow on her elevated leg. In a business-like manner, she said, "I've thought this over and this is what I can offer you - your current pay, plus your room in the dorm. I talked to Lola and she is alright with it because she has picked up some other cleaning jobs for now."

I couldn't believe my ears. I was getting paid, plus a place to stay! I never imagined I could be so lucky. This was music to my ears. I jumped up from my chair throwing the paper to the ground. "Yes, I'll do it! Here, give me a hug!"

Patrice looked at me in surprise. She seemed a little embarrassed at my request, but she seemed resigned to oblige me.

I took a few steps towards her and wrapped my arms around her and gave her an enthusiastic squeeze. "Thank you. You have made my day. I just love working here so much, and I can't believe I get to stay!"

After all my worries and frets about finding a job, I finally had one. Now I knew that I could stay in Fort Lauderdale. It was such a relief to know that I didn't have to go back to Ohio. I could start thinking of Fort Lauderdale again as my home. I was ecstatic. I never imagined that I could be so happy to have a job cleaning.

I was beginning to change my way of thinking about my

career choices. Why couldn't I work this job as long as it suited me and then move on to something else once it all played out? I had had numerous jobs in my life and found it difficult to stay for any length of time in one job. I always got bored and wanted to try something new. Our culture encourages job stability whereas I seemed to thrive on instability. I wanted to work at something that suited me. Wasn't this a better way; a better existence? I just got a job that was part-time with no benefits, but my rent was paid, and I would have enough money to live on. I didn't have to drive my car to work every day. All I had to do was roll out of bed, put on my clothes, and go out my door to work. I was happy as a clam to have a job at the hostel and I didn't care if I had to clean toilets. To me, I was living in paradise.

Chapter 7

Let's Be Friends

Flush with excitement from my new job, I cleaned with unrestrained exuberance. Nothing was off limits. Donning a pair of latex clothes, I started with the appliances in the kitchens. I cleaned the stove tops, replacing the tattered aluminum foil that lined the burner pans. Next I tackled the ovens, spraying each one with a liberal coat of oven cleaner and then letting them set for a few hours while I cleaned out the refrigerators. I rooted through the refrigerators, tossing out long forgotten bags of now mold infested foods some of which were unrecognizable. I delighted in throwing out old containers of condiments, salad dressings, jellies and jams, margarine, and almost empty soda pop and water bottles. I stuffed long forgotten half eaten sandwiches and leftovers into large garbage bags. Determinedly I dug through each shelf until I reached the back of the refrigerator which had not seen the light of day for some time. To my satisfaction, the mound of trash bags grew higher and higher. Then in a stroke of victory, I pulled them all out back and dumped them into the trash hopper. Next, I pulled everything out of the cupboards, tossing out old boxes of rice, spaghetti, noodles, and spices. I washed out the cupboards and the silverware drawers wiping up mouse droppings and dead cockroaches.

Early the next morning as I started my daily cleaning rounds,

I had an unexpected visit from Dwayne. As I mopped the floor of the downstairs kitchen, I suddenly heard Dwayne's voice as he called my name. I turned around to see him standing inside the doorway of the TV lounge with his hands on his hips. He had a stern, agitated look on his face. In a confrontational tone, he asked, "Lu, did you throw away those jars of jam that were in the upstairs refrigerator?"

"Well, yes, I cleaned out the refrigerators yesterday, but I checked the expiration dates before I threw anything out." I looked at him in disbelief. Everything I had thrown out was outdated. I never imagined anyone was eating it.

"What about my brown paper bag with sugar in it?"

I opened the refrigerator door and pulled the bag of sugar from the shelf on the door and handed it to him. "It's right here."

He grabbed the bag of sugar out of my hand and abruptly turned and walked out of the room, leaving me to stew over what had just occurred. It seemed that I had inadvertently discarded some of the leftovers that he relied on for food. As I replayed the scene in my mind, I began to see another side of Dwayne. We had gotten along well together often sitting in the courtyard talking for hours. I realized that I had been fooled by his easy going, friendly manner. I was beginning to learn that some of the guests were not who they appeared to be. It was painfully clear to me now that he was a mooch. He still didn't have a job, and from what I could see, he had no intention of looking for one. I had never seen him bring food into the hostel, only twelve packs of beer that he carried in hoisted over his shoulder. On a few occasions, he had complained to me about other guests stealing his food. I jokingly told him he should put a note on his food that said: 'Warning: This Food Is Radioactive' so that no one would dare take it. After his angry outburst, I had to wonder exactly what he considered as 'his food.' I suspected he was checking the refrigerators for leftovers which he then claimed for his own. Taking other guests' food was grounds for getting kicked out of the hostel. The incident upset me, and I thought it best to bring this to Patrice's attention. Little did I realize it at the time, but my relationship with Dwayne would take an even more menacing turn.

I finished my cleaning for the day and went to the office to speak with Patrice. The office door was closed. Patrice didn't always stay in the office, preferring sometimes to work out of her room which was conveniently located right next door. There was a bell on the office door that the guests could ring to summon her to the office. I walked up to the office door and rang the door bell. I stood back as the sound of the chimes echoed through the hostel. Instantly I turned to see Patrice's door inch open as she popped out from around the backside of the door to see who was there.

"Hi, do you have a few minutes?" I asked.

She replied, "Sure, let me get my keys," then disappeared back into her room returning a few moments later with keys in hand.

We stepped into the cool air conditioned office. It felt good to get out of the hot, humid air. Patrice went around the counter and sat in her office chair. I leaned on the counter as I described to her the incident with Dwayne. She listened with a bemused expression on her face.

"Lu, you can always tell who is stealing food. It is the guests that you never see bringing bags of groceries into the hostel."

"I never thought of that. Come to think of it, I've seen Dwayne bringing in beer, but never any bags of food. He must be eating the food that guests have left behind. I am upset about his belligerent attitude towards me when I was just doing my job."

"Lu, let me tell you something. There are two kinds of people that I have the most problems with running this hostel: black people and Americans who come here trying to use the hostel like it was their apartment." With one hand she reached over and ran her fingers along the top of her other arm. "Look, I am black, but I can tell you that I've had a lot of black people come here that caused trouble because they have a chip on their shoulder."

I listened to her in silence, surprised at her forthrightness. When she mentioned the problem with Americans, I unintentionally tapped the floor with the tip of my toe as I thought of my pile of belongings stashed in my room since I had first arrived here.

I didn't want to cause any problems for Dwayne, but I felt better knowing that Patrice was aware of the situation. Up until this time, Dwayne had always treated my kindly, but that was when we were both guests. Now I was in a different position. Although I stilled lived in the same dorm room as I had since arriving, I was now an employee. I was beginning to see that this was going to change the dynamics of my relationships with the guests.

Thinking our conversation was over, I stepped away from the counter towards the door. Seeing that I was about to make an exit, Patrice held up her hand and said, "Wait, there is something that I need to talk to you about."

I turned back around to face her. "Yes, what is it?"

"Here, these are some additional jobs that I want you to start doing which will give you some extra hours."

With an appreciative nod, I reached over and took the piece of paper from her hand. "Thank you!" was all I could manage to utter. I glanced down in a daze to read what she had scrawled on the paper. The duties that she added included sweeping the terraces, parking lots, courtyard, and back lot; cleaning Carlos's office along with weeding the entire property and putting the trash out for pick up on Wednesday evenings. I was already doing many of the things that she had listed. I looked up at her and said, "Sure, this is fine. I'll be glad to take care of all of this."

"Good. Don't forget, you need to clean Carlos's office on Mondays." The phone rang and Patrice reached over to answer it, dismissing me with a wave of her hand as she did so.

I took the hint and went out the door floating on cloud nine. To have gone through so much turmoil and insecurity with job hunting and to now have such luck was almost more than I could comprehend. I felt that I was going to burst with happiness. I was learning that if you gave life a chance and took risks, it could lead to things that you never could have imagined in your wildest dreams.

That afternoon as I ate my lunch, I started to add some of my own ideas to the list of duties that she had given me. For starters, I wanted to wash a few of the shower curtains each week on a rotating basis. I also thought that the shower stalls, tubs, and sinks should be scoured out with cleanser once a week. I started sketching out a form to type up on my computer, listing the days of the week and all the duties that needed to be performed on the corresponding days. I was starting to give a structure and organization to the job that didn't exist before I came along.

That evening I sat at my outdoor office desk, typing up the forms. I included everything on the list that she had given me along with the tasks I had added. I printed out the forms and made copies for Patrice so that she would have a record of exactly what I was doing each day. The next day I handed her the stack of forms and went over each day's tasks with her. She seemed pleased with my efforts. It was important to me to feel that I was doing everything I could to earn my keep. The next day I started using my new forms. I felt a great sense of satisfaction as I put a checkmark in the corresponding box beside each task as I completed it.

That evening Patrice stopped by my room to give me some avocados that she had bought at the store that day. I could tell that she wanted to show her appreciation for all of my hard work. Her small gesture meant a lot to me, and I felt that we were off to an auspicious start on a good working relationship.

Everything was going exceedingly well with my work life, but my personal life was in shambles. As much as I tried to ignore Elliot, I couldn't seem to get him out of my head. I thought about him day and night. The sound of his voice set off an inner tempest of emotions of an unfulfilled longing. I was hopelessly attracted to him, and there was no way for me to get away from the source of my agony. As time went on, I began to notice that the situation with Elliot was affecting my relations with the other guests. I became sullen and withdrawn, no longer caring to sit outside in the evenings to chat away the hours. Instead, I sought out a deserted corner of the hostel to wallow in grief over a lost love that could have been. After about a week of feeling this way, I knew I had to do something to shake myself out of this. I was beginning to relent to the idea of being just friends with him, although, there were signs that he, too, wanted more than this.

At times I thought perhaps I was making more out of the situation than there was, but I couldn't help but notice that Elliot often parked his car right next to mine. I didn't use my car very often except to go to the store. He was in and out every day. There were enough parking spaces in the front of the building and on the side that he had his choice of parking spaces. I found it peculiar that he usually chose to park next to my car.

Then there was the matter of our groceries in the refrigerator. Seeing how much I liked ice tea, Elliot had started buying gallon jugs of ice tea that he kept in the downstairs refrigerator. I would open the refrigerator door to find Elliot's jug of tea nestled between my two bags of groceries that I kept on the bottom shelf. Since I had just cleaned out the refrigerator, there was plenty of room on the other shelves. I couldn't help but wonder what Freud would make of it.

Picking up these subtle cues, I had a hunch that Elliot would probably be receptive to my overtures of friendship. I just couldn't bear this deadlock any longer. It was difficult for me to swallow my pride and accept that I couldn't have a relationship with him on my terms. Weary from my emotional turmoil, I decided it was best to apologize to him so that we would at least be on speaking terms and could develop our friendship. I was willing to wager that, in time, it might lead to something more. I felt that it was best to give Elliot the freedom to make up his own mind whether or not he wanted to pursue a relationship with me and to let him make the first move. This was difficult for me to do since it is my nature to be assertive, but I knew in my heart that it was the only way. I would have to take a chance knowing full well that he may or may not decide to become more than just friends with me. I finally was able to come to terms with this and to willingly accept the outcome.

I hadn't yet told my family about my feelings for Elliot not wanting them to know that I was interested in a man who was involved with another woman. On a number of occasions, my thoughts drifted back to the conversation I had with my oldest daughter, Laura, over the Christmas holiday when she had predicted I would meet someone soon. She had accurately foretold that I would meet someone with darker skin who was from another country. The only part that was different was that she predicted he was in a hospital. Hospital . . . hostel, I couldn't deny the similarities in the words and that they were both comprised of beds. On one of my weekend calls to her, I finally decided to confide in her. I told her all about Elliot. Then I just had to ask her, "Laura, exactly what did you see that made you think he was in a hospital?"

Laura replied, "Well, I don't see things. I feel them."

"Oh, well then, what made you say hospital? Did you pick up on that he was in a place with a lot of beds, because hostels and hospitals both have beds?"

"Sorry, mom, I know I'm not being a lot of help, but I'm just not sure why I said hospital."

"Well, maybe it's not even him. I guess time will tell."

I made up my mind to apologize to Elliot the first chance I got. I even rehearsed what I was going to say to him. All I had to do was to wait for the opportune time to speak with him. That was easier said than done. At times the hostel would be completely deserted, but Elliot was nowhere in sight. Often when he was there, other guests would be sitting with him or standing nearby.

One morning as I was walking into the upstairs kitchen to mop the floor, I ran into a guest, named Bryan, who I had seen around lately, but didn't know very well. He was a young man in his mid-twenties originally from Pennsylvania who was staying at the hostel while he looked for work. Bryan was tall and lanky with shoulder length blonde hair. When he walked, he swung his arms wildly back and forth as if they helped to propel him forward. He was soft spoken with a quiet, easy manner. His light blue eyes were set in a long face with a firm jaw. He had an air about him that alluded to a troublesome upbringing. As I mopped, Bryan sat quietly in his chair looking down at his folded hands. I was surprised to hear him say, "Lu, you probably don't, but would you have a quarter I could have?"

I was startled by his request since he had hardly ever spoken to me. I had gone to get a newspaper earlier and had some change in my fanny pack, but for some reason I replied, "No. I'm sorry, but I don't have any change on me." And I kept mopping the floor. I always had a difficult time with people asking me for money. I was raised with a strong sense of self-reliance. I would never have the nerve to ask someone I didn't know for money, even a quarter. If I didn't have it, then I would do without. For days afterwards, every time I thought about Bryan asking me for a quarter, I felt horrible about myself and still do. For all I knew, he needed a lousy quarter for bus fare to look for work, and I didn't even have the decency to help him out.

Usually I would have the hostel all to myself until Nathan came home from work. His timing got to being annoying after awhile, since about the time I was ready to bake my chicken or fish, he would show up with one of his frozen pizzas to bake. I often found myself racing to the oven to get to use it first.

Frozen pizzas were an unexpected perk that came with Nathan's new job. He would arrive at the hostel after work with his outstretched arms stacked high with boxes of frozen pizzas, egg rolls, and cinnamon sticks that were passed their expiration date and couldn't be sold in stores, but were still good enough to eat. He filled the freezers in each of the kitchens and shared them with the other guests.

The guests in the hostel were very appreciative of Nathan's bounty. A lot of them were young people who were on a very limited budget. Having this extra food, free of cost, was a gift from heaven. They ate pizzas for breakfast, lunch, dinner, and late night snacks. This was true for the long-term guests as well as the foreign university students who were there for only a night or two. This extra stock of food went a long way towards alleviating the problem of guests' food disappearing. There had been numerous complaints through the summer of food and drinks, especially beer, disappearing from the shared refrigerators.

Everyone at the hostel was responsible for doing their own dishes. If anyone got caught leaving dirty dishes in the sinks, it was cause for immediate removal. Most guests complied with this rule, but there were always a few who felt they didn't have to do their dishes, leaving them for someone else to do. Lola never did the dishes when she cleaned, but I would do them as long as I felt I wasn't being taken advantage of. But after a while, someone began to leave more and more dishes in one of the kitchen sinks. I put a note on the sink politely asking the culprit to obey the rules and do their dishes. This went on for a couple of days. As I mopped the floor in the kitchen, Dwayne came out of his dorm room. He walked into to the kitchen and looked at the dirty dishes in the sink.

"Hey, Lu, aren't you going to do these dishes? They've been sitting here for days."

"No, I am not supposed to do the dishes."

Sarcastically, he replied, "Really . . . are they just going to sit in this sink from now on? The guests that dirtied them left days ago."

Since my first altercation with Dwayne over cleaning out the refrigerator, I had kept my interactions with him very brief and to the point.

"Dwayne, I will discuss this with Patrice."

Dissatisfied with my reply, huffily he retorted, "I'll go and talk to her myself about this. You should be washing those dishes!" And with that he took off for the office. I shrugged my shoulders and finished mopping the floor. I was sure I would hear from Patrice about this later.

I finished mopping the common rooms on the second floor when all of the sudden I heard Patrice calling my name. I walked out to the railing and shouted down to her. "I'm up here!"

She had money clutched in her hand and was waving it back and forth. "Will you go pick up my lunch?"

I ran down the steps. "Sure, where do I need to go?"

She handed me a hundred dollar bill and a business card of a Caribbean restaurant over in Lauderhill Mall.

As I took the money, I asked, "Do you want me to go now?"

"Yes, just pick up my stuff and get out of there - quick."

I knew what she meant. I had accidentally taken the wrong bus one time and ended up at Lauderhill Mall where, for once in my life, I knew what it felt like to be in the minority. Everyone on the bus and at the mall was black. Not that I minded being around black people, actually I enjoyed it. I liked cultural diversity and, to me, skin color was no different than people having different eye colors, but I was aware of the crime in the area and had no desire to get mugged.

Curious to know if Dwayne had spoken with Patrice, I asked, "By the way, did Dwayne talk to you about the dirty dishes in the kitchen?"

Patrice replied, "Yes, but I will handle it. I'll ask around and find out who is leaving their dishes in the sink. If it is him, someone will tell me."

"Okay. I never thought about asking the other guests."

I took off my latex gloves to retrieve my keys out of my fanny pack. I looked at my watch. It was already half past one. Walking out to my car, I felt slightly annoyed. It would take a good hour to get to the restaurant and back during this time of day. I could have been done cleaning by then. Not only that, I was a mess. I was sweating profusely, as usual, and my clothes and my hair were soaking wet. I was embarrassed to be going into a restaurant looking like this. On the other hand, it was nice to be able to take a break in the middle of the day and go for a drive. I decided to make the best of it and enjoy running my errand. I cranked up the air conditioner in my car and turned on the radio.

I got back to the hostel an hour later and promptly knocked on Patrice's door, holding her bag of food out to her when she opened the door. When I handed her the change, she fished out a twenty dollar bill and handed it back to me. We both smiled at each other, pleased with our respective bounty: she had her ethnic food, and I just made some extra cash. I went back to cleaning the hostel. Later Patrice came out and handed me a meat pie covered in a light paper wrapper. "Here, try this." I was always eager to sample ethnic food. I carefully unwrapped the meat pie and pulled it out of the wrapper. It was the size of a small sandwich in a half moon shape with a flaky golden crust crimped at the edges. As I bit into it, I found that it was filled with a spicy meat. I finished it off, savoring the delicate crust and the spicy filling.

That evening as I sat outside to relax and read the paper, I noticed Patrice and Elliot sitting at the picnic table in the courtyard talking together in hushed tones. I had seen them talking a number of times in the office and the courtyard. They appeared to be confiding in each other about something, but I couldn't imagine what it could be. If I approached them to ask Patrice a question, they would abruptly stop talking. I even began wonder if they were talking about me. It would be some time before I would know the topic of their conversation and an even longer time before I knew the full implications of it.

Elliot finished speaking with Patrice and got up to go into the TV lounge. He passed by me looking straight ahead as I sat at my outdoor table writing a card to my cousin Gene. Nathan was in the kitchen baking pizzas for dinner. Elliot and Nathan sat talking while the pizza was in the oven. I started to write out my card, but I didn't know what the date was. I found that I lost track of the date while working at the hostel. I knew what month it was and the day of the week, but it just didn't matter to me what the actual date was. Nathan pulled the pizza out of the oven and sliced it into pieces offering one to Elliot.

As I chewed on the end of my pen trying to remember the date, I was surprised to suddenly hear Elliot's voice call out my name. "Lu, would you like a piece of pizza?"

Astonished, I turned to look at him through the window. "No thank you. I already ate my salad."

I turned back around and looked down at the card opened up in front of me. Suddenly, I felt an urge to reciprocate with a question of my own. I looked back at him again through the window. "Uh, Elliot, do you know what the date is?"

He reached into his pocket and pulled out his cell phone to look for the date. I thought I felt the earth shift slightly beneath my feet. For the first time in weeks, Elliot and I finally spoke to each other. It would only be a matter of time before I made my concession speech to him.

The opportunity presented itself the very next morning. As I stood in the courtyard examining the calluses forming on the palms of my hands from mopping floors, I looked up to see Elliot making his way down the flight of steps. I looked around me quickly. No one was in sight. This was my chance. I felt the distinct flutter of butterflies in my stomach.

I stood waiting for him at the bottom of the steps. As he reached the last step, I asked, "Elliot, can I talk to you for a minute?"

He looked at me in surprise and replied, "Yes, of course."

I motioned towards the TV room. "Let's go in there." I stepped just inside the door and once again, like actors in a play, we found ourselves on our familiar stage, acting out the next scene in our relationship. I turned to face him. He looked at me expectantly, eager to hear what I had to say.

In a shaky voice, I said, "I just want to apologize for my

behavior. I am sorry I hurt you and hope you can forgive me." As a goodwill gesture, I extended my hand towards him. "I hope that we can be friends," I said as I held my breath, waiting for his response.

"Yes, that's beautiful! Thank you. Of course we can be friends." Elliot grabbed my hand enthusiastically and squeezed it. He seemed happy with my overtures of friendship, and I was relieved that our impasse was finally at an end. He was on his way out, and I had cleaning to do, so we wished each other a good day and went about our business. As I watched him walk towards the gate, my heart did a little hop, skip, and jump of joy.

The 2008 Summer Olympics had started in Beijing, China, and the guests started to gather each night to watch the coverage on TV. We each had our favorite events, and we would periodically check in to see which ones were on for the night. I liked watching the gymnastics and the diving. Elliot seemed to enjoy all of it and sat each evening in the TV lounge watching that night's coverage. I started to join him, sitting for awhile beside him and commenting on the performances.

Saturday evening as we watched the girls' beach volleyball coverage, I asked him if I could go to church with him the next day. I was a bit nervous about asking him. I remembered how upset he had been with me when I stopped going to church with him. The spiritual growth I had experienced in our brief relationship was important to me, and I hoped that we could rekindle this once more. When I asked him, his reply was somewhat curt, but he didn't let me down. He agreed to meet me for mass in the morning. A few minutes later, he excused himself, saying that he had some things to take care of. I continued watching the coverage for a little while longer and then decided to run down to the corner convenience store to buy some ice. I walked up the steps to Elliot's dorm to ask him if he needed anything from the store. As I got to the top of the steps, I saw him standing in the computer room, waiting to use the computer.

I stood in the doorway. "Elliot, I'm going to store for some ice. Do you need anything?"

He walked over towards me with a serious look on his face. "Lu, I was just thinking . . ."

There was something about the way he said this that made my heart suddenly lurch. He looked down at the floor absorbed in thought, as if he was carefully planning what it was that he wanted to say. I waited in silence, as if my life hung in the balance. I had an uneasy feeling that this had something to do about my earlier request to accompany him to church. The thought crossed my mind that he might have had a change of heart and didn't want me to go with him after all. He must have seen the apprehension in my eyes and thought better of it. He suddenly reached into his back pocket and pulled out his wallet. Handing me some money, he said, "Would you get me a large cola slushy?"

The next morning, I got up early and took out all of the trash and shut off the night lights. Sundays were my light cleaning days, so I only had a few hours of work to do. With the trash out of the way, all I had to do after church was clean up the kitchen and TV lounges and perhaps a dorm room or two, if needed. I was excited at the prospect of getting dressed up and going to church again with Elliot. There was a spring in my step as I quietly went about getting dressed. I went out into the TV lounge to dry my hair so as not to wake my sleeping roommates. Going back into the bathroom, I styled my hair and put on my makeup. Stepping back, I gave myself a once over in the mirror with an appraising look. My large, wide eyes fringed with long, lush eyelashes set in a darkly tanned face stared back at me. A coat of shimmering bronze lipstick glistened on my full, pouty lips. An almost imperceptible touch of blush on my golden cheeks completed the desired effect. I stepped back from the mirror to get a better look at my outfit which consisted of a black skirt and a colorful floral blouse that was dainty and feminine. Satisfied at my appearance, I slipped on a pair of black dress sandals and went outside to eagerly wait for Elliot to descend the stairs to go to church. At the appointed time, he emerged from his room. Walking down the stairs to greet me, he stopped at the bottom. He looked at me and said, "I've asked Nathan to come to church with us. He will be right out."

My heart sunk. The vision of having Elliot all to myself quickly evaporated in the early morning sun. I plastered a smile on my face and said, "Oh, that's nice. I'm glad to hear that Nathan is going to church." Somehow I had the feeling that Elliot didn't want to go to church with me alone. I felt that in his own way, he was punishing me for my past indiscretions. Nathan finally made an appearance, looking a little shaky. He had been up late partying and had a hangover. At church, we made our way to our regular pew where I sat between Elliot and Nathan who reeked of alcohol. As the time for communion approached, Elliot leaned over and whispered in my ear to tell Nathan that he couldn't go to communion because he wasn't Catholic. Elliot was a strict traditionalist and followed the rules of the church to the letter. Personally, I didn't see anything wrong with Nathan going to communion. After all, we are all children of God, regardless of what church we belong to. I shook my head 'no' to Elliot and said, "I'm sorry, but I can't tell him that." Elliot then reached over and tapped Nathan on the shoulder to tell him himself. Nathan sat out communion.

Mass was over and we went back to the car. Elliot offered to take us out for breakfast at a nearby diner. I liked Nathan, but I wanted Elliot's undivided attention and resented that I had to share him with Nathan. At the restaurant, the waitress led us to a booth, and I wondered for an instant whether I should sit with Elliot or Nathan. I slipped into the booth and Elliot sat down beside me. We ordered breakfast and started talking about the Olympics. We finished eating, and Nathan and I waited by the door as Elliot went to the register to pay the bill. He had offered to take us out to eat, so neither Nathan nor I thought to offer to help with the bill. Although we were some distance from the register, I suddenly looked up to see Elliot leaning over the counter with a pen in his hand scratching something off of the bill. I could clearly hear the waitress's voice as she said, "If you had a problem with your food, you should have said something when you were served!" She deducted the item from the bill anyways, and as Elliot paid her, I heard him say, "It's no problem." As we left the restaurant, I acted as if I hadn't heard their exchange of words at the cash register. Later after getting back to the hostel, I had a strong urge to go back to the diner to talk to the waitress to find out exactly what had happened. There wasn't anything wrong with our food, and we had eaten everything that we were served. I ignored my impulse to go back, and in a fit of denial, swept it under the proverbial rug.

As soon as we returned to the hostel, I changed into a pair of shorts, tank top, and tennis shoes and went back to cleaning. There had been a lot of partying the night before since it was a Saturday night and the kitchens were a mess. The upstairs kitchen was in the worst shape. Pots of food were still on the stove and there was a sink full of dishes. I thought to myself that the cockroaches and mice had had a feast in this kitchen last night. Since it was my light day, I decided to do the dishes in the sink, but I left the pots on the stove, thinking perhaps the guests would get the hint to clean up after themselves. Everyone was informed of the rules when they checked into the hostel, and for those who had a lapse of memory, there were signs posted in each of the kitchens in large lettering that read, "Please wash your dishes. Failure to do so will result in immediate removal from the hostel." I left the kitchen and didn't think anymore about it for the rest of the day, confident that the problem would be taken care of when I returned to work the next day.

On Monday morning when I went to clean, I was greeted with the sight of one remaining pot still sitting on the upstairs stove half full of rice with a spoon handle sticking out of the middle of it like an iron post set in concrete. After two days of sitting in the heat, the rice was a discolored blob of goo. A stack of dirty dishes strewn with pieces of leftover food towered above the top of the sink. Emitting a deep sigh, I shook my head in disgust. Returning to the kitchen awhile later, I tackled the mountain of dishes, washing them in hot, sudsy water. Turning a blind eye, I shunned the pot of putrid rice like a disgraced outcast, leaving it to sulk on the burner. I moved the tables and chairs against the wall and started mopping the floor. Engrossed in moving the heavy mop back and forth across the floor, I was suddenly startled by the sound of a man's voice. I turned around to find Dwayne standing by the stove.

He looked at the pot of rice and then at me. "Aren't you going to clean up this pot of rice? It's been sitting here for two days now." Dwayne was making it a habit to check up on my work as I cleaned. Before I started this job, I never saw Dwayne until early evening. Now he started making regular appearances early in the day. It seemed he had nothing better to do.

Pushing the mop under a table to wipe up some spilled wine, I averted Dwayne's gaze as I replied, "Yes, Dwayne, I realize that. But the guests know they are supposed to clean up after themselves."

In a gruff voice, he retorted, "Yeah, well they're not." Then he abruptly turned and left the room. I stopped mopping and leaned on the mop handle, deep in thought. I was beginning to get very agitated with his negative attitude towards me; for him to treat me so rudely completely perplexed me. He seemed to get some sort of perverted pleasure from finding fault with my work. My mind flashed back to a time when I first started cleaning. Dwayne had stopped to ask me how I was doing with my new job. It was a hot and humid day, and I was drenched in sweat from mopping the floors. As we talked, he looked me up and down from head to toe, and said, "You're a mess!" Perhaps I made him feel inadequate or guilty because I worked so hard. Dwayne had no desire to work. He was trying to cut me down to assuage his own insecurities. I tried not to let it bother me and went back to mopping the floor. But that was not to be the end of the rice fiasco.

The next morning, I walked up the steps slowly to the second floor kitchen in no hurry to discover the status of the pot of rice. I stepped through the doorway of the kitchen and immediately I glanced at the stove top. The pot was gone. There was not a dirty pan or dish in sight. Cheered by my propitious discovery, I walked over to empty the trash can. Not many of the guests had used the kitchen the night before, so the bag was only half full. As I pulled it out of the trash can, something caught my eye in the bottom of the can. I leaned over to get a better look. To my dismay, dumped squarely in the corner of the can was a clump of rice in the shape of the pot it had been ejected from. I stepped back in surprise and looked at the trash can. Before I pulled the trash bag out, it had been securely tied at the corner to keep it in place. It slowly dawned on me that someone had purposely taken out the trash bag and dumped the rice on the bottom so that I would not only have to scrape the rice out, but would also have to wash the trash can. My thoughts immediately went to Dwayne. He must have come back into the kitchen the previous day after I finished cleaning to commit this malicious deed. I picked up the trash can and took it downstairs to the back of the hostel to clean it out. All the while, I mulled over what I should do about this latest transgression. I rinsed out the can with the hose and set it in the sun to dry. Wiping off my hands, I walked to the office to find Patrice. I had had enough of Dwayne's antics.

I peeked through the window of the office to see if Patrice was there. She was sitting at her desk, engrossed in some paperwork.

I opened the door with determination and walked in the office. "Patrice, you are not going to believe what someone just did in the upstairs kitchen!"

Patrice listened intently as I filled her in about the pot of rice.

"Patrice, I think Dwayne did this."

She replied cautiously, "Are you suuuure?"

"No, I will never know for sure. But he came into the kitchen twice over the last few days when I was cleaning and was getting on me about the pot of rice on the stove. Did you ever find out if he was the person leaving the dirty dishes in the downstairs kitchen?"

"Yes, I asked a few of the guests, and they said they saw him leaving dirty dishes in the sink. I had a little talk with him about it."

It all made sense now. Patrice had reprimanded him about his dirty dishes, and he knew that I was the one who brought the problem to Patrice's attention. Now he blamed me for getting him into trouble. I was at the end of my rope with Dwayne.

"Patrice, I have always liked Dwayne as a friend. We used to sit together and talk for hours when I first came here. I don't know what his problem is lately. He has complained about the old food I threw away when I cleaned the refrigerators, the dirty dishes, and now this pot of rice. He seems to have it out for me. I am trying to get along with him."

Patrice didn't say a word, but I saw a subtle flicker of conviction flash across her face, as if she had just made up her mind about something. Our conversation over, I turned to go out the door to get back to work. It would be a few days before I would come to know just what she had made her mind up about.

As I walked out the office door, the man from the exterminator company was coming through the gate on his monthly rounds to spray for rodents and insects. I greeted him cheerfully as I told him I would unlock the doors to all the rooms while he started spraying in the common areas. I went from room to room, knocking on the doors to alert the guests.

The only guest that I found in his room was Jerome, a young African-American man in his late teens. When I told him that his room was getting sprayed, he quietly replied that he would go up to the computer room for awhile. Jerome had been staying with us for a few weeks. He had a private room which was unusual for someone his age. Jerome had a slight build and was always dressed in a neatly pressed short sleeved shirt and long pants. His kinky hair was cropped closely to his head, and he wore a pair of wire framed glasses that gave him a studious look. Quiet spoken and polite, he mostly kept to himself, passing the time by reading a book or working on the computer. I never saw him sitting and talking with the other guests or drinking alcohol. When I cleaned his room, I was amazed at how neat he kept everything. His bathroom counter was a model for neatness. His shaving cream, deodorant, and cologne were neatly lined up against the back of the counter. In the middle of the counter, he had three razors lined up at an angle, all evenly spaced apart. His shoes and slippers were placed in a row under his bed, and his clothes folded and put away or hung in the closet. Nothing was out of place. I always looked forward to cleaning his room because I knew that I would find it neat and orderly, which made my job easier.

That evening, Elliot and I sat side-by-side as we ate our dinner while watching the Olympics in the TV lounge. As we ate, Elliot must have had business on his mind because he started to tell me a little bit about his work. I had no idea what Elliot did when he disappeared all day. He appeared to have money to live on, so I assumed that he was doing some type of work through the day, although, there was that incident concerning our bill at the diner the previous Sunday.

"You know, I have an office not too far from here for my mortgage loan company. I pay them a set rate every month for an office that has everything I need. They have phones, computers, a fax machine, copy machine, and even a conference room that I can use. I'll have to show you where it is sometime."

Nodding my head as I took this all in, I said, "Oh, what exactly do you do?"

"I help people get loans from banks, and then I make a percentage from what they finance."

"How's that going for you with the economy is such bad shape? I hear that banks aren't doing much lending right now."

He shrugged his shoulders and nonchalantly replied, "Not too bad. I have a few things in the works."

Not wanting to get too personal, I didn't inquire any further about his business dealings.

I had firmly resolved to keep all conversation with him on an impersonal level so as not to overstep my boundaries. I did want to resume praying the rosary with him, so I asked him if I could join him that evening. He wholeheartedly agreed, and told me to meet him upstairs at half past nine. Later that evening, we prayed for about an hour. The night was warm with barely a hint of a breeze. I always found it difficult to go inside on such a sultry evening. I thought it best not to linger after we finished, thinking perhaps it wise to take things slowly. I was having a hard time adjusting to our new relationship, and I wasn't quite sure how I should act around him. In the past when he spoke to me, he often reached over and would touch my arm. Now he never touched me. We sat side by side, but I felt we were miles apart.

Our rosary finished, I unzipped my rosary case, carefully tucking my rosary inside and zipped it back up. Elliot leaned his head on the back of the chair and sighed. I looked over at him. He seemed preoccupied with something, and I wondered if it had something to do with me.

I asked, "Is everything okay?"

"Yes, I was just thinking about when I lived in Lexington, Virginia."

Curious to hear more, I asked, "How long ago did you live there?"

"I lived there for ten years, but I left almost five years' ago."

"What on earth made you move to Virginia? I'm surprised that you would want to live in the north, where it is cold in the winter."

"I was sent there along with a number of other families by a prophet. It is in the 'safe area' that will be protected by the angels in the upcoming nuclear holocaust. I will go back there someday to live again. I have a map of the 'safe area.' Let me go get it and I will show you."

Elliot stood up and left to go to his room. While he was gone,

I thought to myself about how much progress we had made in a single day in getting to know each other. Elliot seemed eager to confide in me about things that were on his mind. Maybe this friendship thing wasn't so bad after all. Still, it bothered me that he was careful never to touch me. When he came back, he motioned for me to come into the computer room where there was some light. I watched as he unfolded the map and placed it on the round plastic table in the corner of the room. Leaning over, he pointed to an area on the map in the shape of a triangle that was formed from three points consisting of the cities: Cambridge, Ohio; Altoona, Pennsylvania; and Lexington, Virginia. This area was one of three safe areas in the United States to be protected by angels in the upcoming nuclear war. Elliot chose Lexington because it was the southern-most point, and therefore, likely to not be as cold during the winter.

He pulled a pen and a small notebook out of his pocket. He opened the tablet to write something down. "Here, let me give you the website of the prophet so you can read about him."

He finished writing the website down and tore the sheet from the notebook handing it to me.

I glanced at the scribbled handwriting on the paper and then folded it in half and stuffed it in my back pocket. Trying to sound convincing, I said, "Oh, sure. I would really like to read about him." I was trying my best to mask the skepticism I felt about what he had just told me. I had read about prophets in the Bible, but I had no idea that any existed in the present time. I thought it was rather bizarre that a prophet, in this day and age, would send people to live somewhere. I found it even more bizarre that people would actually uproot their families and move them to where they were told to go. One of the reasons I was attracted to Elliot was because of his deep religious faith, but his devoutness had a cult-like inclination that I felt a little uneasy about.

Lying in bed that night propped up on my pillow, I kept trying to get interested in a book I was reading, but my thoughts kept drifting back to Elliot. I wondered where things would lead with us. It was clear from our conversation that evening that Elliot was much deeper into our religion than I was. In fact, he was downright fanatical. To me, being a good Catholic was going to church on Sundays and saying my prayers. I wondered who this man was and why God brought us together. I believed that God brought people into our lives for a purpose; usually to teach us something. I felt there was some significance to our relationship. I was so caught up in my thoughts that at first I didn't notice a faint offensive odor. I wiggled my nose and sniffed a couple of times. It smelled like urine. I thought perhaps it was coming from the bathroom. Too tired to get out of bed to investigate, I put away my book and fell asleep.

The next afternoon after I finished cleaning, two new roommates from Switzerland arrived. I was in my room changing my clothes when they came in. They introduced themselves and quickly set about making their beds. As they tucked and pulled their sheets across their mattresses, one of them stopped and said, "Do you smell urine?" I was surprised at how well they spoke English.

They both climbed off their beds and started to walk around to locate the source of the odor. I crossed the room to join them in their search. It didn't take long for us to determine that it was coming from the mattress on the top bunk against the wall; it was Aylin's bed. She obviously had wet the bed. I examined some clothing draped over the railing at the foot of her bed. They also smelled of urine. She must have washed them out in water and hung them there to dry. The girls looked at me and nodded in agreement. "I will speak to Aylin about this," I said. "She needs to wash her clothes in detergent. And I will have Patrice change this mattress."

It was out of character for Aylin to pee the bed. I had been her roommate for two months, and she never had done anything like this before. Lately, I noticed that she was hanging around with a young man named Makalo, from Trinidad, who had recently been staying at the hostel. He liked to party and flirt with all the girls. He especially liked Aylin. One evening he had confided in me that he liked her, but complained that she was a "good girl." He then tried to flirt with me. I was old enough to be his mother, and I shooed him away. In the days that followed, I noticed that Aylin started staying out late at night with him and then would sleep until mid-afternoon, not bothering to get up to go to work. I wondered if he had given her alcohol or drugs that had caused her to pass out and urinate in her sleep. I went to get Patrice and we removed Aylin's mattress, replacing it with one from another room. I didn't say anything to Patrice about my suspicions, deciding to keep them to myself. I already had enough problems dealing with Dwayne. I didn't need someone else upset with me.

 The next day while taking out the trash, I couldn't help but notice that the dishes were done in all of the kitchens. Evidently Patrice had gotten after the guests to make sure they cleaned up after themselves. As I went to take out the trash from the upstairs kitchen, I found a little gray squirrel rooting around inside the trash bin. When it saw me, it scampered out of the trash can and ran across the room, stopping suddenly in the doorway to look back at me in a sulky manner for disturbing its quest for breakfast. It was a small gray squirrel with a thin wispy tail. I had seen it around the hostel a number of times scampering through the common areas and climbing on the palm trees in the back of the building. Some of the guests would give it bits of their food, and it was tame enough to eat out of their hands. One morning, I saw the squirrel in the courtyard under the shade of a leafy plant eating a whole piece of white bread. It sat back on its hunches, clutching the bread on each side with its front paws. I was amused at its almost human-like appearance, as it nibbled daintily at the top of the piece of bread.

 When I went to clean one of the downstairs TV rooms, I noticed a stack of black baggage in the corner near the door. Not thinking too much about it, I wondered if a new guest had arrived. Check-in time wasn't until noon, and if a guest came in before their room was ready, they would store their luggage in a common area until they could get into their room. Later that morning, I saw Dwayne walking out of the TV room towards the gate with a black bag in each hand. Puzzled at first by his actions, it suddenly dawned on me that he must be leaving. Going about my work, I kept my distance as he took his remaining bags out to the waiting taxi in the parking lot. Later that afternoon, when I walked by a group of guests sitting in the courtyard, I overheard one of them say that Dwayne had gotten kicked out of the hostel. I silently walked past them, acting oblivious to their chatter. I was relieved that he was gone, but I was also a little sad for how things ended between us.

That afternoon I stopped in the office to give Patrice a list of cleaning supplies that I needed. Handing her the list, I said, "I hear Dwayne got kicked out of the hostel."

She looked up from reading the list and simply said, "He is not a nice person."

I gave her a slight nod of agreement and walked out the door to go to the beach. Not having been to the beach for a number of days due to stormy weather, I was stunned by the dramatically altered beach. It was the height of hurricane season and a number of hurricanes had passed by us, churning up the sea. Even now, a stiff wind and rough waves pounded the shoreline. Looking out over the water as far as my eyes could see, were cascading rows of white caps in the choppy water. Merciless waves had carved out a cliff of sand, running down the middle of the beach, leaving a two to three foot drop off to the ocean. Angry seas had spewed out large mounds of tousled seaweed at the bottom of the sandy cliffs. In bare feet, I slid on my heels down the steep embankment of sand and tiptoed carefully over the tufts of seaweed making my way to the rough water. The high waves and strong undercurrent prevented me from going out very far. When I turned around to go back, a powerful wave pushed me down, and I went sprawling on my hands and knees. I quickly hopped back over the mound of seaweed and up the sandy embankment, to take refuge on an undisturbed strip of beach further back on the shoreline.

That evening, in what was now our nightly routine, Elliot and I met up together in the TV room to watch the Olympics. It was still early, and we were the only ones in the room. During the commercial break, Elliot turned to me and said, "I hear Dwayne got kicked out of the hostel today. I can't believe that he had to leave because of dirty dishes!"

I thought I detected an accusatory tone in the sound of his voice. Word must have gotten around the hostel that I had something to do with this.

I replied nonchalantly, "Everyone has to pull their own weight around here. If you don't obey the rules, then you have to leave."

He gave me a disagreeable look and went back to watching the TV. I wasn't in the position to discuss it further with him. Now that I was an employee, I had to watch what I said to the guests because of the issue of confidentiality. Being in this new position was taking a little getting used to. I was still friendly with all the guests, but I kept a little distance from them, preferring not to gossip or talk about anything that was going on in the hostel.

It was a peculiar situation to live and work in the same place. I was never really off duty. Even the guests had a difficult time drawing the line between when I was working and when I wasn't. One evening, Nathan had complained to me that there wasn't any dish detergent in the upstairs kitchen. I knew I had filled it earlier in the day. Even though I wasn't working, I went to get my key to the supply closet and took some upstairs. It was just one of the little inconveniences of living and working in the same place. But the advantages far outweighed the disadvantages.

Chapter 8

Lovers

No two days were ever the same at the hostel. Anything could happen through the course of the day. One morning as I went to mop the walkway outside the kitchen, I was surprised to see Patrice standing outside Jerome's room with the door wide open. Curious to find out what was going on, I set my mop down and walked over to her.

Patrice motioned for me to go into the room. "What do you think, Lu? It smells like something died in there."

I stepped inside the room and, immediately, a putrid stench filled my nostrils. "Phew!" I said, "What is that smell?" I walked around the room, trying to determine exactly where the smell was coming from.

Patrice replied, "I think a rat must have eaten some poison from the traps and died in the wall somewhere."

I tried standing in different parts of the room, but the smell was the same everywhere I stood. I turned to Patrice and said, "What can we do about the smell?"

Patrice shrugged and replied, "Not much. Carlos has some strong air freshener that he is going to spray in the room. The smell will eventually go away in about a week. I will have to move Jerome to another private room."

That afternoon Jerome gathered up his belongings and moved

into his new room. On my way to the office, I noticed that he had the door wide open, and as I walked by, I could see him inside stacking a pile of books on his night stand. I walked over and stood in the doorway to his room.

"Jerome, how do you like your new room?"

Distracted by my voice, he stopped what he was doing. "I like it. It smells much better in here, and I like the bigger bed." Jerome's room had the only queen-sized bed in the hostel. All of the other rooms had twin beds.

Pointing to his books, I said, "It looks like you enjoy reading."

"Yes, I do. I want to finish these books before my classes start. I won't have time to read then. I'm staying here until I move into my dorm room at my university next week."

Wanting to learn more about him, I asked, "What is your major?"

His face beamed with pride as he replied, "Political Science."

"I've always enjoyed that subject," I exclaimed. "I'm a news junkie and I like to follow politics. I can't wait until the general election this year. Well, I better get back to work and let you finish getting settled into your room." Jerome smiled at me as I turned to go.

Clouds were building in the sky, and it looked like a storm was coming at any time. I wanted to finish my outside cleaning before the rain began. I heard Patrice's voice calling after me, as I started up the stairs weighed down by the heavy mop bucket.

"Lu, can you pick up my lunch?"

"Yes, just let me take this upstairs and then I'll go." I grumbled to myself as I plopped the bucket in the corner of the computer room. I was slightly irritated at her request. I didn't mind going to pick up her lunch on occasion, but this was becoming an almost daily event and it was cutting into my cleaning time. So much for getting done before the rain started. Oh, well, it would be an extra twenty dollars in my pocket.

I ran back down the stairs and went to find Patrice in the office. She was standing at the counter waiting for me.

Slightly out of breath, I said, "Okay. I'm ready to go."

As I tucked the money Patrice had handed me for her lunch into my fanny pack, she said, "Lu, I wanted to tell you that I'm getting complaints about Sam stealing food. You need to keep an eye on him."

Sam had been staying at the hostel for about a week. Although in his early twenties, with his short stature and crew cut, he looked like an adolescent. He was constantly in motion, running from room to room in the hostel, getting in peoples' faces. After overhearing some of his conversations with the other guests, I didn't think he fit in very well. He was loud and obnoxious with an abrasive manner that came across as being confrontational. He didn't have a car, but rode a bicycle everywhere. He was a bit of a misfit that seemed to drift from one part of the state to another, staying in hostels.

I was curious if Patrice had noticed Sam's behavior. "Patrice, have you heard how he talks to the other guests? He is rude to them and then laughs it off like it was a joke. I don't think he's doing this intentionally. Maybe it's just how he talks, but he rubs people the wrong way when he talks like that."

Patrice gave me a quizzical look. "No, I haven't noticed that."

I knew Patrice well enough to know that she would check on this for herself by inquiring into the matter with the other guests. I wasn't surprised to hear that Sam was suspected of stealing food. Nathan's supply of frozen pizzas had run out, so it was open season on the guests' food. From what I could tell, Sam didn't have a job, or if he did, it was odd jobs that he picked up on the side.

One of my job duties was to observe guests' behavior. It wasn't a new duty that I could add to my neatly typed up list of duties, but something that I had to keep in mind. At first, I found that I had to remind myself that I was supposed to keep an eye on Sam. In time, this would become second nature, and I would become quite adept at it.

With Sam's arrival in early September, I began to notice a

change in the type of guests staying at the hostel. Summer season was winding down, and the flush of European students turned into a trickle as many of them returned home to spend time with their families before classes started. This left somewhat of a void that was filled by locals who came to the hostel looking for cheap lodging. Many of them paid a weekly rate with the intention of living there as long as possible. For a nominal fee by Fort Lauderdale standards, a guest could get a shared room with a bed and a bathroom. The common areas had cable TV and there was free wireless internet for guests with laptops although this new influx of guests didn't come equipped with laptops; they couldn't afford them. They were misfits ranging in age from late teens to senior citizens; mostly men, but also some women, who didn't have steady jobs or were on disability. Many of them drank in excess and reeked of alcohol. They couldn't afford an apartment on their own and most did not own a car. The hostel offered an affordable alternative and it was located right on the bus route. The only stipulation in staying there was to follow the rules and not cause any problems. At one time, a guest was required to have a passport to stay at the hostel, but that was no longer a requirement.

 Thankfully, Patrice had ordered food from a nearby restaurant, so it didn't take me long to pick it up and get back to work. I was beginning to notice a pattern in Patrice's eating habits. She would find a restaurant that she liked and then would order food from there for days at a time until she got tired of it and wanted to try something different. Still, I didn't like having to stop what I was doing to go pick up her lunch, even though I got paid extra for it.

 The storm blew in just as I finished my work. The rain came down in torrents, soaking my already sweat-drenched clothing as I threw the rags into the laundry room. I stepped outside to relish the cool drops of rain pelting my flushed skin while deeply inhaling the fresh scent of rain. A haze of misty steam rose from the hot pavement. A sudden flash of lightening swiftly followed by a loud crack of thunder sent me running for cover.

I made a dash for my room where I peeled off my wet clothing, showered, and changed into a nightgown. This was a perfect afternoon to curl up in bed with a good book. My roommates were all out for the day, so I had the room to myself. I climbed into bed, pulling the covers up around me, feeling snug and dry. Reaching under my bed, I pulled out a book I had been reading. The steady patter of rain against the window above my head was lulling me to sleep. My eyelids grew heavy as I struggled in a futile effort to focus on the words in front of me. Finally I surrendered to a peaceful slumber as the book slipped from my hands, falling to my chest.

The next day while cleaning, I found myself talking to the squirrel that made a regular appearance at the hostel looking for food. The squirrel was friendly and remarkably tame. I ran into my room and dug out a package of almonds that I kept on hand for a snack. When I went to lay the nuts on the ground, the squirrel came right up to me in an attempt to eat from my hand. Afraid of being bitten or scratched, I quickly laid the almonds down in front of it. The squirrel grabbed an almond with its two front paws and sat back on its hunches to eat it. Looking at the squirrel's belly, I could tell she just had a litter and was nursing. I decided that since she was going to be a part of our family, she needed a name. As I watched her finish off the small stack of almonds, I tried to think one. I always loved the names of the starlets from the golden era in movies. For some reason, the name Greta Garbo came to mind. As I said the name, "Greta" she looked up at me with her big, round eyes. I thought the name suited her well.

While I was sweeping the courtyard, I looked up to see Patrice walking towards me, clutching something in her hand.

"Lu, here's your paycheck."

Laughing, I took the check from her and said, "Oh! . . . I'm having so much fun working here that I forget that I get paid for this!"

Hostel by the Sea

"Someday you can run this hostel for me. I want to retire in five years, and I'm going to live over there!" she said as she pointed at the towering condo building across the street.

Frowning, I replied, "Ugh! Why would you want to live in that big box? You'd be way up in the air, cut off from everything. Look at all those windows and not one of them is open!"

"Ohhhh, but it is sooooo beautiful inside."

"When you move in there, then I will come see how beautiful it is. But I still think it is like living in a big box."

I looked across the street at the upscale condo building that sat on the beach. I had heard from some locals that it was very pricey. People paid millions of dollars to live there and the tenants included some well-known celebrities. I just looked at Patrice. I couldn't believe what she was telling me. First, she was buying the hostel, and now, she wanted to buy a beachside condo. I couldn't understand where she was getting her money from. I knew that she had run the hostel for a few years for her Uncle Carlos, but how much money could she have saved from working here? She didn't dress like she had a lot of money. She didn't even have a car. But every time I went to pick up her lunch, she usually handed me a hundred dollar bill. It crossed my mind that perhaps she came from a family with money. It didn't seem appropriate for me to ask her, so I just stared back at her in surprise. She wasn't done just yet.

Turning back to face me, she said, "Would you like to start working in the office on Wednesdays for me? That is my day off, and Carlos fills in for me. He usually stays until about ten o'clock at night, but then he doesn't get home until late because he lives quite a ways from here. I can work the office until you finish cleaning, and then you can take over for me. I will pay you extra for it. Do you want to think about it?"

Practically jumping up and down with glee, I said, "I don't have to think about it! I would love to work for you on Wednesdays. When do you want me to start?"

"Well, let me talk to Carlos. I think perhaps it will be next week, but I need to check with him first. I will let you know."

"I can start this Wednesday, if you want me to," I said eagerly.

"We'll see. I will need to show you a few things in the office. I can do that one day this week after you're done cleaning." The sound of the doorbell chimes filled the courtyard as Patrice finished speaking. A new guest had arrived, and Patrice walked away to open the gate.

I went back to my sweeping. Patrice didn't get much time off. The hostel office was open seven days a week from early morning until late at night. I don't know how she managed to work such long hours with only one day off a week. I could help relieve some of her burden by working in the office. Since I had worked in a hotel before, I knew how to take reservations and check-in guests. I liked having variety in my work. In a large hotel, the division of labor is more compartmentalized, whereas, in a small property like the hostel, employees had to wear many hats and that suited me just fine.

I sailed through the rest of my work, and for once, Patrice didn't ask me to pick up her lunch. I showered and changed into clean clothes. That particular afternoon, I wanted to go to the library to get some new books to read, but I also had something else in mind. As much as I loved living and working at the hostel, it was my whole world, and I felt the need to branch out a bit. I wanted to start volunteering to teach in the library's adult English as a Second Language (ESL) class. Walking into the library lobby, I noticed an ESL poster off to the side. I walked over and scanned the poster. To my delight, in the corner of the poster in small print I saw a notice for volunteers on Tuesday and Wednesday evenings. Wednesdays were out because I would soon be working for Patrice in the office, but Tuesdays would be a good night for me.

Time passed quickly as I wandered from floor to floor browsing through the prodigious collection of books neatly arrayed on seemingly endless rows of shelving. Looking at my watch, I realized that it was almost dinner time. Satisfied with my selection of books, I made my way to the counter to check them out. I needed to get back to the hostel to get ready to pray the rosary with Elliot later that evening.

On my way to the kitchen to make my salad, I caught Sam unawares. The refrigerator door was open and he was stooped down, rummaging through packages of food. When I walked in the room, he promptly stopped what he was doing, shut the refrigerator door, and then walked out of the room. He didn't even look at me when he passed by. I found his actions very suspicious, and I didn't like the looks of it.

That evening, Elliot didn't show up at his usual time to watch TV and eat dinner. I kept myself busy reading the news on my laptop. When I looked up from my reading, I was surprised to discover that dusk had settled in. I glanced at my watch. It was almost half past eight and there was still no sign of Elliot. I put my computer away and walked through the courtyard to peek out into the parking lot. His car was in the front parking lot, right where it had been when I had returned from the library hours earlier. Worried about him, I decided to knock on his door. This was not like him to stay in his room all evening. I ran up the steps and breathlessly came to a stop at the foot of the door to his room. I rapped sharply on the door a couple of times and waited. No answer. I tried again and waited a few more seconds. Just as I turned to walk away, the door opened and Elliot stuck out his head, looking half asleep and wearing his pajamas.

I started to laugh at the sight of him and said, "Hi, are you okay? I was worried about you."

Looking somewhat startled, he replied, "I'm fine. I didn't sleep very well last night, so I was taking a nap."

"Oh, I'm sorry I woke you up. I just wondered if we are praying the rosary tonight?"

He glanced down at his watch. "I didn't realize I slept so late. Thanks for waking me up. I'll meet you on the terrace in an hour."

"Okay. I'll see you then." I walked back down the stairs.

A warm, salty sea breeze caressed us as we sat on the terrace to pray. A full moon hung in the sky, suspended like a luminous pendant between the top floors of the towering condo buildings across the street. As we prayed, out of the corner of my eye, I stole furtive glimpses of Elliot as he sat with his head bowed reverently, his fingers nimbly moving from one tiny bead to the next, working their way through the rosary strewn across his lap. I was mesmerized by his demeanor. Steadfast in his faith; he was a rock. Spellbound by the moonlit night, we lingered afterwards not yet ready to relinquish this enchanting ambience. Elliot was wide awake now and in the mood to talk. I was learning that he liked to reminisce after we finished our prayers.

Looking at me with a sideways glance, he said, "I would like to start a prayer group here when I get my apartment. I had a prayer group when I lived in Virginia. Once a week everyone from my group would come over to pray. Some of them didn't like how I prayed and after a while, one by one, they stopped coming over until, eventually, I was the only one left. They said I was a fanatic."

He stopped talking, lost in thought. I didn't know what to say. I felt a surge of pity for him. He was very devout and I admired him for that. Finally, I said, "Why did they think you were a fanatic?"

Taking a deep breath, he replied, "I had a certain way that I thought everyone should pray. Not everyone agreed with me. You have to understand that when the prophet sent us there, he wanted us to change the church."

I wondered to myself how you can change the Catholic Church. I had been to masses in different Catholic Churches, and they all followed the same format. Finally, I asked, "Change the church how?"

"We changed it to the more traditional mass. They didn't even have benches to kneel on. Some of the things I wanted to change, they didn't do. I still believe that you should kneel when you receive communion."

"Oh, I never noticed. I'm always in front of you in line, so I didn't realize you were kneeling."

"Yes, I do, although it's getting harder to do so as I get older." He gave a slight chuckle and continued, "Someday, I'm afraid I won't be able to get back up again."

I laughed at the thought. He was a big man and was carrying a little more weight than he should. Jokingly, I replied, "I'm sure the priest would help you."

I tossed my head in his direction expecting an amused reaction to my retort; instead his face was set in a somber mask, his eyes clouded over with a faraway look. The magical aura of the evening had dissipated under the weight of melancholy memories. Perhaps this was a good time to call it a night. I stood up. Looking down at him sitting quietly in his chair, I said, "Thanks for letting me pray with you. I hope you get your prayer group together again someday."

He looked up at me and softly said, "Yes, I hope so, too."

September also brought the height of hurricane season. It had been an active hurricane season already with a number of hurricanes passing to the east or south of us in the past month. The first part of September the most ominous hurricane to date, Hurricane Ike, started to form with its preliminary track placing South Florida directly in its path. Talk turned to plans for evacuation. Patrice stopped to talk with me after work one day to inform me that if the hurricane did come our way, as was expected, the guests would have to evacuate.

"Lu, you will have to evacuate, also."

"Patrice, I don't want to evacuate. Since I am an employee, can't I stay here? There will be plenty of work for us to do to get ready for the hurricane and then with cleanup afterwards."

She replied, "It's a liability issue with our insurance. You would have to sign a waiver if you stay."

"I'll sign a waiver. Let's wait and see what happens. Hopefully it won't even come this way."

I had no desire to go inland to a hurricane shelter. I had never been in one before, but from what I had seen of them on TV, I had no intention of going to one unless I absolutely had to. Hurricane shelters conjured up images of people crammed into a large room, sleeping on cots or, more likely, the floor. I would rather take my chances and face the hurricane; at least I could sleep in my own bed.

In preparation for Hurricane Ike, I made a trip to the store after work. The parking lot was overflowing with other people who were on the same mission. I circled the lot three times before I could even find a parking place. Inside the store, there was an excitement in the air as shoppers urgently stocked up on essentials. I filled my grocery cart with bottled water, cans of fruit, beans, and tuna fish. If the electricity went out, at least I could subsist on canned food, although I didn't find the thought very appealing.

The weekend came, and as we held our breath, Hurricane Ike continued on a westerly path taking it past the southern tip of Florida. We were no longer in its direct path, but on the outer edges of the hurricane, which produced heavy rains and high winds. As the winds picked up, I ran around the hostel securing the furniture, placing all of the plastic tables, chairs, and trash cans into the TV lounges and kitchens. Strong gusts of wind ripped out some of the plastic ceiling tiles that covered the fluorescent lights in the downstairs kitchen, sending them careening through the air and skidding across the floor. I promptly shut all the doors and windows to keep the wind and rain out. With everything closed up tight, the rooms seemed small and confining, and I felt cut off from the outside world.

Surprisingly, all of the guests that had reservations showed up despite the stormy weather. The new guests blended in with the old, forming a new found family that huddled together in the common areas talking, laughing, and watching TV, oblivious to the wind whipping through the trees outside the door, and the rain thrashing up against the side of the building. Although using the barbeque grill was out the question, they used the stoves to prepare elaborate meals by each contributing food they had stored away in the refrigerators and cupboards, then sharing it amongst themselves. A sense of camaraderie pervaded the hostel as everyone pulled together to make the best of the inclement weather.

Thinking that my ESL classes would be cancelled due to the weather, I called the library on Tuesday afternoon. Looking forward to going to my class, I was relieved when the woman on the other end of the phone replied that there weren't any cancellations. Class started at six o'clock in the evening, so I ate my dinner early and then took a shower. I dabbed on some makeup and dressed in a denim skirt and white top that showed off my tan. As I walked out the door, I opened my umbrella, expecting an onslaught of rain. Stepping outside, I was surprised to find that the rain had slackened off into a faint drizzle. I ducked into the TV room hoping to talk to Elliot before I left. As I opened the door, I found him talking with a group of guests. I stepped inside the room and smiled at him. Elliot stopped talking and, as he turned to look at me, his eyes transformed into luminous orbs; the 'look' had returned. I hadn't seen him look at me like that for quite some time. Puzzled by the sudden change in Elliot's expression, everyone stopped talking and stared over at me. My face flush with embarrassment, I took a step backwards towards the door.

Amused by my apparent discomfort, Elliot spoke reassuringly, "You look nice tonight."

Regaining my composure, I replied, "Yes, I'm going to the library to teach English as a Second Language this evening. I'll be gone for a couple of hours."

"Who's in your class?" he asked.

"There are adult students of all different ages from all over the world."

I thought I detected a slight hint of jealousy as he said, "I'll bet the men will really like you tonight!"

Casually with a light note so he wouldn't recognize my

delight, I replied, "I'm going there to teach English, not to pick up men! I have to get going. I'll see you later!" Amused by my repartee, the guests broke out into laughter as I swung around to walk out the door, making a dash through the rain for my car.

Only two students showed up that night because of the weather. There were more volunteers than students. I paired up with a young woman from China who was trying to improve her English so that she could get a better job. The evening went by quickly as I helped her with her reading and pronunciation. Driving home that night, I was filled with a deep sense of satisfaction from my efforts. I found teaching to be a rewarding experience and enjoyed it immensely. Besides that, it was a nice change of pace to mix with other people besides the guests at the hostel. I promised myself that I would continue going every week.

Within a few days the relentless rain and wind finally ceased, giving way to bright sunshine. Relieved that it was all over, I opened the rooms back up and dragged the outdoor furniture and trash cans to their rightful places in the fresh air and sunshine. We suffered only minor damages with the loss of a few kitchen ceiling tiles and some blown down palm tree fronds, which I gathered up and tossed into the dumpster. It could have been a lot worse.

I walked through the common areas picking up the extra rugs I had laid down so that the guests wouldn't track wet sand through the rooms. Sam was at the counter making a sandwich. I had seen him a few times in the past couple of days going through the refrigerators again, but no one had complained recently about stolen food, so I just made a mental note of what he was eating. I didn't confront him to find out if he had bought the food he was eating; that was Patrice's job. She was the manager, and I knew she would want to handle the situation in her own way. My job was to just observe him.

After all the excitement from the hurricane, the rest of the week passed by on a rather dull note, and I looked forward to my light day on Sunday. Saturday evening Elliot and I sat in the TV room discussing where we should go to eat after mass. We liked trying out the different ethnic restaurants in the area, and he had taken me to a nice Greek restaurant the previous Sunday. Not feeling comfortable with him paying each time we went out, I offered to treat him this time. At first he resisted the idea, but I insisted that I was fine with the arrangement. I was making decent money, so I didn't mind paying when we went out. I had been single for a long time, so I was happy just to have someone to go out to eat with. The money didn't matter to me at all. Besides that, I knew that his savings wouldn't last forever. As we spoke, Patrice came walking through the room. Overhearing our conversation about restaurants, she recommended that we try the Sunday brunch at the Seagull Inn which was located just down the street.

Sunday after church, we climbed in Elliot's car eager to try the brunch that Patrice suggested. Before going to the restaurant, Elliot needed to stop at the drug store. As he drove down the boulevard toward the store he suddenly slowed down and pointed past me at a building.

"Lu, that's where my office is."

Nodding my head in acknowledgement, I said, "That is a nice building and it is so close to hostel."

"I'll tell you something, but you have to promise me you won't tell Patrice I told you."

Looking over at him, I replied, "Okay. I promise."

"I'm helping her to get financing for the hostel. If she can't get financed, then I'm going to buy the hostel and put my office there."

"Oh," was all that I could manage to say, and I let it drop at that. Perplexed by what Elliot had just told me, I stared out the window as we drove down the street. This didn't make sense to me. Patrice had recently confided in me that she was in the process of buying the hostel from her Uncle Carlos. Now Elliot was telling me that he might buy it. The way Patrice threw cash around, I was sure that she had money stashed somewhere in a bank account, but I wasn't quite so sure about Elliot. He couldn't even afford to take me out to eat every Sunday. My mind reeled as I thought about how he had told me a number of times about his plans to make his movie and buy real estate, but I couldn't understand where all this money was going to come from. He was living off his savings from when he had worked as a waiter on a cruise ship, but how long could that last? He didn't strike me as the type that had a stash of money hidden away in a bank.

Elliot ran into the drug store while I sat waiting in the car still pondering what he had said about buying the hostel. Although what Elliot told me didn't add up, I chose to shrug it off. All that mattered to me was that Elliot and I were going out to lunch together. His errand completed, we made our way to brunch. The Seagull Inn was an upscale hotel located right on the beach. When we pulled up to the wide, sweeping entrance, a valet on each side of the car opened our doors for us. Elliot handed over his keys, and we walked up a broad set of steps that led into a well-appointed lobby. Awed by the grandeur of the hotel, I practically floated down the hallway to the dining area. A woman at the hostess station asked if we had reservations. The dining room was full, so they took our name and told us we would have to wait for at least a half an hour to be seated. The hostess handed me a beeper that would light up when our table was ready.

I turned to Elliot and said, "That's alright. We can go outside on the veranda and wait."

Elliot suddenly grabbed me by my elbow and pulled me aside. "Lu, did you see how much the buffet costs?"

"No, I didn't. Why? How much is it?"

"It's thirty-five dollars per person. I know you said you would treat this time, but that's a lot of money for brunch."

I swallowed hard. Patrice had neglected to tell us how much it cost, and I didn't think to ask. Since she regularly tossed around hundred dollar bills for lunch, she probably didn't think anything of paying thirty-five dollars for brunch. Luckily, before leaving for church, I had taken some extra money out of an envelope in my locker. For some reason, I had a feeling I might need it. I planted a smile on my face and nonchalantly replied, "That's okay. It's not like we eat out at expensive restaurants all the time. I can splurge this one time."

Eyeing me skeptically, he conceded. "Alright, Lu, if you're sure you're okay with this."

In a reassuring tone, I said, "Come on. Let's go sit out on the veranda and look at the ocean."

We sat on a wicker love seat padded with thick tropical print cushions. The wide, spacious veranda overlooked the beach, giving a clear view of the ocean stretching out before us. Large, cascading waves, remnants of Hurricane Ike, somersaulted onto the eroded beach. Elliot and I sat idly looking out at the choppy water crowned with frolicking white caps that gleamed in the bright sunlight. The hem of my flowing skirt fluttered in the gentle breeze as we sat quietly waiting for the beeper nestled in my lap to summon us to eat. Half an hour passed without any indication that our table was ready for us. Thinking we had been overlooked, Elliot excused himself to check with the hostess to find out if our table was ready. Returning a few minutes later, he stood in the doorway motioning for me to join him. Our table was ready.

As the hostess led us to our table, we passed by buffet tables piled high with sumptuous offerings. The hostess directed us to a private booth where Elliot and I sat opposite of each other. Ravenous after a long morning, we eagerly started to make our rounds to each of the buffet tables. Wanting to sample as much as possible, I was careful to take only a small serving of each dish. Even with small helpings, my plate filled up quickly from the sheer variety of food in the buffet. I made my way back to the table where Elliot was patiently waiting for me. After I sat down, he reached his hands across the table to hold mine as he said grace. Formalities taken care of, we dug into the well laden plates in front of us, savoring each delectable bite.

As we ate, our conversation drifted towards family. Elliot talked about his parents' relationship when he was growing up. Between bites, Elliot spoke about his father.

"My father had a mistress. My mother wasn't very happy about it, but there was nothing she could do. All of us kids knew about it. My mother said that things were better financially for us before my father started seeing this other woman. I guess he was helping her with money, which took away from us. The woman lived not too far from us. I used to hate her until one day when I was walking down the street, she passed by me and said 'hello.' I wasn't going to respond to her, but I did. That was the first time that I had seen her up close. She seemed like nice lady. She even went to the same church as we did. My mother sat on one side of the church, and his mistress sat on the other side."

Fascinated, I listened in silence as I went about tackling the mounds of food on my plate. I couldn't imagine what it must be like knowing that your father had a mistress. As Elliot spoke, I could tell that it bothered him a great deal that his father had a mistress. He seemed anxious to tell me about this, as if in some small way, it helped lighten the burden of shame and guilt that he must have felt and carried with him into adulthood. In time, I would come to see that his father's actions had a great psychological impact on Elliot views regarding sex and religion.

I reached across the table and lightly touched his hand where it rested on the table. Softly I said, "I'm sorry. I know that must have been difficult for you. Sometimes parents do things that we can't understand. They are human and have reasons for doing things, just as we have done things for our own reasons."

Nodding at me, he continued, "I know that my father loved us. He was a good provider. He saved money and built our house. When he got paid, he would bring back big sacks of food for us. He loved my mother, too. But they didn't get along very well. They fought a lot, especially after he took a mistress. Eventually they split up. They're both gone now . . . "

I looked down at my plate. Thoughts of my father raced

through my mind. There were very few people in the world that I could really open up to, but Elliot's easy, compassionate manner compelled me to confide in him about some of my own internal torments.

"My father's mistress was the bottle. He drank too much. Ever since I could remember, he drank. And he didn't take very good care of himself. He would drink and smoke cigarettes all day and hardly eat anything. He was a disabled veteran from World War II. I know his drinking hurt my mother and us kids. I'm sure there was some reason that he drank so much, but I don't really know why."

Elliot's kind, dark, brown eyes radiated a compassion that encouraged me to also confide in him about some of the regrets that I carried with me for my past actions. It was as if he was assuming the role of benevolent priest, and I, the penitent sinner.

"And, I know I've done things that have hurt my children. Not intentionally, but looking back, I can see that I was very selfish and self-centered. On the weekends, I drank beer, smoked cigarettes, and sometimes went out to bars when I should have been home with my children. I've never seemed to be able to find stability in a relationship with a man, a job, or even living in one place for very long. Eventually, my children went to live with their fathers because they made better money and could offer them a better lifestyle – and stability. My relationship with my middle daughter, Rachel, is especially strained. Even though she came back to live with me during her teenage years when my life was more settled, she barely has anything to do with me. I feel like I have let her down." My mouth dry from stirring up painful memories, I stopped to take a sip of water. Looking up at Elliot, I continued, "I regret that I didn't take them to church more and teach them how to pray the rosary. I can never right the wrongs that I did, so I have to live with this for the rest of my life." I quickly wiped away a tear in an effort to hide my emotions. Our mood had turned somber, and I suddenly groped around for a way out to a lighter note.

I seized on the subject of work. "Did I tell you that Patrice wants me to start working in the office for her on Wednesdays?" I said with a forced, upbeat tone.

As I filled him in on the details, the somber mood lifted as we became caught up in the excitement of new possibilities. When we finished eating and got up to leave, Elliot stood beside our booth and suddenly raised his arms towards me. "Here, give me a hug," he said.

Slightly dazed by his request, I stared at him for a few moments as he stood with outstretched arms. He very seldom ever touched me and now he wanted a hug. I momentarily froze as I took a sudden, unexplained interest in his attire. His striped yellow and white shirt was stretched tightly across his expanding midriff, pulling on the buttons down the front; the untucked tails of his shirt draping over the top of his black dress pants. A pair of black high-top tennis shoes ballooned out from under the tapered cuffs of his pants. I took a sudden fancy to the ends of his shoe strings which were pulled forward under the crisscrossed laces, the crimped ends coming to a rest on the top of his toes. Shaking myself out of my stupor, I stepped forward and gave him a quick, clumsy hug.

As I pulled away from him, he said, "Lu, thank you for treating me to such a wonderful meal. You didn't have to do that. We could have gone somewhere less expensive to eat. That was very nice of you."

His sincere expression of gratitude suddenly made me feel shy. Blushing, I smiled up at him and mumbled, "You're welcome." Somewhere deep inside I knew this was a turning point in our relationship. My efforts to win him over were beginning to make head way, and nothing could have made me happier.

The start of a new week ushered in the next phase in my life at the hostel. That morning as I swept a large puddle of water from the second floor terrace, I could hear Patrice's voice rising from somewhere down below.

"Luuuu! Luuuu! Come down here! I need to talk to you."

Hostel by the Sea

Patrice had a habit of running through the courtyard to summon me, loudly calling out my name.

I propped the broom up against the side of the terrace and went downstairs to the office.

"Yes, Patrice, what's up?"

"I spoke with Carlos, and he doesn't want to work on Wednesdays anymore, so I want you to start this Wednesday. I will work in the office until you are done cleaning and then you can take over for me. You will need to work until midnight. Are you okay with that?"

"Yes, that's fine. I'm looking forward to it."

"I will pay you extra to work for me on Wednesdays. Is that acceptable?" She eyed me closely to see what my response would be.

"Yes, that's absolutely fine." I could hardly contain myself at the thought of making some additional money. I felt like I was rolling in dough. I would get my regular paycheck plus the money I made running to get her lunch and now this extra bonus from working in the office. I had to pinch myself to make sure I wasn't dreaming. I had wads of money stuffed everywhere: there was a handful of folded twenty dollar bills in my fanny pack, an envelope full of cash in my locker, and money in my wallet. I didn't even bother counting it anymore. I never had so much money.

"Lu, I need you to stop in the office after work today, so I can show you what you need to do in here."

"Alright, I should be done about two o'clock," I replied. "I'll see you then." Smiling to myself, I went back upstairs to the terrace. As I swept, I wondered how much money Patrice had been making when she ran the hostel for Carlos. It seemed like she was doing very well for herself financially, and I could tell that she wanted the same for me since she was being extremely generous to me. Running the office was a lot of responsibility, so I knew that I would be earning my keep. Wednesdays would be a long day for me starting at nine o'clock in the morning with cleaning and then working in the office from early afternoon until midnight, with just a two hour break at dinner time.

Later in the day, after I finished cleaning, I ran to my dorm room to shower and change clothes. I arrived in the office at two o'clock sharp, bursting through the door eager to start my training. Patrice was on the phone. I browsed through the brochures in the office while I waited for her to finish taking a reservation.

Finished with the reservation, she set the phone down. She motioned for me to come around the counter to her desk, where she sat with the reservations book opened in front of her.

"Lu, you need to write down all the reservations in this book. Make sure you don't miss any. High season is coming, and we don't want to sell more beds than we have, or a guest won't have a place to sleep when they get here."

I had worked in a reservations department before in a hotel, so I was very familiar with the importance of recording reservations. I had my share of unpleasant experiences from guests showing up at the front desk with no record of their reservations, or the wrong arrival date on a sold out night. One concern I had was that Patrice didn't use a computerized reservation system, instead relying on written records which I felt were inadequate. I liked to be able to print out reports from the computer, but this would have to do.

As Patrice stood up, I stepped out of her way, so that she could get to the cupboard. The office was small, and it was a tight fit for two people. She opened the cupboard door. "This is where the sheets and towels are kept. When guests check-in, you need to give them each one of these."

Shutting the cupboard door, she picked up some envelopes lying on the counter under the cupboard. "I keep the mail here on the counter. Sort through the mail and give the guests their mail when you see them. Outgoing mail goes in this basket." She stepped over to the guest check-in counter and opened a drawer. "This is the cash drawer. When the guest pays, you need to put the money in here. We don't accept checks." Turning around and pointing to the wall opposite of where we stood, she continued, "Also, the credit card machine is mounted on the wall over there."

She turned to look at me. "Any questions?"

"No, I'm sure I'll be fine. I can always call you if something comes up that I don't know how to handle."

"Oh, Lu, one more thing. There is a website that I retrieve reservations from, but I will show that to you some other time. I don't want to overwhelm you with too much at one time."

My training completed, I went to run errands. I needed to go to the store to buy some salmon and rice to make for lunch the next day. As I drove along Ocean Boulevard, I looked over at the crowded beach filled with tourists enjoying the sunny day. A few ships anchored off shore in the harbor were waiting to unload their freight in the port. Above the sparkling sea, I could see planes on their final approach, coming in to land at the airport. This city had everything: beautiful beaches, a busy shipping and cruise port, and an international airport that was less than ten miles from the hostel. I marveled at how lucky I was to be living here.

Wednesday afternoon finally arrived, and Patrice was waiting for me outside the office. She stood by the door with a backpack slung over her back. Elliot was standing beside her. As I approached, she held the office key out in front of her.

"Lu, here is your office key. You need to go in the office and get the phone to carry with you. You don't need to stay in the office all the time."

I took the key and held it in my hand.

"There are only two guests arriving later this evening after six o'clock. If you get any walk-ins, I left a note on the desk of the rooms that have available beds in them. If you need me, I have my cell phone."

"Okay. Hopefully, I won't have to call you. I'm sure you would like to get away from here for a while and not be bothered with business. So, where are you off to this afternoon?"

With glee, she replied, "I'm going to the casino!"

"Good luck. I hope you win something!"

Patrice walked off with Elliot trailing behind here. Evidently she had enlisted him to take her to the casino, as I had done in the past. I put the key in the office door and walked inside. Stooping over the desk, I looked in the reservations book. With only two reservations, the day would be a quiet one unless there were some walk-ins. I picked up the phone to take with me to the kitchen. In an effort to relieve Patrice as soon as possible, I hadn't had time to eat. I heated up my fish and rice in the microwave, then sat outside at my corner table to eat my lunch. I leaned back in the chair, enjoying the mid-afternoon solitude. The only noise came from the cars passing by on the busy street in front of the hostel. All of the guests were out sightseeing or at the beach, and the long-term guests were at work or sleeping. The atmosphere was so laid back that I didn't feel like I was actually working at all. I spent the rest of the afternoon in the office surfing the internet and checking my e-mail until my dinner break arrived at four o'clock. I decided to lie down for a few hours to rest up for my evening shift. Setting my alarm for slightly before six o'clock, I drifted off into a light sleep. Waking before my alarm went off, I freshened up and then went to wait in the coolness of the air conditioned office for my two guests to arrive.

At six thirty, I heard the familiar chimes from the door bell as the guests waited at the gate. I went outside to let them in. Opening the gate, I said, "Hello, do you have reservations?"

Two bleary eyed young men stood slightly stooped over, weighed down with large backpacks. In a heavy German accent, one of them replied, "Yes, we do. My name is Peter and this is Hans."

Opening the gate wider, I said, "My name is Lu. Come into the office with me." We went inside so that I could make a copy of their passports and fill out their registration forms. Pointing to the lower half of the registration form, I said, "You need to read these rules and then sign and date at the bottom." As the guests finished filling out the form, I made a copy of their passports.

"Where are you from?"

Leaning on the counter, filling out the form, Peter replied, "Germany."

"Did you just arrive here?"

"Yes, we are very tired. We had a long flight."

"Well, let's finish up here so that you can get to your room and relax. I just need you to pay for your two-night stay."

In a befuddled fashion, they both started digging through their pockets in search of their wallets. Jet lag and weariness from waiting in lines at airports and a lack of sleep due to cramped airline seating had taken a toll on their senses, leaving them in a somewhat discombobulated state. Finding their wallets, they handed over the money which I carefully placed into the cash drawer. I walked over to the cupboard and pulled out two sets of sheets and towels from off the shelf.

"Oh, I almost forgot your room keys. I pulled out two keys from a row of plastic cups lined up on the counter, each neatly hand-marked with a room number. Handing them their keys and linens, I said, "You are in room #6. I'll take you to your room." I opened the door and waited for them to walk outside, shutting the door behind me. As we walked through the courtyard, I pointed out the kitchens, TV rooms, and computer room. We crossed the courtyard to door #6. Flipping through my master set of keys, I found the key to their door. I slipped the key in the lock as I knocked on the door and opened it. Stepping inside, I said "This is your room." Pointing to an empty set of bunk beds, I continued, "These are your beds here. You can set your backpacks in the closet or up against the wall so that no one will trip over them. There are lockers in the corner by the closet, but you need to have your own lock."

Peter and Hans nodded patiently as I spoke, but I could tell that they were eager to get settled in and relax.

"If you need any information about where to get something

to eat, let me know. I will be in the office until midnight. If I'm not in there, just ring the buzzer on the door." I walked out of the room and shut the door behind me. I had just checked in my first guests.

By now, most of the guests had returned to the hostel and were cooking their dinners, or sitting in the courtyard drinking a few beers. I went back to the office where I sat behind the counter, watching the guests through the large window that overlooked the courtyard. Before long, I saw Tim coming towards the door. Tim was an American who was renting on a weekly basis. I didn't see very much of him. He slept most of the day since he worked midnights as a cook at a restaurant on Las Olas Boulevard. The only time I saw him was when I quietly cleaned his room, while he slept soundly in his bunk. During the evenings before he went to work, sometimes he would sit outside to talk to the other long-term guests, but he seemed to shy away from the international guests. He was so quiet that, sometimes, I forgot he was even here. I smiled expectantly at Tim as he opened the door.

"Lu, I lost my key. Can you give me another one?"

"Yes, Tim, but you know you have to pay $5 deposit on the new key."

Tim dug through his pockets as I searched through the row of plastic cups to find another room key for him. As he handed over a crumpled five dollar bill, he said, "Sorry about that. I can't imagine what happened to my key. I had it this morning when I got back from work."

"That's okay, Tim. It will probably turn up. If it does, just bring this key back and I will give you back your deposit."

I followed Tim out the door and closed it behind me. It was getting dark outside, and I needed to go to the laundry room to turn on the night lights. I walked briskly towards the back of the hostel. Suddenly, I realized that I had forgotten to take the phone with me. I was supposed to carry the phone with me at all times in case someone called to make a reservation. I turned around and ran back to the office. I reached into my right pocket for the office key, but there was no key to be found. I frantically rummaged through my other pockets and the fanny pack secured around my waist. Coming up empty handed, a sudden realization dawned on me: I must have forgotten to put the key back into my pocket the last time I unlocked the office door. The key was probably sitting on my desk. I thought to myself: "Great! The first day that I work for Patrice in the office and I lock myself out! How embarrassing!"

I glanced at my watch. It was half past nine. Patrice probably wouldn't be back for hours, maybe not even until midnight or after. I couldn't call her because her cell phone number was written on a piece of paper in the office. I sat dejectedly on a railroad tie bordering the empty flower bed outside the office, casually looking over at the guests gathered in the courtyard. I didn't want them to know that I had locked myself out.

Thankfully it was a quiet night since there weren't any more reservations and the chances of getting walk-ins at this time of night were slim, although not impossible. I decided to wait it out and see what happened. Many years ago, a girlfriend once told me that when you don't know what to do about a problem, it is best not to do anything. I had taken her advice on a number of occasions and found that she was right. Many times a problem would work itself out in time. I took her advice again. A half an hour passed and suddenly I heard Patrice's voice as she came walking through the gate with Elliot. She stood with a bag of food in her hand, looking down at me sitting on my little stoop.

My face red with embarrassment, I said, "Patrice, I locked myself out of the office!"

Patrice doubled over in laughter. "Lu, I leave you alone for the first time and you lock yourself out?! That's okay, I do it all the time." As she spoke, she took her key and unlocked the office door for me. I went inside and retrieved my key from the desk right where I had left it earlier. I held up the key in front of me and said, "I am putting this on my personal key ring right now so that this will not happen again!" I slipped it onto the key ring that held my room and car keys and then tucked them securely into a zippered compartment of my fanny pack.

I looked over at her as she stood in the office doorway. "Alright, now go eat your dinner!" I ordered her playfully. The rest of the night went by uneventfully. At midnight, I shut off the office lights and locked the door. Going to my room, exhausted, I climbed into my bed ready for a much deserved rest.

Rhoda and I had planned another Friday night out for dinner at the same seafood restaurant. I enjoyed Rhoda's company and was looking forward to our night out. We had planned dinner together a few times, but I found it peculiar that I was always the one to initiate a night out. I would usually e-mail her earlier in the week to which she always promptly replied that she could meet me for dinner. I didn't know her very well and hoped that in time we would become better friends. We had so much in common that I couldn't imagine why we wouldn't. We were about the same age, divorced, and from Ohio. Living in a big city without knowing anyone can be scary. I found that the hardest part of moving to a new city was establishing new friendships. I could find a job and a place to live, but I often felt lost and lonely without having an established social network of family and friends nearby.

I didn't see Elliot all day on Friday. He was gone when I went in to clean his room. I noticed his pajamas were not in their usual place on his bed. I thought perhaps he had gone to the laundromat. I pushed aside all thoughts of Elliot and concentrated on my night out

That evening I got dressed up and met Rhoda at the restaurant. We ate our dinner sitting at the bar while listening to the band. Rhoda seemed interested in a man sitting on the other side of her, and I encouraged her to talk to him. Rhoda didn't have a steady boyfriend, so I thought perhaps she could hook up with him. Nothing panned out with him, so we finished our dinner and danced for awhile. A younger crowd started to stream into the restaurant for a night of partying. With no prospects for male

Hostel by the Sea

companions our age, we decided to call it a night and went our separate ways. We waited as the valet brought her car around and I watched her as she climbed into her car and waved goodbye. I didn't know it at the time, but that was to be the last time I would see Rhoda. I handed my ticket to the valet and waited while he retrieved my car.

Driving home, I wondered what Elliot was up to. When I pulled into the parking lot, I noticed his car was gone. He had been at the hostel the last few weekends, but I instinctively knew he was in Port St. Lucie. Disappointed that he was gone for the weekend, I went to my room and went to bed.

Saturday morning I was washing dishes in the upstairs kitchen when Patrice suddenly appeared through the doorway. "I have a proposition for you," she said. "You can have your choice of getting paid extra for working for me on Wednesdays, or you can have your own private room."

My mouth dropped open as I looked at her in amazement. I was speechless.

"Why don't you think about it and let me know what you decide." Then she turned and walked out of the kitchen.

I picked up a dirty dish and absentmindedly began to scrub away at dried spaghetti sauce. I didn't have to think about it for very long. The extra money was a nice supplement to my income, but having my own room would be heavenly. I had enjoyed sharing my room with all the international university students that I had met, but I had to admit that there was a certain appeal to having my own room. I wanted to have a place to call my own where I could keep my personal belongings, instead of having them stored away on the shelves and closet in my dorm room and in the trunk of my car. My imagination soared as I thought of how I could decorate my new room and maybe even buy some furnishings to make it more comfortable and cozy. I dropped the dish in the sink and ran down the stairs to the office. I burst through the door. Slightly breathless, I gasped, "Patrice, I've made up my mind."

Surprised to see me so soon, Patrice looked up at me expectantly with raised eyebrows.

My voice filled with excitement, I continued, "I'll take the private room. Which one do you want me to move into?" We had three private rooms, and I didn't care which one she wanted me to stay in.

Patrice replied, "I think room #5 will be fine for you."

Barely able to stand still, I said, "When can I move in?"

"How about today?" Patrice walked over to the counter and pulled a key out of the plastic cup and handed it to me.

"Great! I'll move my things as soon as I get done cleaning."

"There is one thing I must tell you. I am expecting a large group from Switzerland later this month that will need 32 beds. You will probably have to share your room with someone just for two nights."

"Oh, okay, I understand." Slightly dismayed at the thought of having to share my newly acquired private room with someone else, I consoled myself with the thought that it would only be for a few nights. I pushed the thought aside while relishing the feel of the key to my private room that I held in my hand.

I was very familiar with my new room since I had cleaned it many times. The room had two twin beds, two night stands, a black cloth covered futon, a small refrigerator, a flat screen TV, and a set of lockers. I especially liked the bathroom because it had a tub with a shower. I loved to take bubble baths, and I reveled at the thought of luxuriously soaking in a tub filled with mounds of foaming bubbles. Again, I couldn't believe my good fortune. So many good things were happening to me at such a fast rate that I could hardly believe my luck. I thought back to the first day when I had arrived at the hostel. Never in my wildest dreams did I ever imagine that I would live and work here. Life, indeed, can take many unexpected twists and turns.

After I finished working, I went into my dorm room and immediately gathered as much as I could carry at one time and took it over to my new room. Not wanting to waste a moment,

I hastily made four or five trips before I had everything moved. I spent a few hours arranging my room, hanging my clothes in the closet and putting away my toiletries in the bathroom vanity. There wasn't a chest of drawers, so I laid my suitcases on the floor up against the wall, positioning them so that I could just open the flap to take out my clothing. A set of metal lockers provided a good place to store my dishes and canned goods. I retrieved my two bags of groceries from the shared refrigerator in the kitchen and filled my refrigerator. To have my own refrigerator was a luxury. I no longer had to worry about anyone taking my food. I would still have to use the shared kitchen to cook in, but I didn't mind that at all since it gave me a chance to mix with the guests. I made up my bed and laid a blanket over the unused bed. Standing in the middle of the room, I slowly turned around in a circle to admire my new room. This was one of the happiest moments in my life. There are those who would find it odd that I could be happy with so little. After all, I was living in one room with barely any furniture. But I had everything around me that meant something to me: cultural diversity, an upscale city filled with lots of fun things to do, a spectacular beach right across the street, and a job that I loved. I thought my heart would burst from all the joy I felt.

That evening, for the first time in many months, I soaked in a tub full of foaming bubbles then sat down to watch TV. As I sat cross-legged on the futon, I was distracted by prickly sensations on various parts of my legs. Annoyed by this sudden irritation, I stood up and inspected my legs. I couldn't see anything crawling on me. I sat down again and in a few minutes I experienced the same sensation. As I ran my hand across the cloth surface of the futon, I could feel grains of sand that more than likely came from the beach. Suddenly it occurred to me that there must be sand fleas on the cushions. I went to the bathroom and found a towel to sit on. That fixed the problem temporarily, but I needed to buy some flea spray to treat it with.

Sunday morning, I got up and went to church. It felt strange going to church without Elliot, but I was determined to go by myself. After church, I went to the store. The night before, I had made a list of some items that I needed for my room. I bought a little cart with shelves for my kitchenware, a teal coverlet to spruce up my futon with two matching pillows, and a wall hanging depicting a large veranda with a patio chair overlooking a harbor. I wanted to add a few personal touches, so that it didn't look so much like a room in a hostel. I completed my shopping spree with a can of flea spray, a hand-held sweeper, and a DVD player.

Back in my room that afternoon, I pulled the futon away from the wall and gave it a good dose of flea spray, then let it set undisturbed for a few hours. After putting the utility cart together, I set it beside my refrigerator and the metal lockers that I used for cupboards, all of which completed a small kitchen area. I stacked my pots, pans, and dishes on the cart and stood back to admire my work. Everything just fit. I dug out my hammer and pulled an old nail from the wall to use to hang up my picture above the beds. Confident that the fleas were all dead, I ran the sweeper on the futon then pushed it back up against the wall, draping the teal coverlet over the back of it and setting a pillow on each end. I didn't know how to hook up the DVD player, so I decided to leave that for another day. I wanted to find someone to help me hook it up, hopefully Elliot. My decorating completed, I spun around to admire my handiwork. It was starting to look like home.

In the evening, I sat outside my room in a chair overlooking the courtyard, enjoying a refreshing sea breeze. To my surprise, I saw Elliot making his way down the steps from his room. He must of returned from Port St. Lucie while I was busy fixing up my room. He nodded in my direction as he walked by me without saying a word and went directly into the TV room. I found his behavior odd since he usually stopped to talk with me when he saw me sitting outside. The ice cubes in my ice tea had melted, so I got up and walked through the TV room to get some out of the freezer. Elliot sat watching the TV oblivious to my presence. He seemed distant and aloof, and I wondered if he was upset with me for some reason. I walked passed him again on my way out without saying anything to him. Later when he came out of the room, I called him over.

"Elliot, is everything okay? I haven't done anything to upset you, have I? If I did, I'm sorry."

Seeing the concern on my face, he replied emphatically, "No, no. Of course not. You have no reason to be sorry." He stopped talking for a moment as if caught up in his thoughts. Then suddenly he held his arms out to embrace me. "Here, give me a hug."

Again I was taken by surprise at his request for a hug. This was the second time in a week. I stepped forward to wrap my arms around him. I felt so small up against his large chest with his bulky biceps wrapped snuggly around me. My arms only reached to the other side of his shoulders. Afraid to linger in his embrace too long, I quickly stepped back away from him.

"Do you know that I have my own room now?"

His eyebrows shot up in surprise.

"I just moved in this afternoon." I pointed at the room we were standing in front of. "It's right here."

"That's nice, Lu. Do you like it?"

Eager to talk about my room, I said, "Yes, very much. I've been busy fixing it up." There was so much more that I wanted to tell him about my weekend.

"I'm happy for you. Well, I have some things to take care of tonight. I'll see you tomorrow." He started to turn to go.

"Elliot, wait. I wanted to ask you if you know how to hook up a DVD player."

"Yes, I think so."

"Would you help me hook it up tomorrow night?"

"Sure, Lu. I can help you with that."

"Okay, great. I'll see you then."

He went back up the stairs to his room, and I sat down to

finish my ice tea. I was disappointed that he hadn't stayed longer to talk with me, but I looked forward to seeing him the following night. I had an ulterior motive for asking him for help with my DVD player; we would be able to watch movies together in the privacy of my room.

The next evening, while I was sitting in my room reading, there was a knock at my door. I opened the door to find Elliot standing there. "I've come by to help you hook up your DVD player," he said.

"Yes, thank you. Please come in." I walked over to pick up the DVD player off the night stand beside my bed.

Elliot stepped inside and looked around the room. "It looks nice in here."

"It's starting to look like home. There are some other things I would like to do to fix it up more. I want to put a table and chairs in here for a dining area."

"Don't you think it will be too crowded in here?"

"No, I'll just have to move some of the furniture around. It would be nice to be able to eat in my room." I handed the DVD player to Elliot. "I'm afraid I'm not very good at hooking these things up."

Elliot pulled my TV stand away from the wall and placed the DVD player on one of the shelves. I ran around the room turning on all the lights, so that he could see better. Before I knew it, he had it hooked up. He pushed the TV stand back up against the wall. Patrice had given me a couple of movies to watch, so I took one out of the case and slipped it in the DVD player. I picked up the remote control and pushed a few buttons. The movie came up on the TV screen.

"Perfect! Thanks so much for your help, Elliot. Maybe sometime you can come over to watch a movie with me." I stood a few feet away from him, anxiously waiting for his reply.

"Yes, I would like that."

There were a few moments of silence between us, before Elliot spoke again. "I'm going to get something for dinner. Do you need anything from the store?"

"No. Not tonight. Thanks again for stopping by to help me." I stooped over to pick up the box and wrappings from the DVD player off the floor to throw away.

Wondering to myself when I would see him again, I said, "Oh, by the way. I can't pray the rosary on Wednesday evenings anymore because I'm working in the office for Patrice. Can we change it to Thursday evenings?"

"Yes, I pray the rosary every night. You're welcome to join me anytime."

I followed Elliot out the door and watched him as he walked out of the gate. I sighed as the gate closed behind him and went to throw away the wrappings in the trash hopper.

A soaking rain came down all afternoon and evening on Thursday, eliminating any plans for praying the rosary on the terrace. Finding Elliot in front of the TV in the early evening, I suggested to him that we could pray in my room, to which he wholeheartedly agreed. Excited by the prospect of praying in the privacy of my room, I went to freshen up and wait for him. Awhile later, I heard the now familiar knock at my door. When I let him in, he went about pulling two chairs together to face east, giving us a view of the blinds covering the large picture window in my room. When we finished our rosary, Elliot turned to me and said, "You know, Lu, maybe someday things will work out for us to be together."

Shocked by what he had just said, I didn't have time to think about how I should respond. I had spent so much time concentrating on how to be a friend to him that I wasn't sure how I should react to this sudden assertion. In an attempt to avoid talking about anything personal between us, I jumped up to retrieve a small picture of the Madonna holding the baby Jesus in her arms from the shelf underneath the DVD player. I held it out for him to see. "This was my grandmother's. We called her Baba which means grandmother in Croatian. She kept this on a shelf in her living room. I've had it ever since she passed away many years ago. It is something that I treasure. I loved her very much."

Elliot gently took it from my hands to have a closer look. My tiny treasure looked so small and insignificant in his large hands. Then he handed it back to me. I was trying my best to disguise my true feelings. My heart was filled with happiness at what he had just told me, but I was afraid to let him know for fear that it might not come true.

I set the trinket back on the shelf as Elliot stood up to leave. Hesitant to let him leave without some future commitment of seeing each other, I decided to take a chance.

"Elliot, would you like to come over to watch a movie with me tomorrow evening? I have some movies that Patrice gave me to watch. We could watch one of those."

Elliot turned towards me. "Yes. It would be nice to watch a movie for a change."

The next evening before Elliot came over, I rearranged my furniture. We needed a place to sit. The futon was set up against the picture window facing my twin beds. I moved the beds to one side of the room and moved the futon sideways so that it was facing the TV. Just as I finished moving everything, there was a knock at the door. I was nervous. This was like a date, but it wasn't a date. We were watching a movie together as friends. Nevertheless, it was a nice feeling to be entertaining a male companion in the privacy of my own room. Elliot came in and sat down on the end of the futon nearest the window. I put the movie in the DVD player, shut out all the lights, and then sat down on the opposite end of the futon. I tried not to notice the large, gapping space between us.

When the movie was over, I got up to turn on the light. As I reached up to flip the switch, my attention was drawn to the sound of Elliot's voice. "Lu, come sit down here. I want to talk to you."

The tone in his voice made my heart skip a beat. I instinctively felt that there was something important that he was going to say to me, but I dared not get my hopes up too high. I had been disappointed by him in the past, and I didn't want to go through that again. I flipped the switch on and walked over to the futon.

As I approached the futon, Elliot said, "Here, sit down beside me. You don't need to sit way over on the other end."

I almost giggled out loud at how silly it must have looked with the two of us sitting on opposite ends of the futon like children on opposite ends of a seesaw. I slowly sat down beside him, almost afraid at what he might say.

He took my hands in his. I liked the way his hands felt. They were warm and comforting.

"Lu, I want to be with you. I will break it off with this other woman I've been seeing."

Then he leaned over and kissed me.

I pulled away from him slightly and looked deep into his eyes. "I want to be with you, too. I always have."

He pulled me towards him with his powerful arms. Holding me tightly, he gave me a tender, loving kiss.

He whispered in my ear. "Do you want me?"

Embarrassed, I pulled away from him. I said, "No, not tonight. You need to give me some time to get used to all of this." Out of the corner of my eye, I looked at the two twin beds pushed up against the wall on the other side of the room. Somehow they seemed hugely inadequate. Elliot was 6'2" and weighed over two hundred pounds. I winced at the vision of the two of us trying to fit into my little twin bed. We didn't even have a proper bed to make love in.

Disappointed, he replied, "Alright. I understand."

Looking at him in earnest, I asked, "What made you decide now to take our relationship further?"

"You did. Because of the kindness and humility you have shown towards me. Those are the qualities that I look for in a woman."

Satisfied by his response, I pressed my lips against his. We kissed a while longer until Elliot spoke up and said, "I better get going. If I keep kissing you like this, I won't be able to tear myself away from you."

He pulled himself away from me and stood up. Taking my hands, he pulled me up off the futon to face him. He kissed me goodnight, then I walked with him to the door. As the door closed behind him, I stood alone in my room in a daze. I couldn't believe that we finally were going to be together. I pushed the futon back up against the wall and the beds back into their original position. As I rearranged the furniture, the thought occurred to me that things came together in our favor to enable us to develop a romantic relationship. When we first met, we both were in dorm rooms with roommates. We had no privacy to take our relationship any further. With my own room, that was no longer a hindrance.

That night as I lie in bed, my heart was filled with joy. I had a job that I loved, a man that I loved, and my own room. My life could not have been any better at that moment. I felt like I was in heaven.

The next morning as I collected the trash from the courtyard, I saw Jerome coming out of his room with a suitcase in each hand, walking towards the office. I set the trash bags down and walked over to him.

"Jerome, are you leaving today?"

"Yes, I'm moving into my dorm," he replied with a hint of excitement.

I was sad to see him go. "Jerome, give me a hug!"

Surprised, he set down his suitcases. I threw my arms around him in a friendly embrace.

Stepping back, I looked him straight in the eye. "Jerome," I said, "you are a very nice young man. You will do well in college. Good luck with your classes." I felt a surge of emotion welling up inside of me. I found that I was getting attached to some of the guests and, when they left, I often felt like crying. Blinking back my tears, I smiled at Jerome as he picked up his suitcases and went to the office to turn in his key to Patrice.

Later that day, I propped open Jerome's door as I cleaned his room. Patrice saw me in the room as she was passing by on her way to the office. Suddenly she appeared in the doorway. She pointed to the queen-sized bed, the only one in the hostel. "Lu, how would you like to have a queen-sized bed? You will get a good sleep in that bed."

I looked at the bed and then at Patrice. I couldn't believe what she was saying. Was it possible that she knew about Elliot and me and was offering us a bigger bed so that we could sleep together? I hadn't said anything to Patrice about our relationship, but since she didn't miss much, I was sure that she was aware of what was going on between us. Still, I couldn't be sure. We had been very discreet. Even though it had only been a few days, no one knew that Elliot and I were more than just friends.

Trying to hide my excitement, I replied, "Yes, I would really like to use this bed. When can we switch them?"

"How about right now? I have some queen sheets that I will give you to use."

I laid down my mop and peeled off my latex gloves. We hoisted the bed off the frame and carried it to my room, then took the twin beds back to the other room. After setting up my queen-sized bed, Patrice ran to her room and returned with an armful of queen sheets. As I made up the bed, I couldn't help but wonder what Elliot would think about all of this.

That evening, I invited Elliot over to eat dinner with me in my room. I had taken a round plastic table and two chairs from the upstairs terrace to use for a dining room table. Elliot brought his sandwich, and I had made a salad for myself. When he walked into my room, his eyes went immediately to the large queen-sized bed. Astonished, he said, "Whose idea was that?!"

Trying to hide my embarrassment, I simply replied, "Patrice's."

We needed a bigger bed and the very next day after our first kiss, one magically appeared. I wanted to laugh out loud at the absurdity of it all.

After dinner, we watched another movie. It was a nice feeling to sit beside Elliot with his arm placed snuggly around me as we watched the movie. When the movie ended, he excused himself to use the bathroom. I took the movie out of the DVD player and placed it back in its jacket then set it on the shelf. Embarrassed at what he must think about the bed, I firmly planted myself on the futon, waiting to see what he would do when he came out of the bathroom. A few minutes later, he came out and laid on the bed, propping his head up on a pillow. Laying his arm across the empty side of the bed, he motioned to me with his hand. "Come here and lay down beside me."

Obligingly, I crawled onto the bed beside him. Facing each other, Elliot kissed me and caressed my back, pulling me close to him. Before long we shed our clothing and crawled under the covers to make love. I wanted to sleep in arms all night.

Nudging me, he asked, "What time is it?"

I pushed the light on my alarm clock. "It's two o'clock. Will you stay with me tonight?"

Elliot let out a sigh. "No. I don't think that's a good idea. I better go back to my room."

I didn't let on that I was disappointed. "I will miss you tonight." I rested my head on his shoulder, reluctant to let him go. I ran my fingertips tenderly across his forehead and down the side of his clean shaven face.

He hugged me one last time and got out of bed to get dressed. Then leaning over me, he kissed me goodnight and left to go back to his room. I grabbed the pillow he had slept on, pressing my face against it.

The next afternoon, while eating at our favorite Cuban restaurant after church, I brought up the subject of his mid-night trek to return to his dorm room.

"Elliot, why did you go back to your room last night?"

Elliot hesitated and looked down at his plate for a moment as if carefully choosing his words. When he looked back up at me, he said, "I'm concerned about what the guys at the hostel will say."

"Which guys are you referring to?"

"Nathan, for one. And Stuart and Bryan. They're nosy and I don't want them saying things about us."

I was silent for a moment as I considered what the other guests might say if they knew that Elliot and I were sleeping together. I hadn't thought about it before because I really didn't think it was anyone's business. The hostel was a small place and news spread quickly about any gossip. Since Nathan was his roommate, he would be the first to notice if Elliot didn't spend the night in his room and probably would ask him where he had been.

"Elliot, the guys here have always treated me with kindness and respect. I doubt that they would say anything at all to you, or me. Really, I think that when they find out that we are in a relationship there will be some gossip at first, but, in time, it will just be the way it is and everyone will just accept it."

Elliot seemed reassured by my reasoning and picked up his fork to continue eating. After a few bites, he said, "Your right. But I think I will talk to Nathan to let him know what's going on with us. I would feel better if he heard it directly from me."

I winked at him and said, "Then you'll stay with me tonight?"

A smile slowly spread across his face as he replied, "Yes. I'll stay with you tonight."

Monday morning, I stopped in the office to talk with Patrice about the group that was scheduled to arrive on Wednesday. I found her huddled over a list of names, fretting over where to put all the guests.

Twisting the ends of her long, wavy hair around her fingers, she said, "Lu, I am going to have to ask some of the long-term guests to leave for a few days to make room for this group. They're not going to be very happy about that, but they can come back when the group leaves. Also, I need to move some of the remaining guests into other rooms. When you see Tim today, will you let him know that he needs to move in with Nathan and

Elliot?"

"Okay. I'll talk to Tim, but he sleeps through the day, so I probably won't see him until this evening," I replied.

"I'll tell him, if I see him first."

"What time is the group arriving?"

Patrice looked up from her list and replied, "Six o'clock in the evening."

"Patrice, I've been thinking about that since I'll be working that night. When they get here, I will have thirty-two guests to check-in which means I need to make copies of all their passports, give them their sheets and towels, and read the rules and regulations. That will take forever! I think I will put their sheets and towels on their beds a head of time."

"Good idea, Lu. That will save time."

I left her to her list and went off to start my cleaning for the day. Later that morning, I saw Tim carrying bags of clothes to the upstairs dorm. He was usually asleep by this time. He must have come home late from work and Patrice caught him on his way in to tell him to switch rooms.

As I walked by him, cheerfully I said, "Good morning, Tim! How are you this morning?"

I could tell by the look on his face that he was in a surly mood. All I got back from him was a gruff grunt.

I followed him up the steps to his new room. "Are you alright?"

At the top of the stairs, he stopped and dropped his bags down next to the door. Irritated, he said, "No, I'm not very happy about moving to another room. I've been in my room for two months now. You know . . . it's like home to me. It's hard for me to have to change rooms."

Tim fumbled through his pocket looking for his key. I grabbed my master keys, dangling from the clip on my waist. "Here, let me open the door for you."

I opened the door and peeked into the room. Nathan was at work and Elliot was gone. I stepped inside the room. "Looks like you get a top bunk."

Tim threw his bags up against the wall. His face was turning red. "I hate sleeping in the top bunk! I hope that bunk doesn't give way under my weight. And look at that ladder! I will probably break it if I climb up on it. I weigh two hundred pounds. I need to be in a bottom bunk."

As he ranted on about his bunk bed, I lifted up the mattress to check to see how many slats were on the bed frame. I found a solid piece of wood, cut to the size of the frame. "Tim, I think that looks pretty solid. You should be okay up there."

Tim looked apprehensively at the bed frame.

Trying to appease him, I said, "Tim, you need fresh sheets. I'll run down to the office and get you a set." I ran down the steps into the office. Patrice was gone. I went to the cupboard and grabbed a set of sheets. Then I walked over to the refrigerator where we kept candy bars and soda pop that we sold to the guests. I opened the door and took out a candy bar, tossing a few quarters in the petty cash to pay for it. I ran back up the steps to find Tim hanging his clothes in the closet. I walked over and laid the sheets on the mattress, and without a word, I set the candy bar down on top of his sheets as a little gesture of sympathy. I guess he must have found it and ate it, but he never said a word about it. The next morning when I went in to clean Tim's room, a broken, splintered ladder was propped up against the wall. Jagged pieces of splintered wood still attached by nails to the bed frame were all that was left from the once attached ladder. Tim was fast asleep in the top bunk. At least the bed hadn't fallen down.

Wednesday morning, Patrice had all the logistics finally worked out for the incoming group. Since my twin beds had been replaced by the queen bed, I was relieved that I didn't have to share my room with one of them. All the guests that needed to leave had checked-out, and the other remaining eight guests had been moved to their new room assignments. This opened up the necessary rooms for the incoming group, so that they could all be housed together. I stopped by to talk to Patrice first thing in the morning.

When I came into the office, she was blowing her nose. She looked up at me and said, "I'm not feeling well today, Lu. I won't be able to help you when the group arrives."

"That's okay. I can handle it."

With a convincing sniffle, she said, "I'm going to provide breakfast for them. Elliot is going to take me to the store later. I'll put the food in a box and set it in the upstairs kitchen for them."

Although she had a slight cold, I didn't think she was that sick. I had a feeling that she didn't want to be bothered with the group once they got here. She had done her work with the reservations and was leaving the rest up to me. I didn't mind. I liked a challenge and was glad to take over the arrangements.

By mid-afternoon I finished my cleaning and started preparing for the group. I took baskets of sheets and towels and set them outside the doors of the rooms to distribute them, placing a set of sheets and a towel on each bed along with a sightseeing brochure. At four o'clock, I went to take a nap for a few hours. I knew I was in for a long night.

At ten minutes to six, before my alarm had a chance to go off, I distinctly heard the sound of a bus's brakes in the parking lot. The group had arrived. I jumped up and ran to the bathroom to splash water on my face and freshen up. Elliot had been sitting in the TV room and came to my door to tell me the group had arrived just as I was walking out. I looked up to see a flock of students coming through the gate. I ran up to them and told them to get back on the bus. I didn't want them running through the hostel before I had a chance to give them their orientation. With the bus driver's help, I directed everyone back onto the bus. The students back into their seats, I walked up the steps of the bus as the bus driver handed me a microphone. The students listened intently as I gave them their instructions. They had been on the bus for hours having driven down from Cape Kennedy and were eager to get settled in their rooms and get something to eat. I pointed out the common areas of the hostel and read through the rules. Then I warned them about swimming in the ocean. There had been a number of drownings in the past month due to the strong undercurrent from all the hurricanes that season. The water could be deceiving and beachgoers often got caught in rip tides unable to break free. Nathan had a close call recently, and I didn't want any mishaps with the group.

My spiel completed, I walked down the steps of the bus and stood outside the door. As they came off the bus, they handed their passports to me as I handed them their keys and room assignments. Everything went like clockwork. Elliot helped direct the students to their rooms and carried their bags. With everyone off the bus, I gathered up the passports to take to the office to make copies. Elliot was just walking back from helping some of the guests to their rooms as I walked through the gate on my way to the office. He looked at me and shook his head in disbelief. With a smile, he said, "You are really something else!"

I smiled back at him, happy that everything had gone so smoothly. Later the group guide came in to retrieve the passports. He asked where they could all go to eat. I made a phone call to a popular restaurant within walking distance that was located on the intercoastal waterway and made reservations for them. Guests from the group popped in and out of the office, collecting brochures and information on car rentals. They finally all left to go eat so that I had some time to catch my breath. I sat with Elliot in the TV room. With the group out for dinner, the hostel was peacefully quiet.

The next day, I ran into Patrice in the courtyard. Her cold seemed to have entirely cleared up overnight. "Good morning, Patrice. Are you feeling better?"

"Yes, Lu. I took some medicine and fell asleep last night at about five-thirty. I never even heard the group when they got here."

I smiled back politely and said, "Everything went smoothly."

But I had the feeling that she had been awake the whole time, watching through a crack in her blinds in the window that looked out into the front parking lot. Patrice didn't miss much.

After our conversation at the Cuban restaurant, Elliot started to spend every night with me. He would come to my room in the early evening and leave in the morning when I got up to go to work. I noticed his daily routine changed drastically once he started staying with me. He no longer disappeared for the whole day. He used to go to church first thing in the morning and then to his office or to the library. Now he got up and went upstairs to his room to go back to sleep. He would sleep until late afternoon and then come down to watch TV. One morning when I went in to clean his room, he lifted his head off his pillow to look at me as I came through the door. His face had an angelic glow. As I looked back over at him, I thought to myself: "This is the man that I want to spend the rest of my life with." I gave him a slight wave and a smile, and he turned over and went back to sleep.

Chapter 9

Making A Home

In the realm of love there exists an inherent folly in human nature to see only what we want while turning a blind eye to obvious shortcomings, giving credence to the saying that 'love is blind.' Despite some subtle indications that all might not be as it appeared with Elliot, I was willing to give him the benefit of the doubt, choosing to think the best of him and our relationship. I was determined to build a life with the man I loved, confident that fate had brought us together.

More than anything else, I wanted to create a place for us where we could spend time together in comfortable surroundings. With some extra money in my pocket, I started shopping in an effort to transform my austere dorm room into a cozy, tropical retreat. Little by little, my room began to resemble a furnished studio apartment, albeit without a kitchen sink and stove.

The extra money I made working as a driver for Patrice and the guests came in handy to buy some of the items I needed for our room, but eventually as the driving jobs took more and more of my time, I started looking for a way out. Since Elliot wasn't working, I thought perhaps he would be interested in taking them over to make some extra money. I didn't even have the time to discuss the opportunity with him before it transpired on its own one evening as we were getting ready to say the rosary on the terrace. Hearing Patrice calling my name from somewhere below in the courtyard, I got up from my chair just as she came up the stairs and started towards us.

"Lu, I have a driving job for you in the morning before you start working."

"Patrice, I really have enough to do now with cleaning the hostel and working in the office. What about giving the driving jobs to Elliot?" I looked from Patrice to Elliot to see what his reaction would be. He looked pleasantly surprised by my suggestion.

Looking at him in earnest, I said, "Elliot, what do you think? Do you want some driving jobs?" I had a hunch that he would be interested since I knew that he had picked up Patrice's lunch a few times and had taken her to the casino. He seemed to be sleeping away the day a lot lately, and I had the feeling that he could use the money. If he would do the driving jobs, that would lift a burden off me and give him some extra money, along with something to do.

Elliot looked from me to Patrice with a smile. "Yes, I can do that," he said.

Although none of us realized it at the time, with those simple words Elliot became Patrice's personal driver. Patrice filled Elliot in on the details for his driving job in the morning, then descended back down the stairs to the office, leaving Elliot and me to ourselves.

I looked over at him. "I hope you don't mind that I suggested you do the driving."

"No, I don't mind at all. I could use the money and it will give me something to do."

With the driving arrangements taken care of, we started on our hour long rosary. Halfway through, Elliot's cell phone rang. He stopped in mid-sentence and reached into his pocket for his cell phone. He glanced down at the display and shut the cell phone off, placing it back in his pocket. This was the first time I could ever remember his cell phone ringing during our prayers.

I was curious as to who called him, suspecting that perhaps it was his ex-girlfriend. Although we had been together for almost a week, he never told me if he had followed through on his word to break up with her. After our prayers, my curiosity got the best of me. I was almost afraid to ask him if he had broken up with her for fear that he had a change of heart. But I knew that for my own peace of mind, I needed to find out.

The air was unusually still that night as we leaned back in our chairs, gazing up at the stars in the sky. I mustered up my courage and finally spoke, "Elliot, you never told me if you broke up with that woman you were seeing from Port St. Lucie."

Elliot took a deep breath. "Yes, I did. I called her the next day, after I told you I would, to break up with her. She didn't take it very well. In fact, that was her that called me when we were praying."

"Oh." I didn't like the sound of that. "Is she trying to get you back?"

"Now that we are together, I won't go back with her. I still consider her a friend. She is a nice lady and it's not like she did anything wrong. Although, she doesn't know about . . . *you.*"

An uncomfortable feeling crept over me at the way he emphasized 'you.' I was concerned that she might try to cause problems between us if she were to find out that he had broken up with her to be with me.

"Do you think that she will come down here looking for you?"

"I don't know. She doesn't know exactly where I live. She only has a vague idea, so she could come down here and possibly look for my car."

I had been looking at him intently as he spoke, but I now turned away to stare off at some indiscriminate point in the distance. A slight shudder rippled through me as my overactive imagination drummed up a vision of some jealous, irate woman lurking in the parking lot of the hostel, and when spotting me with Elliot, accosting me because I had stolen her man. I didn't like the thought of it, but I knew there was always the possibility that something like that could happen. The wrath of a woman cast aside for another woman could be unpleasant, to say the least. I dismissed the thought from my mind, deciding to deal with the situation, if, and when it arose.

Stifling a yawn, I glanced at my watch. It was getting late, so Elliot and I went downstairs to my room to get ready for bed. While he went to use the bathroom, I undressed and climbed into bed eagerly waiting for him to join me. He walked out of the bathroom and stood across the room from me getting undressed. As he removed his trousers, my eyes were drawn to large areas of dark skin on both of his knees.

"Elliot, what happened to your knees?"

Elliot looked down at his knees and then over at me. Offhandedly, he replied, "Those are calluses from praying on my knees."

My eyes fell again to his knees in wonderment at the thought of how many hours upon hours he must have knelt in prayer to develop such large calluses, displayed like badges of honor. Who was this man who had so willing devoted his life to the service of God? Surely my heart would be safe in his hands. It had been seven years since I had dared let someone get this close to me. I was ready to take a chance and love again. I knew that there was risk involved, nothing was assured, but I felt confident that because of Elliot's deep convictions to God, I would be alright. He treated me well. He was kind and considerate, possessing an easy manner that complimented my fretful nature. I liked how I felt when I was with him. His presence calmed and soothed me.

That night as we lie in bed embracing, Elliot reached up with his hand to stroke my shoulder length hair. As he did so, tears sprung to my eyes, and before I knew it, a soft sob escaped from my lips. Startled, Elliot pulled his hand away. "What, what is wrong?" he asked.

Biting my lip to keep myself from crying, I replied, "It has been a long time since a man has played with my hair like that."

Elliot held me tighter in his arms. He whispered in my ear.

"Sometimes the nicest people are the ones who have the hardest time in life."

I had had more than my fair share of hard knocks in my life, especially with men. I always ended up in relationships with men who drank too much and made a mess of my life. Eventually, I would break free from the relationships, spending years picking up the pieces of my life trying to get it back together, only to do it all over again. This time, I hoped and prayed it would be different. For the moment, the only thing that mattered to me was that I felt safe, secure, and loved in Elliot's arms.

The next morning I got out of bed quietly, so as not to wake up Elliot. He would usually get up after I left for work to go up to his own room and go back to sleep. After getting ready for work, I walked over to the bed and kissed him lightly on his forehead, quietly shutting the door behind me as I went to get started on my day.

I collected beer bottles off the picnic table in the courtyard that were left over from some guests' impromptu party the night before, as Patrice came out of the office en route to the laundry room, toting a basket of sheets and towels.

"Lu, have you seen Elliot yet this morning?" she asked.

Caught off guard, I replied, "No, Patrice, I haven't seen him."

I regretted what I had said as soon as the words escaped from my mouth. I didn't want to lie to Patrice. She kept such a tight watch on the happenings in the hostel that I couldn't believe she didn't know that Elliot and I had started sleeping together. We were being discrete, but by no means were we trying to hide it from her. The more I thought about it, the more convinced I became that I needed to tell Patrice about our relationship before she heard about it from someone else. Since I had my own room, I felt that it was my business if I so chose to have someone stay overnight. Still, I didn't want to get on Patrice's bad side over something like this, so I felt that honesty was the best policy. I waited for Patrice to go back into the office. Once she was inside, I quickly went in after her.

"Patrice, I have to tell you something." Taking a deep breath, I continued, "You know when you asked me if I saw Elliot this morning, and I said I didn't? Well, the truth is . . . he is asleep in my bed." Not knowing what to expect, I winced while waiting for her reply.

As what I said sunk in, she began to laugh heartily as if I had told her some great joke. Then she stopped laughing as suddenly as she had started as if gripped by some innermost thought. She shot me a stern look. "He still has to pay his rent!" she hissed.

Rattled by her sudden change in demeanor, I hastily replied, "Oh, well, yes, of course he has to pay his rent. I just wanted to let you know that Elliot and I are in a relationship before you heard it from someone else."

Before she could say anything else, I left the office as quickly as I had entered it. Since I lived on-site, I felt responsible for keeping her informed about any changes in the circumstances in my life. I wasn't seeking her approval, but, out of respect, I wanted her to be aware of the situation. All I asked for in return was that she respected my privacy and that I be allowed to conduct my life as I saw fit, as long as I didn't break any rules of the hostel. I didn't think it mattered much whether Elliot slept in his bed upstairs in the dorm room or with me. I most certainly didn't expect her to give him free rent just because he was staying in my room. Perhaps she thought that Elliot wanted to live with me so he wouldn't have to pay rent. Unbeknownst to her, Elliot was totally unaware of the arrangement I had with Patrice regarding my pay. He never asked me about the arrangement, and I never told him. I didn't think it was any of his business.

As I swept the courtyard sidewalk, Greta made an appearance looking for food. I was becoming attached to her and looked forward to her visits. I laid the broom down and ran to my room for some almonds. I left the door slightly ajar as I went in to retrieve them from on top of my refrigerator. As I went to grab the bag, I noticed that Elliot was gone and he had neatly made up the bed. When I turned around, I saw Greta sitting patiently on the rug inside my door. Fearful that she might think she could have the run of my room, I shouted playfully, "Greta! You can't come in here! Come on, get going! Out!" I shooed her out the door and followed her outside, laying the almonds down on the low wall across from my room that bordered the courtyard. Greta climbed up on the ledge and sat down to eat. I stood watching her for awhile longer, marveling at her tameness.

Finished with feeding Greta, I started mopping the dorm rooms. The first one I went into had sand all over the bottom mattresses and the floor. I spotted Patrice passing through the kitchen as I swept the sand from the floor. "Hey, Patrice, come here for a minute!"

Patrice walked in the room with an inquisitive look on her face. Pointing to all the sand, I said, "Who was in this room? It looks like they brought part of the beach back with them."

"Oh, it was those guys from the islands. They were probably swimming last night."

As she spoke, she abruptly took off her shoe and swatted something on the wall. "Fucking bugs!"

Startled by her sudden movement, I looked curiously at the wall bearing the crushed remains. She didn't say what kind of bug it was that she had killed, and I didn't think to ask her. Florida was notorious for bugs, especially ants and cockroaches. Even though I kept my room clear of any crumbs, I would still find ants and the occasional cockroach. I kept everything in the refrigerator, even my cereal. Not thinking anymore about the incident, I finished my sweeping as Patrice left the room.

The next morning when I walked through the kitchen, I noticed that there were rags stuffed under the door to the room where Patrice had killed the bug. Later in the morning on her way to the laundry room, she told me I didn't need to clean that particular room. I was beginning to wonder what kind of bug she had killed when my suspicions were confirmed that afternoon by her Uncle Carlos. I cleaned Carlos's office once a week. Usually he wasn't there, but this particular day, he was sitting at his desk when I went in to clean.

Reading a letter at his desk, he looked up at me when I came through the door. "I hear there are bed bugs in room four again," he said matter-of-factly.

I stopped in my tracks and looked over at him not saying a word. I had no idea what he was talking about.

He continued in an irritated tone. "I just got rid of them a few months ago and they are back again."

"Oh. I hear that they are hard to get rid of."

"Well, we have a special spray that we use for them. It's cheaper than hiring an exterminator."

I knew a little about bed bugs from my previous experience working in an upscale hotel where most people would assume there wouldn't be any bed bugs. Unfortunately, bed bugs do not discriminate based on property ratings; they can show up even in the most luxurious of hotel rooms brought in by unsuspecting guests on their clothing or luggage. Once bed bugs get onto a property, it is very difficult to get rid of them since they get into cracks in the wall, bedroom furniture, picture frames, and light switches. They can travel great distances, and if the room they infest is left unoccupied, they will make their way to adjoining rooms. It can cost a property thousands of dollars to pay for an exterminator to spray for bed bugs, and sometimes they end up replacing the furniture in the room after repainting and putting down new carpeting. So when Carlos started talking about bed bugs, I raised an eyebrow.

After letting the room sit for a few days, Patrice asked me to do a general cleaning in preparation for arriving guests. I walked cautiously around the room, acting like it was contaminated with deadly bacteria. I didn't dare touch the bedding, but, out of curiosity, I leaned over to inspect a mattress, and to my relief, didn't see anything crawling around. I cleaned the room as quickly as possible and was relieved when I shut the door behind me. I felt sorry for the unsuspecting guests that would soon be arriving to stay in the room. I thought about how I might feel if

I found out that the room I was staying in had just been sprayed for bed bugs a few days earlier. The thought made my skin crawl, and I quickly put it out of my mind. I consoled myself with the thought that Patrice had handled this type of problem before and knew what she was doing. Patrice never said a word to me about the bed begs; she didn't confide in me about such matters.

That evening I saw Nathan in the TV lounge and asked him how his job was going. A bit tipsy after having a few beers, Nathan was in the mood to talk and conversation flowed freely as he entertained me with tales about his job driving a delivery truck. Caught up in laughter, I didn't notice that Elliot had walked into the TV room until he placed something wrapped in a brown paper bag into my lap.

I put my hands around the package and looked up at him. "What is this?"

"Open it up and see for yourself," he said as he stood looking down at me smiling.

I unfolded the top of the bag and pulled out a large bottle of macadamia nut liqueur. "Oh, thank you. I've never had this before."

"You will like it. We will have some later tonight." Elliot nodded at Nathan and then turned to go. "I'll see you later. I have to go check my e-mail," he said.

I half-listened to Nathan finish his story as I sat with my hands clasped around the crumpled brown bag, my mind preoccupied with thoughts of Elliot.

That night we sat in bed sipping the strong, nutty liqueur from crystal glasses that Patrice had sent over for us to use. Elliot had stopped by the office on his way in to let Patrice know that he had brought in the liqueur since it was forbidden to have hard liquor on premise. Since she was aware that I didn't have much in the way of glassware, she had thoughtfully provided the glasses for us to use. The fiery liquid burned my throat, and in a few minutes, I felt my muscles go limp as a warm glow spread from my head to my toes. We set the empty glasses on our night stands, then turned to hold each other in our arms. I reached up and stroked the wavy coils of Elliot's hair until I drifted off into a peaceful slumber.

Elliot was spending every night in my room. I started to think about asking him to move in with me. It didn't make sense for him to get up every morning to go upstairs to his room to go back to sleep or shower. It didn't occur to me to ask Patrice how she would feel about this. Perhaps I was being presumptuous, but I had my own room, and I felt that I could do with it as I pleased. When you live on-site there are some vague areas regarding how to conduct your personal life. I was used to renting my own apartment and making my own decisions. Many months later I would come to find out how Patrice really felt about my decision to ask Elliot to move in with me.

The opportunity to discuss our living arrangements presented itself that evening at dinner. Earlier in the day, I asked Elliot if he would like pizza for dinner. I hadn't had pizza for a long time because I didn't like to eat pizza by myself. When my children were growing up, we always had pizza on Friday nights, so it became sort of a family tradition. I ordered the pizza and when the deliveryman dropped it off, we went to my room to eat. Elliot and I pulled up our chairs to my little, round plastic table and ate while talking about how our day went. Halfway through dinner without anyforewarning, I came right to the point.

"Elliot, why don't you move in here with me?"

Elliot had just taken a large bite of pizza. I waited in silence while he finished chewing, feeling confident that he wouldn't have any reservations about the idea.

"Uhhhh, I don't think I want to do that right now."

Trying to hide my disappointment, I got up to refill my drink. My fear of rejection kept me from asking him what his reasons were for not wanting to live together. My immediate thought was that he might not want that type of commitment between us. He may have been concerned about what Patrice would think, or perhaps he was uncomfortable with the idea because of his religious beliefs. I will never know, because I didn't ask him. All I knew was that I wanted him to live with me, and I didn't consider what anyone else would think of it, including the church. Elliot and I had a strong spiritual bond that was important to our relationship. The Catholic Church does not approve of sex outside of marriage, let alone living together. That I could admire Elliot for his devoutness, but be so willing to disregard the basic teachings of our faith, makes me wonder where my head was at at the time. I was asking him to go against something he believed in deeply. Since we were already sleeping together outside of marriage, I didn't think that living together would be an issue. I had a lot to learn about Elliot's beliefs.

Regaining my composure, I sat back down at the table. "Well, let me know if you change your mind."

Elliot continued eating his pizza and didn't say another word about it. I had a feeling that, in time, Elliot would change his mind.

I was beginning to see a clear pattern in the differences in how we conducted ourselves. I would think about what I wanted and then take immediate action to get it, not wasting a moment. Elliot, on the other hand, had a different modus operandi. He would think about something for a long time, and then he would act when the mood struck him, or when he eventually got around to it.

Elliot was spending more and more time huddled in conversation with Patrice surrounded in an air of secrecy. One afternoon when I was in the office with Patrice, Elliot came in to talk to her. She asked me to leave for a few minutes, so that they could talk in private. Since Elliot had confided in me about helping Patrice get financing for the hostel, I knew that they were talking about business. Their relationship became even more involved once Elliot became Patrice's private driver. She no longer had to take a cab or the bus. He made himself available to drive her every day at four o'clock in the afternoon until six o'clock when she returned to work in the office. On

Wednesdays, she would call him on his cell phone to let him know what time she was going to the casino, and then he would usually stay there with her until she returned late at night while I ran the hostel. On Wednesday evenings, I ran the office out of my room by taking the phone with me and opening my blinds which gave me a good view of the office and courtyard, so that I could watch TV or read in my room until a guest arrived. I kept my TV volume low so that I could hear the door chimes if a guest was at the gate. At midnight I would shut off the office lights and lock the door then go back to my room to get ready for bed. I had given Elliot a key to my room, so that he could get in if I was asleep.

I was pleased that Patrice was taking Elliot under her wing, just as she had done to me. I couldn't imagine a better arrangement between the three of us. We were a perfect team. We all got along well and helped each other out. There was so much to look forward to in our future at the hostel.

One afternoon, in an effort to show her appreciation for all our hard work, Patrice treated us to lunch. Her original plan was to take us out to eat at an upscale restaurant that she liked to order her lunch from. When the day arrived, she decided instead to have Elliot bring back our food for us to eat at the hostel. In the morning, she gave us a menu to look over and told us to let her know what we wanted to eat. She ordered our lunches and Elliot went to pick them up. I thought we would all eat together. Instead, when Elliot returned, Patrice took her food to her room, and Elliot and I went to my room to eat. Although she was the one who had suggested we go out to eat together, there was something that held her back from letting us get too close to her. Perhaps she felt uncomfortable since Elliot and I were a couple and she was alone, although I can't imagine why that would bother her. The three of us were at the hostel all day long together. Since she was my boss, we weren't close friends. We liked and cared about each other, but we both seemed to have a reserved nature that kept us from getting too close to each other on a personal level. There was a certain safety in the emotional distance between us.

When we talked to each other, it was about work; she didn't confide in me about business matters. We talked about what needed to be done around the hostel or issues with guests. That I had an intimate relationship with Elliot, and Patrice had a business relationship with him, put me in an awkward situation with Patrice. After Patrice found out that Elliot and I were a couple, she made it a point to tell me that what went on in the hostel was confidential, and I was not to discuss it with him or anyone else. Matters became more complicated when Elliot confided in me about business dealings with Patrice. I was caught in a delicate position between the two people who were the dominant forces in my life.

Elliot and I sat in my room enjoying our lunch, both of us in high spirits from our good fortune. We had a generous boss who treated us well, and we had each other. As we laughed and ate, Elliot's talk turned to business.

"Hey, baby, I've got some good news. Patrice is interested in financing my movie with her investment group from Tobago. Looks like before long I will be heading to Los Angeles to make my movie."

I stopped chewing long enough to let his words sink in. I swallowed my food quickly so as to respond. "You're going to Los Angeles?"

"Well, sure. That's where I'm going to shoot my movie."

"What about us? How long will you be gone?"

"Only for a year or so. It shouldn't take that long. You can come visit me."

All of the lightheartedness from our festive lunch evaporated into thin air. I was not happy to hear that he had plans to leave me to go to Los Angeles. No wonder he didn't think it was a good idea for us to live together. He must have known about Patrice's interest in financing his movie when I first asked him about living together and didn't want to jeopardize the project by doing something that might upset Patrice.

My appetite vanished. I pushed my plate aside and looked up at him with an anguished expression. "I don't want a long distance relationship," I said defiantly. I took a deep breath daring to say what I felt. "Look, the way I feel about you is more than just liking you." I hesitated for a moment fearful of revealing my true feelings for him. I tossed all reservations aside and poured out my heart to him. "This is love . . . I love you."

I waited to see how he would respond to my ardent profession. His gaze held mine for an interminably long time. I saw kindness and compassion in his eyes, perhaps even a hint of love.

Quietly in his easy, laid back manner, he said, "Thank you for your love. That means a lot to me."

"Well . . . That's how I feel about you."

We finished our meal in silence. I didn't regret that I told him that I loved him. I was disappointed that he didn't respond the way I would have liked, but I couldn't make someone love me, nor would I want him to tell me he loved me, if he didn't. I was proud of myself for having the courage to say how I felt. I found that as I got older, I became more vocal about my feelings. Life is too short to waste by not being upfront about how you feel towards someone in a relationship. It is better to risk rejection than to keep your feelings bottled up inside of you, leaving the other person guessing as to how you really feel.

Elliot must have needed time to sort through his feelings about me, or his guilt for not holding up his end of the deal got the better of him. The next evening it was his turn to profess his feelings for me. As I rested my head on his shoulder while watching TV, he reached over and took hold of my hand, caressing it with his fingers.

"I wanted to thank you again for your love. I can't just tell someone I love them because they say it to me. I can only say it when I feel it. So when I do tell you that I love you, then you know it comes from my heart and that I mean it."

"That's okay, honey. I understand."

"What I notice about you is that you love deeply and with your whole heart. You have a lot of love to give."

"It is not easy for me to love again. I have been hurt a lot by men that I have loved. You are the first man that I have loved for a very long time; too long. It is a lonely life when you don't have someone to share your love with."

He stroked my arm tenderly as if trying to soothe away past hurts. He softly said, "I do love you, too."

I climbed into his lap and wrapped my arms around his neck, resting my cheek against his. It was good to feel loved again. I was sure this time it would last forever.

Having found love again after being on my own for so long made me somewhat clingy. Once while we were eating dinner, I had to leave momentarily to retrieve something from the kitchen. As I made my way to the door, I suddenly turned around and gave him a tentative look. "I'll be right back," I said.

He started to laugh and replied, "Don't worry. I'm not going anywhere!"

I blushed with embarrassment at how I must have come across to him, as if I thought he was going to disappear into thin air while I was gone.

At night I would wake up and frantically search for him, lifting my head off the pillow to see where he was at in the bed. Spotting him on the other side with his back to me, I would wiggle my way across the bed until I was right up against him and wrap my arm snuggly around him, holding on to him for dear life.

When I turned out the lights at night, I was ready to go to sleep. Elliot, on the other hand, liked to talk before he went to sleep. I would try to force myself to stay awake by blinking my eyes determinedly, but slowly my eyelids would begin to droop, lulled to sleep by his incessant chatter which was as effective as a lullaby. One night before I had a chance to drift off into a dreamy sleep, he suddenly said, "I wonder what our child would look like. I think about that sometimes."

Suddenly wide awake, I looked over at him. I had never had a man say that to me in my life, and I had three grown children. I reached over and squeezed his hand. "Well, we'll never know. I can't have any more children. It's a shame that we didn't meet when we were younger."

"Yes, it is a shame. We would have had a beautiful child."

I drifted off to sleep snugly wrapped in Elliot's arms, my head filled with the laughter of a small child with sparkling brown eyes set in a face of smooth skin the color of brown sugar and framed by tightly coiled ringlets of coal black hair, who picked up seashells to show us as we walked arm in arm along the edge of the sea.

A few days later Elliot decided to move in with me. He casually announced it as we were eating dinner. I asked him what had made him change his mind. He simply responded, "You did. You asked me to move in with you." I found his response to be lacking in substance, but I didn't push the issue any further.

Once he moved in, I succumbed to the innate desire to build a nest; in this case, a love nest. Going against my tendency to spurn material possessions I went on my biggest shopping spree yet, buying a dinette set with two cushioned chairs and a recliner. To make room for everything, Elliot helped me move the futon into one of the TV rooms for the guests to use. When I pushed the recliner into place not too far from the TV set, I was pleased when he said, "I can see I'll be sitting in that a lot." I wanted him to feel comfortable in our new home, even if it was just one little room. I didn't have a lot of room to work with, but I made the best use of the available space, making an area for the kitchen, dining room, living room, and bedroom all in the space of one good-sized room. For added comfort, I even bought a feather mattress to put on top of the regular mattress and two new pillows. Patrice was kind enough to contribute a dresser and two matching night stands for our little nest. She seemed to be going out of her way to make sure that we were comfortable and had everything that we needed. I cleared out half of my closet and Elliot brought down his clothes from his dorm room, filling his side of the closet and dresser. In the bathroom I cleaned out one of the drawers in the vanity for his shaving supplies, but to my dismay Elliot left his shaving bag on the counter unpacked. There wouldn't be a day that went by that I didn't look at that unpacked shaving bag with an uneasy feeling that I tried to casually dismiss from the back of my mind.

I was happy at how Elliot and I's relationship was developing. Little by little, our lives began to totally revolve around each other, as we became set in our daily routines. There was one thing that prodded at my conscience: I noticed that Elliot had stopped going to communion when we went to mass on Sundays. I would rise up from the pew at the appointed time to get in line for communion, while Elliot remained firmly entrenched in his pew, kneeling in prayer. I figured he had his reasons, and, at first, I didn't say anything to him about it. This weighed heavily on my mind one Sunday morning as I dressed for church. I decided that if Elliot didn't go to communion that morning, I would ask him about it. Yet again, he stayed behind while I went up to receive communion.

I waited until we went back to my room after our usual Sunday dinner to discuss the matter with him. Elliot picked up a newspaper and sat on the recliner absorbed in reading. I changed my clothes and sat down in the chair from the new dinette set.

"Honey, I noticed you haven't gone to communion for the past three weeks."

Elliot slowly reached up to remove his reading glasses, as he carefully laid the newspaper down in his lap. Staring straight at me from across the room, he replied, "I can't go to communion because we are sleeping together. You shouldn't be going either," he said matter-of-factly.

I felt my face turning red with anger. "What? You went to communion before when you were seeing that other woman!"

"That was different. I went to confession before I went to communion with the intent of not doing it again."

"But you did do it again with her!"

Where I was emotional and quick to anger, Elliot conducted himself in a calm and deliberate manner, stopping to think before he spoke. Patiently, he explained, "This is different because we are living together in sin, and unless we get married, we cannot go to communion."

I wasn't ready to give up yet. "Well, what if we go to confession every Saturday?"

Elliot narrowed his eyes in exasperation. "Do you really believe it is right for you to go to communion?"

His reproachful tone caused me to squirm in my chair. "No, not if you follow the laws of the church it isn't. But what is the point in going to church if you can't go to communion?!"

"You can do a Spiritual Communion. The prayer is in the blue prayer book that I gave you."

My temper subsided as I thought about what he was saying. I had to admit that he was right in his thinking. I didn't have any qualms about bending the rules of the church to suit my own style of living, but I couldn't expect the same from Elliot. One of the things I loved about him was his strong religious faith, and I just expected him to toss it aside to suit me. We were sleeping together outside of marriage, while praying the rosary almost every night and going to mass every Sunday, and I thought we should still be able to go to communion.

I was the first to admit when I was wrong about something, and this time I was blatantly wrong. I looked at him sheepishly. "I'm sorry. You're right, of course. I won't go to communion anymore," I said.

"There is another way, Lu."

"What do you mean?"

"We can give up sex as a sacrifice to God."

"Give up sex?"

"Yes. When I was engaged to my fiancée many years ago, we talked about living a married life together without being intimate, as a way to please God."

As he spoke, in my mind's eye I saw a young man dutifully sitting beside his mother in church, slyly looking out of the corner of his eye at his father's mistress, demurely seated on the opposite side of the church. In his own misguided way, Elliot was trying to pay for the sins of his father.

I shook my head in disbelief. I couldn't believe what Elliot was suggesting to me. I struggled to control my temper as I tried to reason with him. "Elliot, I thought that God gave us marriage so that we could be intimate with each other. I have never heard of married people giving up sex for God! Only priests do that! You should have been a priest!"

"I told you before that I didn't feel that I was worthy enough to be a priest."

"You know, I have to be honest with you. If this is how you feel about being in a relationship, then you need to find someone who shares your vision. I'm sorry, but I can't be that kind of woman for you."

"I respect your feelings."

"You do realize that withholding sex in a marriage is grounds for divorce? I mean, if we were ever to get married, I wouldn't want this to become an issue with us."

"It won't."

"Okay, enough of this. I am going to the beach this afternoon. What are you going to do?"

"I am going to take a nap."

I got up and changed into my bathing suit, as Elliot picked up his newspaper to begin reading where he left off.

On my way out the gate, I ran into Patrice. "Lu, did you hear the fight last night?"

"What fight? Where?"

Patrice smiled broadly. "Last night in the upstairs kitchen, Nathan caught Sam stealing some of his food and wanted to punch him out. I told Sam to get his things and get out."

"Well, that's for the best. He has caused a lot of problems here."

I was relieved to hear that Sam was finally gone. I had tired of spying on him. After that, I would see Sam on occasion riding his bike up and down the street. I figured he had moved on to raid another refrigerator from some unsuspecting guests in another hostel.

I never tired of watching the pelicans as I sat in my chair at the beach. They would fly overhead in a V-formation; a pattern so perfect that they would be the envy of any flight formation pilots such as the Blue Angels. I marveled at how they knew to space themselves so evenly apart and at the right angles, wondering how they decided who should be the one in front to lead the flock. Other times, I would see them gliding, one in front of the other, with outstretched wings a few feet above the sparkling water. Circling over the water in search of their dinner, they would swoop down head first with a splash, momentarily submerging themselves into the sea to pluck a fish from its depths with their long, slender beaks. Then bobbing back up to the surface, they would float on top of the water, savoring the freshly caught fish. I envied the simplicity of their life. All they had to do all day was glide over sparkling seas, stopping to feed from the vast kettle of fish when hunger struck. They lived their lives completely in tune with the rhythm of nature their days guided by the sun, the starry night, and the ebb and the flow of the tides.

After Elliot moved in with me, Patrice started to make a habit of knocking on our door every afternoon after I got off from work. Elliot liked to take a nap in the afternoon, and I would often crawl into bed with him to while away the afternoon. We would just be getting comfortable when there would be a loud rap on the door. Elliot or I would get up and get dressed to answer the door. Patrice, meanwhile, would be waiting patiently outside. She usually had some question for me about work that day, or would tell Elliot what time she wanted to leave for errands later in the afternoon. Elliot would close the door, remove his clothes, and climb back into bed. One afternoon as he sat on the edge of the bed slightly irritated at another interrupted afternoon nap, he looked over at me and said, "I think Patrice is jealous that we have each other."

It must have been hard for her to see the two of us always together. Patrice was by herself most of the time, since Madeline lived in Denmark and could only come to visit a couple of times a year for a few weeks at a time. I don't know how they managed to keep their long distance relationship intact. She talked to Madeline on the phone every day and kept her picture prominently displayed on her TV stand.

I'm not sure exactly when it was that I first realized Patrice was a lesbian. She had mentioned Madeline on numerous occasions and, at first, I thought they were just good friends. Patrice never insinuated that Madeline was her significant other, nor did she drop subtle hints. I began to put the pieces together when Patrice had asked me to clean her room, and I noticed a picture of Madeline on her TV stand. There was something about where the picture was placed on the bare shelf that caught my attention. The stark black and white photo of Madeline in a mid-sized silver frame was placed on the edge of the shelf so that Patrice would have full view of it when she sat in her sofa chair to watch TV, which she often did. It had a place of honor.

My feelings toward Patrice didn't change at all after I finally figured out that she was a lesbian. Her sexuality was her private business. I thought of her as a person, first, and then as my boss. Neither the color of her skin nor her sexual orientation had any bearing on how I acted towards her. But then, that is my attitude towards anyone that I meet.

If Patrice wasn't knocking on the door, she would look for me by running through the hostel loudly calling out my name because she wanted to ask me some mundane question relating to work. One afternoon after I finished working, I was taking a shower. The window to my bathroom overlooked the back of the hostel, and I could hear her voice coming from somewhere outside. I yelled back that I would be right out, then jumped out of the shower and quickly put on some clothes. When I found her in the courtyard and told her I had been in the shower, she looked at me somewhat embarrassed and replied that she thought I was out back in the laundry room. The constant interruptions were nerve racking at times. I was finding out that there was little privacy living and working in the hostel. I never really had my own time to myself.

Now that I had my own room, I didn't see Aylin as much as when I roomed with her. She still had another month to go at the hostel before she returned to Turkey the latter part of October. I would sometimes see her outside the gate standing very close to Makalo, her petite form dwarfed by his tall, lanky frame. I could tell that they were lovers from how they looked at each other. Patrice had gotten rid of Makalo because he was smoking in the computer room, and when he drank, he would cause problems with some of the other guests. She didn't kick him out; she simply told him there wasn't any space available when he went to pay for another week's rent.

Since I started working in the office, I quickly learned how Patrice regulated the long-term guests in the hostel. She would let them pay for a few days or a week and then observe them around the hostel. If they obeyed the rules and didn't cause any problems, she would let them continue to stay. The foreign guests stayed at the hostel for a few nights since they were just passing through on their way to another destination. There were seldom any problems with them except for occasional late night partying. I think she would have preferred to just cater to international guests, but since she couldn't count on them to always fill all the beds in the hostel, she rented to Americans to ensure a steady income. As she explained to me, "They are what keep us going when things are slow." Many hostels require the guests to have a passport as a way to keep out riffraff looking for cheap lodging.

Aylin was spending a lot of time on the house computer causing the other guests to complain. Guests were limited to using the computer for half an hour at a time. Even Elliot was getting upset with her, which was unusual for him. It took a lot for him to get upset. Things came to a head one Wednesday evening when a guest complained to me that Aylin had been on the computer for over two hours. I went up to the computer room to talk with her.

"Aylin, how long have you been on the computer?"

She looked at me sheepishly, and replied, "Oh, just for an hour or so. If someone comes in to use the computer, I let them use it."

"No, Aylin, one of the guests said you have been on the computer for hours. You can't always see them waiting because your back is to the door."

"No, I always see them and let them use it," she insisted.

"I want you to sign off the computer right now, and you can't use it anymore tonight. You need to talk with Patrice in the morning before you use the computer again. We are getting too many complaints about you."

Aylin's face turned red as she fought back tears. She logged off the computer and quietly went down to her room. I felt bad for having to reprimand her, but it was my job to enforce the rules of the hostel and handle complaints. That was the most difficult part of my job. I had been friendly with Aylin for months, treating her like my daughter. And now, as I had done to my own daughters in the past, I had just grounded Aylin.

After working all day, I was looking forward to getting a good night's sleep. Elliot brought Patrice back from the casino around midnight, so we climbed into bed together exhausted after a long day and fell right asleep. After what seemed like only a brief time later, I was roused from a deep sleep by loud voices in a heated argument. I pushed the light on my bedside clock which read shortly after two o'clock. I climbed wearily out of bed and quickly threw some clothes on, trying not to wake up Elliot in the process. He stirred just as I finished getting dressed. I looked over at him, and said, "I'll be right back. Someone is fighting." My room was located between the two downstairs TV lounges.

As I opened my door, I could hear loud voices coming from the TV room closest to my door. When I made a quick entrance into the room, everyone scattered except for Toby, a tall, skinny African-American who had been staying with us for about a week. He was always polite and well behaved around me, so I was surprised to see him there. He had pulled the TV out away from the wall and stood holding the plug in his hand.

Angry at having been woken from a deep sleep, I barked, "What is going on here?!"

"Nothing. I am just turning off the TV. It was too loud and I couldn't sleep."

"Who were you fighting with? I could hear you in my room next door!"

"I asked them to turn the TV down and they wouldn't, so I unplugged it and they got mad."

"Put the TV back where it belongs and go to your room!"

"It's not my fault. They wouldn't listen to me. I just . . . "

"Go to your room now, or get your things and get out!"

He pushed the TV back in place and quickly walked out the door to go to his room. Whomever he had been fighting with had taken off to hide in their rooms, or in some dark corner for fear of getting into trouble also. I shut the light off in the room. Peace and quiet had been restored, so I crept back into my room, and snuggling up to Elliot, I fell back asleep. The next morning I filled Patrice in on the middle of the night melee. A few days later, I noticed that Toby was gone.

On weekend evenings, Elliot and I started watching movies. At first, we watched movies that Patrice had given us from her collection which, although entertaining, weren't quite our style. One evening over dinner we talked about the kinds of movies that we liked. I asked Elliot what some of his favorite movies were and he mentioned that he liked *Casa Blanca* and *A Street Car Named Desire*, along with some other classic movies which I had never seen. Although I was familiar with the titles and actors in the classic movies, I had never gotten around to watching them. I printed out a list of the top classic movies from a web site, and I would pick up one or two from my list to watch every weekend. The first one that we watched together was *Casa Blanca*. After that, every evening before eating our dinner, Elliot and I would raise our glasses in a toast and he would say, "Here's to you, baby!" A slight twist on our favorite line from the movie.

Elliot had a penchant for rum and raisin ice cream. One evening after we finished our rosary, he asked me if I would like some ice cream. He ran down to the convenience store to pick up a pint of rum and raisin ice cream which we shared that night while watching a movie. After that, to the distress of my expanding waistline, one of us would pick up a pint of ice cream for our movie night. Weekend evenings we would sit up in bed propped up against our fluffy pillows, relishing our bowls of ice cream as we contentedly watched a movie.

Now that Elliot filled my days and nights, I no longer asked Rhoda out for dinner. I never heard from her again since I was always the one to initiate contact. I always wondered if she ever thought about what had happened to me. It had been an odd relationship from the start.

I continued with my ESL classes, making my weekly trek to the library on Tuesday evenings for a few hours. I enjoyed the students and looked forward to going to class. Besides going to the beach, it was the only thing that I did without Elliot.

I was content to have a man around to share my life with. I had fixed up a home for us where we could live in comfort. In our room, with the door shut and the blinds drawn, we didn't feel like we were in a hostel at all, but in our own private cocoon shielded from the outside world. If we wanted to be a part of the hostel, all we had to do was step outside our door and we were immediately drawn into another world.

I had used all my own money to buy furniture and fix up my room. I didn't ask Elliot to contribute to household expenses and he didn't offer, although, he continued to pay his rent as he did when he was in his own dorm room. I suspected that he didn't have much money, even though he talked about his mortgage business and making his film. My intent was to make a home for us that we could live in for an undetermined period of time. I never discussed this with Elliot, preferring to think that he was of the same mind. I had a tendency to go about things my own way without considering other peoples' thoughts or feelings, assuming that they wanted the same things that I did. Sometimes I think that I must be off in my own little world somewhere.

   This was evident in an incident that occurred one evening as I was puttering around the room setting the table for dinner. Elliot was stretched out on the bed watching me as I was setting the table for dinner. I felt his eyes on me as I set in place the dishes, napkins, and silverware. In an amused tone, he said, "It looks like you are playing house." His statement struck me as odd, and for a brief moment, I stopped what I was doing. In the back of my mind, I wondered what would make him say such a thing.

Chapter 10

Rifts

All of the excitement from the past few months settled down into a routine that brought with it a contentedness like the flame from a match that at first flares up and then subsides into a steady burning flame. But that flame eventually flickers and dies out, much like the excitement in life, extinguishing the flame of happiness.

Running late one morning, I dashed out of my room to shut out the night lights. Turning to go through the open door of the TV room, I ran into Greta as she was coming out of the door. We both stopped in our tracks and I let out a screech of surprise as Greta turned and ran the other way. Realizing what had happened, I burst into laughter as I watched Greta run across the room to the door on the other side of the room.

"Greta, come back here! It's just me. I'm sorry I scared you." I shouted after her.

Greta stopped at the door and turned to look at me with her big, dark eyes full of fright. I took a few steps towards her. "Wait! I will get some almonds for you." I quickly retrieved them from my room, and when I came back out the door, she was patiently waiting for me. She scampered towards me as I set down the nuts on the walkway. I left her to her snack while I went about my cleaning. I was eager to finish my cleaning early since it was

Wednesday, and I had to fill in for Patrice for the rest of the day.

    I liked that working in the office gave me the opportunity to meet many of the new guests when they arrived. It was the end of October and a whole new group of guests were arriving in time for the international boat show. All of the hotels and hostels in the area were sold out for the event. People come from all over the world to go to the convention center or to the marinas to look at the boats on display. A few of the guests that arrived for the boat show were younger people looking for work on yachts. The boat show offered an opportunity to meet with owners looking for crew members, or there was always the chance of finding work on a yacht through networking with crew members who were staying at the hostels.

    Sarah was one of the guests coming in from New Zealand to look for work on a yacht. I had answered an e-mail she had sent to us a few weeks before to make arrangements for her transportation from Miami Airport to the hostel. I had enlisted Elliot to pick her up. She e-mailed her arrival time to me along with a brief description of herself, so that he could pick her out of the crowd at the airport. I jotted down her description on a piece of paper and handed it to Elliot. Her flight was due in at ten o'clock at night, so it would be almost midnight before they got back to the hostel. Elliot had taken Patrice to the casino earlier in the day and planned to pick her back up after he dropped off Sarah. I had everything ready for Sarah since she would be a late arrival. Wednesdays were my long day, and I didn't want to have to work past midnight. I was watching TV in my room when I looked out the window and saw them walk through the gate. I got up and went out to meet them.

    Quiet spoken and polite, Sarah was a petite young lady in her early twenties with light brown hair pulled up into a pony tail and hazel eyes. She had a girlish quality about her that made her seem much younger. I peered across the counter at her as she filled out her paperwork, admiring her courage to come so far all by herself at such a tender age. I checked her in quickly and gave her a room key. She had her hands full with all of her luggage, so I carried her sheets and towel as we made our way to her room while chatting about her long flight. I tiptoed into the room and turned on the bathroom light so as not to disturb her roommates and pointed out her bed to her. Bidding her goodnight, I closed the door quietly behind me. It was time to close up the office and go to bed. Elliot had left to pick up Patrice and wouldn't be back for another hour.

A young married couple, Ethan and Hannah, from Australia arrived about the same time as Sarah. They looked remarkably alike with their dark hair and tall, gangly physiques. Ethan was a chef looking for work on a yacht and his wife was looking for work as a cabin stewardess. Every evening, he cooked up a delectable meal while she assisted him. I would walk by the stove and stop to ask what he was making, and he would rattle off the name of some fancy French dish. I don't know how they managed to stay so thin with all the sumptuous meals that they ate. They slept in one of the dorm rooms that had been sprayed for bed bugs, and every time I looked at them, I couldn't help but hope that all the bed begs were gone. They were such a nice, friendly couple that I couldn't bear the thought that bed bugs might be feasting on them while they slept. When I walked by them, I would look at their unexposed skin for signs of bite marks. To my relief, I never saw any.

The guests looking for work on the yachts would leave during the day in search of employment. I would listen to them talking to each other when they came back at night. Many of them returned discouraged at night with tales of yachts running with skeleton crews, or owners trying to sell their yachts because of the bad economy. Some of these guests eventually left, unable to find work. Those that stuck with it, and were persistent, eventually did find work. Sarah found a job and so did the young couple. Ethan was such a fabulous cook that I knew someone would snatch him up relatively quickly. The couple left to crew on a yacht while Sarah stayed at the hostel while she did cleaning or went out on a few overnight trips.

Evelyn, a young woman in her late twenties, from London, England, arrived at the hostel to look for work. She was a tall, leggy, brunette with a long face set with doe-like eyes and spindly legs that she showed off by wearing a short, black skirt that came to just below her derriere. She wore the same skirt night after night and often the same black and white stripped top with it. She liked men and booze, and like Stuart, she could talk to anyone. She sat happily chatting away to whomever she could find to talk to. She would drink the night away, and I would often find her passed out on the futon in the TV room in the morning when I went in to clean. One morning she was sprawled out on the futon with her back facing outwards, her panties protruding from under her skirt which was pulled up around her hips. Patrice came into the TV lounge to ask me a question, and when she saw Evelyn's backside immodestly exposed, she went to find a blanket to cover her up with. Another evening when Evelyn had too much to drink, Patrice took her to her room and put her to bed.

Patrice didn't like drinking, but she catered to the guests that did, often going out of her way to accommodate them. She had a sensitive nose and the smell of alcohol on a person upset her. She took a disliking to some of the older men, mostly drifters, who reeked of alcohol, but she seemed to be drawn to the younger, long-term guests who like to party and have a good time. She was tolerant of their drinking, as long as they didn't get out of line and they paid their rent on time.

Eleanor, a French Canadian, also arrived to look for work on a yacht. Curly, golden locks of hair framed her round face set with lively, blue eyes and small mouth. At first sight, she looked pleasant enough, but as soon as she started talking, I was appalled by her foul language. She sprinkled expletives generously throughout her conversation as if talking that way made her sound cool. Her laugh was loud and brash and seemed a bit off color, as if she was always laughing at some bawdy joke. She sounded like she had just gotten off a ship after spending months at sea with hardened sailors. I felt sorry for her that she thought it becoming to conduct herself in such an unpleasant manner. Despite her crude manner, she was outgoing and got along well with everyone except Evelyn. They took an immediate disliking to each other, and Patrice had to put them in separate rooms to keep them from bickering and arguing with each other. Eleanor took a liking to Matt, a boyish young American guest, and I would see the two of them talking with their arms around each other. I sometimes wondered if the relationship between Matt and Eleanor was the cause of friction between the two of them.

Ramon arrived at the hostel looking for a place to live while he worked as a chef in a downtown restaurant. Originally from Columbia, he had been living in the states for many years and spoke fluent English with a heavy Spanish accent. He was in his late forties, with a stocky build. Ramon was always pleasant and eager to please. He would bring salads and cookies home with him from work to give to me and Patrice. He was kind and thoughtful and went out of his way to be friendly. I sensed that he wanted to fit in and be accepted by the group, adopting us as his surrogate family. He roomed with Stuart, Tim, and Bryan.

Tim had moved out of the room with Nathan and in with Stuart and Bryan where he, again, had a bottom bunk to sleep in. They were all long-term guests, so they didn't have to deal with the constant flow of short-term guests coming in and out of their room at all hours of the day and night. Tim was much happier in his new room which was evident by his demeanor. He was more relaxed and at ease with everyone, and I noticed him spending more time talking to the guests in the TV room and courtyard. I often stopped to talk to him, and through our conversations, I found out that he was taking classes in graphic design at a local university and sailing lessons. It seemed like he had gone through a hard time and was now in a much happier place in his life.

Nathan shared his room for a few weeks with a young Asian

doctor. Although from looking at him, I never would have guessed that he was a doctor. Dressed in a faded tee-shirt, shorts, and sandals, he looked like a college student. When I went into his room to clean, he would either be asleep in bed or talking to someone in a language that I couldn't identify on his laptop webcam. He was always pleasant and would say 'hello,' but that was the extent of our conversation. He kept mostly to himself. Elliot told me one evening after taking him to the airport that the guest was a doctor who was going to Texas for an interview at a hospital.

Evelyn and Aylin roomed together and everything was going fine until Patrice put Sophia, a middle-aged woman from Italy, in their room. The woman took a disliking to Aylin. She stopped by the office to complain to me that Aylin was going in and out of the room repeatedly late at night and slamming the door while she was trying to sleep. I was familiar with Aylin's late hours from rooming with her, but she had always been considerate in keeping the noise to a minimum. I promised the woman that I would speak to Aylin. I caught up with Aylin when I saw her go into her room, and she politely agreed to keep the noise down. An hour later, as I passed by their room on my way to the laundry room, I could hear loud voices coming from a partially open door. I stepped inside the room and found the two of them face-to-face, arguing with each other. Sophia was speaking in Italian with a few words of English sprinkled in. Aylin's face was red, and I could tell she had been crying.

I stepped between the two of them fearful that a fistfight would ensue. "What is going on here?!"

Sophia flailed her arms about as she rattled off a list of her complaints in Italian.

Aylin ignored her and turned towards me. "She should have said something to me about the noise instead of complaining to you!"

Sophia continued her rant, waving her arms back and forth and smacking her hands together sharply to simulate the sound of the door slamming shut.

I turned to Sophia trying to get her to calm down. At the top of my voice, I yelled, "Wait! Stop!" I took a deep breath, trying to gain a sense of control over the situation. "Sophia, I talked to Aylin, and she said she would keep the noise down."

"No, no. She go back and forth all night long. I can't sleep!"

"Sophia, you only have one more night here. Do you want me to put you into another room?"

"Why should I go to another room and move all my bags? I want to sleep here!"

"Fine. You go to sleep now and Aylin will come outside."

I turned to Aylin. "Why don't you go outside for awhile and let her go to sleep. She will be leaving in the morning."

Aylin looked at me defiantly. "Good. I'm glad she's leaving!"

"Alright. That's enough." I pointed at Sophia and then to her bed. "You, go to bed." Then I turned and pointed to Aylin and then to the door. "You, please go outside. Now!"

Aylin picked up her handbag off her bed and walked out the door. Sophia, still muttering under her breath, went to get ready for bed.

Sophia left early the next morning before I started work. I never saw her leave, but I assumed she got a good night's sleep since I didn't hear any more of a disturbance coming from their room. Aylin left for Turkey the following week to return to her university.

Elliot had taken Patrice to the casino one Wednesday afternoon, and I didn't expect him back until after midnight. I was eating my dinner at the table in our room with the blinds partially opened, so that I could keep an eye on the office when I saw him coming through the gate. I thought perhaps Patrice was coming back early, but Elliot came into our room and told me that she needed more money. Patrice had given him a key to her room, so he went to get some more money out of her dresser drawer and then he hurriedly left for the casino. I sat thoughtfully chewing my salad as I watched him walk out of the gate. It was

only dinnertime and Patrice was already out of money.
    This became a regular weekly occurrence. Patrice would go to the casino armed with a wad of cash, and when that ran out, she would send Elliot back to her room for some more. Patrice always talked about how much money she was winning at the casino, but it was plain to see that she was spending more than she was winning. She had once made a comment to me that she came from a family of alcoholics and gamblers. Although I had never seen her drink, I was concerned about the amount of money she was spending on gambling. I was not a gambler. The most I would ever spend at a casino was a couple of dollars. For someone to spend hundreds of dollars on gambling seemed like such a waste of money when it could be put to better use buying food or household items. The consequences of her actions would soon become apparent.

Once a week after I finished cleaning, I would take inventory of the cleaning supplies and make a list of what Patrice needed to purchase. After completing my list one afternoon, I went to the office and handed it to Patrice. She took the list from my hand and scanned it quickly.

"Lu, I wanted to talk to you about these supplies. I don't think we need two kinds of cleaner, do weeeee? Why can't you use the bleach cleaner on everything?"

I was puzzled by her line of questioning. The items I requested were the same ones that I had been ordering since I started the job. I had been using a general household cleaner for some cleanup jobs and bleach cleaner for others. Suddenly, I felt like I was being unreasonable in requesting what would be considered my usual supplies. I didn't quite know what to make of this sudden change in her thinking.

Groping for an answer, I found myself stammering, "Uh, well, these are the cleaners that you told me to use before. I suppose we could do with just one."

"And what about this shower cleaner? Do you really need that? Can't you use the bleach cleaner in the showers, too? And the same with the cleanser."

Now I felt like I was being extravagant in my supply request. These were the supplies that she had previously instructed me to use. She took a pen and scratched off half of the list of supplies. I shrugged my shoulders and walked out the door still perplexed by her conduct.

Usually when I gave her a list of supplies that I needed, I would have them in a day or two. Days went by and I still didn't have them. My cleaning supplies were dwindling at an alarming rate. I found myself rationing the supplies. Where before I would use a liberal amount of cleaner diluted with water, now I was using a few ounces. The morning that I had to add water to the bleach bottle to rinse the remaining cleaner from inside the bottle, I went to look for Patrice in the office. I couldn't possibly clean without the necessary supplies and the situation was getting desperate. Patrice was in the office putting sheets away in the cupboard.

"Patrice, I have just used up all of my cleaning supplies including the bleach cleaner. I really need some for tomorrow."

She swung around to face me. Vehemently, she said, "That fucking mortgage is killing me!"

Stunned by what she said, I just looked at her. Meekly, I said, "I can make do with just one bottle of bleach cleaner."

"I'll have Elliot take me to the store on my break to get some for you. Also, I was thinking that I might start washing the sheets and towels at the laundromat. The washer and dryer use so much water and electricity that I think it would be cheaper to do them there. Do you think Elliot would be interested in doing the laundry?"

"Yes, I think so. Why don't you ask him this afternoon when he takes you to the store?"

The next day Patrice filled up six large plastic garbage bags with sheets and towels. I noticed a little spring in Elliot's step as I watched him gather up the bags and load them into his car. He didn't say much about it, but I could tell that he was more than happy to take on the laundry. Three hours later he brought them back. After that, every four to five days Elliot went to the laundromat. Laundry in the hostel piled up fast and clean sheets and towels were a necessity for the guests checking-in, as well as for the long-term guests who received fresh linens once a week. A few weeks later, I found out Patrice changed her mind about the laundromat when I stopped by the office to drop off some cards to my family in the outgoing mail.

"Lu, I decided not to have Elliot go to the laundromat anymore. It's just too expensive. I think it would be better to wash and dry it here. I offered to pay Elliot to do the laundry, but he doesn't want to do it here."

I nodded at Patrice and left without saying anything further about Elliot and the laundry. At times, I wished I could confide in Patrice about such matters, but I felt it would be inappropriate. I kept to my unspoken rule of not interfering in their relationship or any business dealings between the two of them.

Although, curious to find out why Elliot had turned down her offer, I did ask him about it. He offhandedly replied, "It just doesn't make sense to do it here. It's much quicker and easier to do it at the laundromat."

I lowered my eyes to stare at the food on my plate, too preoccupied with my thoughts to respond. This was coming from a man who had no full-time job and who needed the extra money. All he had to do was to go back to the laundry room every so often to load and unload the washer and dryer, and then fold the linens in the comfort of our room. I couldn't believe that he was turning down Patrice's offer. I didn't argue with him about it. I didn't say anything. Elliot was a grown man who could make his own decisions, but I didn't think he had made a wise decision.

I found out Patrice had other plans for the laundry when I saw her the next day.

"Lu, I want you to start doing a few loads of laundry every day."

Unsuspectingly, she had touched on a raw nerve of resentment that had been building up over the past few weeks. My schedule was already so full from cleaning and working in the office that I couldn't believe that she was giving me more to do. She also had started to leave the hostel with Elliot in the early afternoons to do errands, instructing me to keep an eye on the place while she was gone. Usually I finished cleaning at two o'clock, but now I had to watch the office almost every day until four o'clock. Little by little, she was piling on more duties and taking more of my time. I had went along with this because I knew that she had worked the hostel on her own for a long time and really needed a break from it, but now I felt like I was being taken advantage of.

I struggled to keep my temper in check. "Patrice, when am I supposed to have time to do the sheets and towels? I'm already washing the rugs and the rags along with cleaning, doing the yard work, and filling in for you in the afternoons. I don't know how much more I can handle!"

She relented and slightly reworded her request. "All you have to dooooo is just *start* the laundry for me in the morning. Juuuust put in one load of sheets and towels first thing in the morning. I will take them out and fold them."

My voice wavering, I replied, "Well, okay . . ."

To further ease my displeasure, she said, "You don't have to dooooo the weeding anymore. I am going to have someone else do the yard work, so don't bother with that anymore."

"That's fine, but I still have the parking lot and courtyard to sweep."

"Well, not doing the weeding should lessen your load."

"I spent a lot of time weeding to get everything to look nice around here. I hope you find someone to keep up with it. It doesn't take long for it to all grow back."

I walked out of the office somewhat dejected. I had spent weeks diligently weeding the flower beds in and around the hostel. I had my doubts that Patrice had really found someone to do the yard work. All my hard work weeding was all for naught.

When I told Elliot that I had to start doing the sheets, a smug, subtle look of victory crossed his face like he had just won a secret, little battle with Patrice over the sheets, but it was at my expense.

Perhaps Elliot didn't think he needed the money to do the laundry since he was getting plenty of driving jobs from not only Patrice, but the other guests as well. Most of his driving jobs were taking guests to and from the airport. His day sometimes started at five in the morning, and at times, his last run was after midnight. He never complained about the erratic schedule, grateful for the opportunity to make some extra cash. The money that he made as Patrice's driver was enough to pay his weekly rent, and the rest of the money went for food and gas.

I went to the grocery store once a week to buy groceries. Elliot would give me some money to help out with the groceries, slipping me a twenty dollar bill at the most, and when low on cash, just five or ten dollars. That didn't go far in helping to pay for all the groceries, but that he at least made an effort was all that mattered to me. I was generous to a fault in paying the brunt of the grocery bill. If Elliot gave me a twenty dollar bill, I spent a hundred dollars. I would ask him what he wanted, and even if what he gave me didn't cover his requests, I would buy what he asked for and much more. I liked having someone to cook for again and to share dinners with. That was more important to me than the money.

Elliot enjoyed cooking and we often spent the evenings together in the kitchen, cooking our dinner. We cooked simple, hearty meals. One evening, the menu for our dinner included barbecued chicken, coconut rice, and an artichoke. Before we barbecued the chicken, he soaked it in white vinegar and squeezed a lime over it to give it a fresh, citrusy smell. He showed me how to make the coconut rice, a dish that his mother used to make when he was growing up in Belize. He rinsed the uncooked rice in water to wash off the starch and then put it in a pot with a can of coconut milk and left it to simmer until the rice was tender. I didn't have a cookbook, so I asked Ron, a middle-aged, unemployed chef staying at the hostel, how to cook the artichoke.

Elliot often shared food that we had cooked together with guests who happened to be sitting in the TV room. I, on the other hand, was more conservative with our food to the point of being stingy. When cooking in a communal kitchen there was always someone around, and I didn't want to get into the habit of giving food away. I would bake pans of corn bread or cookies and walk right passed guests on my way to our room without offering them anything. One evening, I lifted a prodigious pan of lasagna out of the oven while a group of guests watching TV diverted their attention to the tantalizing aroma of steaming lasagna paraded before them, as I made a beeline for my room.

After dinner one evening, I sat outside our room drinking a glass of ice tea while Elliot drove some guests to the airport. Patrice saw me on her way to turn on the night lights and walked over to where I sat on the low wall across from my room.

"Lu, Madeline is coming to visit for two weeks in December. Do you think you would be interested in covering the office for me then?"

"Of course I will."

"She is coming sometime in the middle of December and staying until after New Year's. We will probably go to Key West for a weekend. We will talk more about it later."

"That's fine with me, but what about the cleaning?"

"Don't worry about that. I will have someone else do the cleaning. I might have Lola come back. I talk to her once in a while, and we are still on good terms."

"Oh, good. I like Lola. I hope she comes back. I would like to see her again."

She turned to go, and then hesitated for a moment, turning back around to face me.

"I'm thinking about making an apartment in the hostel for Madeline and me. I could knock out the wall between my room and the office, so that we will have more space and move the office into one of the TV rooms. What do you think?"

"Oh, I thought you were going to buy a condo across the street?"

"No, they want too much money. I can fix us up a place here for much cheaper."

"I think that is a wonderful idea. That will give you and Madeline more room, and we will have a bigger office."

"Good. I think so, too."

She left me alone to stew over my thoughts. First, there was the reduction in cleaning supplies, now she wasn't buying the condo. I also noticed she no longer spoke about retiring. I think she had a rude awakening when she took over the hostel and had to start paying the mortgage and all the bills. She had a construction business in Tobago at one time, so I assumed that she was familiar with how much it cost to operate a business. There was money to be made in Fort Lauderdale, but it was not a cheap place to live or conduct business.

Conspicuous tears were beginning to show in the fabric of life at the hostel, but I was too caught up in my good fortune to realize the true significance of them. Elliot's indifferent attitude towards working and Patrice's financial struggles made worse by her willingness to gamble away the profits were serious defects which I chose to shrug off, telling myself it was none of my business. I was happy and making money, so all was right with the world.

Out of the blue, Elliot started talking a lot about past girlfriends. He would mention them casually in a conversation dropping their names while telling me some of the things they used to do together. I was dumbfounded as to why he would do this and wondered if he was trying to make me jealous. I would quietly listen to him and then change the subject until one Friday during dinner when I decided to call him on it.

Friday night was tuna fish night. Elliot didn't eat meat on Friday's on a regular basis as a form of abstinence that is normally practiced during the season of Lent. In an effort to become more in tune with his religious practices, I also abstained from meat on Friday's. This made sense not only for religious reasons, but also because we were preparing most of our meals together, so Friday night became tuna fish night. He liked the albacore tuna mixed with mayonnaise. Elliot would pick up a loaf of French bread from the bakery in the afternoon, and I would prepare the tuna fish salad.

Elliot spread a liberal spoonful of tuna on an open slice of thick, crusty French bread and then folded it over and took a bite while I did the same. As we ate, the conversation drifted from Patrice to some of the guests. He mentioned that one of the female guests from France, who was short and plump, looked like a woman he used to date.

"Honey, it sounds like you have had a lot of girlfriends."

Puffing up with pride, he responded, "Well, yes, I have had quite a few girlfriends over the years."

"I really don't like hearing about your old girlfriends. I don't understand why you keep bringing them up."

He shot me a vexatious look. "Why wouldn't I talk about them? They were a part of my life, so I like to talk about them sometimes. All you ever talk about is stuff that happens now. You never talk about your ex-husbands. It's like they never existed. Sometimes I wonder if you would do the same thing to me if we ever broke up!"

"I don't talk about my ex's because they are in the past. When you talk about people it brings them alive in the present, and I don't want to do that because it stirs up bad memories. If I wanted to keep them in my life, I would have stayed with them."

Quietly, with conviction, he said, "It won't ever happen again."

True to his word, Elliot never spoke about his ex-girlfriends again. I don't think he actually was trying to make me jealous; he was just sharing information from his past. We had different ways of dealing with our past memories. I preferred to keep mine to myself and concentrate on living in the present. It was hard for me to understand why he would want to drudge up past memories of women who were no longer a part of his life. Perhaps his memories were more pleasant than mine. The deeper I could bury mine, the better. I never had much luck with men and past relationships were unwanted reminders of my failures in life. I had my share of bad dreams which did that.

That night as we prepared for bed, I watched as Elliot peeled off his undershirt that he usually wore to bed, exposing a religious cloth medallion that he always wore around his neck.

"Honey, why do you always wear that thing around your neck?"

He reached up and reverently grasped the medallion between his fingers, pulling it away from his chest. "It's a Scapular. I am made to understand that if you are wearing this when you die, you will go straight to heaven."

I peered closely at the insignia mounted on a small, rectangular piece of brown felt the size of a small wafer depicting the Blessed Mother holding baby Jesus, her outstretched arm handing a small object to a figure on bended knee which I later learned represented the first Brown Scapular she gave to Saint Simon Stock. A corresponding cloth medallion bearing the Scapular Promise hung on his backside and the two cloth medallions were attached by brown strings resembling shoe laces.

That I was born and raised a Catholic and never heard of a Scapular until I met Elliot made me wonder what I had been learning in Sunday school and church for all those years. Elliot removed the Scapular from around his neck and carefully placed it on the nightstand beside his bed. There was only one thing for which Elliot took off his Scapular. I removed my clothes and climbed in bed beside him.

The weather began to change as the rainy season transitioned into the dry season. The days became less humid as the dry air settled in. Clear blue skies and stiff ocean breezes reminiscent of blustery, sunny spring days in the north began to take over. The weather was more conducive to working outside, and I hummed a tune as I walked through the hostel unlocking doors for the exterminator man on his monthly visit. Matt stopped me as I walked by him on my way to sweep the sidewalk.

In sotto voce, Matt said, "Lu, is that man here to spray for bed bugs?"

I stopped dead in my tracks. I hesitated for a moment to make sure that I heard him correctly. "Bed bugs? . . . No, he is here to spray for cockroaches. Why are you asking about bed bugs?"

"Because I think I have them in my bed."

"What?"

"Yeah. Come to my room and I'll show you."

I followed him to his room where he stooped over his mattress on the bottom bunk and pulled back the bottom sheet. Using his index finger, he poked around in the crevice on the edge of his mattress until he found a small brown speck. With his finger in front of the bug, he said, "There." Then he got up, and smoothing his sheets back in place, he pointed to spots of blood where bugs had left trails after feeding on their way back to their nest.

"We need to get Patrice," I said.

I ran to the office and found Patrice sitting at her desk. When I told her about what Matt found, she got up and hurriedly walked to his room. As we stood by Matt's bed discussing the bugs, one was crawling up the wall. Patrice reached over and squashed it. There were three other long-term guests in Matt's room. Patrice moved them all to another room. Matt washed all of his clothes to get rid of any bugs that might be lurking in them which could cause another infestation in his new room. As his roommates came back from work later that day, they moved their belongings to their new room. Not everyone was as careful as Matt about washing their clothes before they took them into their new room. I wondered how long it would be before the bugs would show up in there, too.

We now had bed bugs in a room on the opposite side of the building from where we first had found them. An uneasy feeling crept over me when I realized that my room was located between the two rooms. I knew it would only be a matter of time before they showed up in my room, too.

Lola's husband, José, came the next day to dismantle the wooden bed frames from Matt's room and placed them along with the mattresses out back near the dumpsters. While I was cleaning, he came to find me and motioned for me to come out back with him. I stopped what I was doing and followed him to where he had been cutting the frames into pieces to put into the trash bins. He pointed to a long, wooden piece of frame where bed bugs were clustered into two separate, massive heaps. I looked at José and said, "Malo. Muy malo."

"Sí," he said. I walked away as he picked up a spray can with a long hose equipped with a nozzle and sprayed the bugs with the insecticide.

A few days later, in the early morning, I walked over to the refrigerator to get some milk for my cereal, and when I turned around, I looked over at Elliot who was sound asleep on his side with his arm outside the covers. From across the room, I could see three red welts in a row on his upper arm. I knew instinctively that they were bed bug bites.

Then I discovered a red, itchy bump on the front of my neck while I was cleaning. I ran to my bathroom and examined the bump in the mirror. The red bump had a hole in the middle. I had never seen anything like it before, and I knew that I was the next bed bug victim. It was not a pleasant experience to get bed bug bites. There was an unsettled feeling that accompanied the thought that something was crawling over my body, feasting on my blood while I was asleep. Being a helpless victim in the depths of slumber seemed unfair and overly intrusive.

A firm believer that knowledge is power, I went to the internet to look up information on bed bugs. The best defense to combat them was to have an exterminator come in and treat the entire property. Considering that I couldn't even get much needed cleaning supplies, I suspected that that would be out of the question. I thought back to Jinty, a woman from South Africa that I used to work with at a hotel, who had a problem with bed bugs in her apartment. She was unaware of the problem until one night, when she was reading a book in bed, she happened to look down to discover them crawling towards her. She couldn't afford an exterminator, so I had gone with her to the hardware store to buy some spray. She tried to treat the bugs on her own, but in the end she had to hire an exterminator.

I also found out that I could buy vinyl mattress and box spring covers that had zippers on them, trapping the bugs and the eggs inside. The covers had to be kept in place for a year since that was how long the eggs could survive. Confidant that Elliot and I had both been bitten by bed bugs, I went to show Patrice the bite on my neck.

"Luuuuu, no, no, no! Bed bugs bite more than once in a row. You don't have a bed bug bite. You probably got bit by something at the beach."

"Patrice, Elliot also has bite marks on his arm, three in a row."

Her eyes narrowed, emphasizing the dubious look on her face. "Are you suuuuuure?"

"Yes, just ask him. I'm sure he will show them to you. Anyways, I am going to buy some spray and covers for my mattress and box springs."

"Alright, but that is a preventative measure. I don't have to do this, but I will reimburse you for the cost of them. Just bring me the receipt."

"Okay. I will."

Despite her misgivings, I went to the store that afternoon and bought the vinyl covers and pillow casings. Then, as Jinty had done when I was with her months earlier, I went to the hardware store to buy two cans of bed bug spray. Returning home, I spent the afternoon tearing apart my bed and spraying the entire room and every crack and crevice with bed bug spray. I left it set undisturbed for two hours while I went to the beach. I came back and slipped the covers over the mattress, box springs, and feather mattress and then put the bed back together. Elliot was gone on a driving job so he was not there to help me. By the time he returned later that evening, I had everything back in place.

The vinyl mattress cover, even with a sheet pulled over it, was uncomfortable. It trapped my body heat and made me sweat. Every movement was accompanied by a rustling sound. Despite the discomfort, I slept soundly knowing that at least there wouldn't be any bed bugs that night.

The next day when I went into the bathroom, I saw something lying on the floor up against the bottom of the bathtub. I stooped down to get a closer look. My heart sank when I realized it was a dead salamander; an unintended victim of the bed bug spray. Unlike Charlie, who had a penchant for sleeping on my suitcase in my dorm room, I had seen this little guy a few times behind the TV stand when I mopped my floor. I hadn't seen him for awhile and had forgotten all about him. I retrieved a broom and dust pan and swept up his tiny little body. Then I went to the supply closet and pulled out my little shovel that I had used for weeding. I dug a shallow hole in an empty flower bed on the concealed side of the hostel where I had pulled all the weeds in what seemed like a long time ago. I placed the salamander in the hole and covered it with dirt. I made a cross out of some small twigs and placed it on top of his grave, shedding a few tears as I did so.

Elliot was sleeping a lot. I began to wonder if he was depressed. He stayed in bed sleeping when I got up to go to work in the morning. When I went to our room to get my piece of fruit for my late morning snack, he would be sitting in the recliner with his prayer book and rosary. After he finished his prayers, he would walk down and get the newspaper and then come back to read it. At two o'clock when I went to eat my lunch after I finished working, I would find him back in bed asleep. I would eat my lunch in silence, trying not to make any noise so as not to disturb him. Then I took a shower and joined him for a nap until four o'clock when he had to get up to drive Patrice.

His sleeping habits became more erratic when he began to get up in the middle of the night. He would go to bed with me at my usual eleven o'clock bedtime, but I would wake up in the middle of the night to find myself alone in bed. I would find him back in bed asleep when my alarm went off in the morning. One morning when I asked him where he had gone during the night, he told me that he went upstairs to use the computer. He liked to while away his days and nights on no particular schedule; sleeping, praying, and reading with the occasional driving job in between.

As if Patrice didn't have enough problems, the washer started acting up. First thing in the morning, I put a load of sheets in the washer. When I came back later, I reached into the washer and pulled out a handful of soaking wet sheets. The washer had not spun them out properly. I put them through another cycle, and when I went to take them out, found that they had spun out properly the second time. The washer would work for a load or two and then act up again. I dreaded bringing up the subject of the washer to Patrice, but I knew it needed repaired. After putting the same load through a cycle three times, I went to the office to tell Patrice and received the usual response, "Are you suuuuuure? Maybe you had an unbalanced load."

She went to the laundry room and wrestled with the soggy sheets rearranging them in the washer and then putting them through another cycle. When I checked back on them later, they had spun out properly. There was only one washer in the hostel and it got a lot of use. We washed four or five loads a day and the guests used it in the evenings. I could tell by the looks of it that it had been there for awhile. The washer acted up frequently, and each time Patrice would attempt to fix it, which resulted in washing the same load two or three times until it finally spun out properly on its own accord. We had a lot of laundry to do and only so much time to do it. What we really needed was a new washer, but I knew better than to mention it.

I was perplexed and frustrated by Patrice's continual tendency to minimize or challenge any concerns that I brought to her attention. She reacted with an air of doubt, bordering on denial, which left me feeling dejected. Her refusal to adequately address problems created a wall between us that was difficult to break through.

Now that I had a steady man in my life, I looked forward to going out for an evening. I browsed through the brochures in the office and found a local dinner theater. At dinner that evening, I showed Elliot the brochure and asked him if he would like to go there with me. I offered to buy the tickets since they were somewhat expensive. Elliot flipped through the brochure and agreed to go. He had a driving job on Friday evening so we decided to go on Saturday. I called and ordered the tickets. Saturday arrived and I breezed through my cleaning in eager anticipation of our night out. After work, we took a short nap and then got up to get ready to go.

Holding hands, we strolled down the street towards the dinner theater. Once inside the well-appointed lobby, I glanced around at the other customers and noticed that most of the people were white, middle-aged couples or seniors. Considering the cultural diversity in Fort Lauderdale, I was somewhat surprised by this. The hostess led us to our table on an elevated platform in the back of the room, overlooking an array of tables that stretched out before us all the way to the foot of the stage on the other side of the room. We sat side by side with our backs to the wall, glancing around us to take it all in. The waiter promptly arrived at our table, and as he handed us our menus, he explained that he was part of the cast and that they would be serving our dinners before performing in the show. Elliot and I looked at each other in delight. We looked over our menus while our waiter went to get our glasses of wine. With an air of refinement, the waiter placed our wine glasses on the table, and after taking our orders, left Elliot and I to sip our wine while engaging in idle chitchat. In a lull in our conversation, Elliot reached up and motioned for one of the waiters to come to our table. The waiter dutifully appeared at the other side of our table.

Elliot leaned towards him and in a confidential tone, he said, "There is a producer in the audience. Spread the word to the cast."

The waiter nodded and smiled, giving him a rather curious look, then walked away.

Appalled by Elliot's outright lie, I said, "Honey, why did you say such a thing?!"

"Hey, baby, if they think there is a producer in the audience, they will perform better."

"These people are professionals!" I exclaimed. "They always give their best performance!"

"Oh, you didn't like that I did that?"

I shot him a look of disbelief. "No! I didn't!"

I turned my head away in disgust and looked past the tables in front of us towards the stage. I couldn't believe that Elliot would say such a thing. I wanted to crawl under the table and hide from embarrassment. His behavior was deceitful and cruel and was in such stark contrast to the image of him with his rosary and prayer book in hand, fervently praying. As I had tailored my religious beliefs to conform to my views regarding living together and sex, he applied his own spin to the meaning of honesty.

I couldn't bear to look at our waiter as he placed my dinner in front of me, wondering if he had gotten wind of the fabricated rumor. As we dined, our conversation resumed its lighthearted tone, but the glow of the evening had been tarnished. The house lights dimmed and Elliot put his arm around me as we sat to watch the show. The show was spectacular and we applauded wildly. I always wondered if the waiter had spread the rumor, rousing the cast members to perform at their utmost best, sure that this was their big break. I will never know. But they did give a superb performance.

Elliot accepted a driving job to take a group of guests from Germany to Orlando. They planned to stay there for three days and then have him return to pick them back up. Orlando was three hours away and Elliot toyed with the idea of staying in a hotel there until it was time to drive them back. I didn't like the idea of him being away for two nights, but with the amount of gas and the time that it would take to drive back and forth, it did make sense for him to just stay there. Elliot packed some clothes and took his shaving bag from the bathroom counter. He dug out his movie screenplay and gave it to me to read while he was gone so that it would give me something to do in the evenings. I kissed him goodbye in the morning when he left and kept busy with my work. I missed him terribly and didn't like sleeping alone. He promised to call me each night.

The first night he was gone, I watched the second presidential debate between Barack Obama and John McCain. I was an avid supporter of Obama and Elliot favored McCain. After the first debate, Elliot and I had many a lively conversation about our respective candidates and the issues. Always an advocate of cultural diversity, I was delighted with the aspect of our first African-American president. I found Obama to be intelligent, articulate, and good looking, but his most striking feature is his eyes. The first time I ever saw him, I was struck by his eyes. He has the eyes of a pharaoh or a wise king.

Elliot was surprisingly conservative in his politics and didn't think that Obama had enough experience to be president. He also believed that Obama was a Muslim. Because Elliot was of English, German, African, and Mayan ancestry, I assumed he would be in favor of a black president. No matter how much we argued, we could not see eye to eye, and decided to just agree to disagree.

I was impressed with Elliot's screenplay and felt that it would make a good movie. I knew how much he wanted to make the movie and how hard he was trying to get financing for it. It meant everything to him and he had spent years trying to get the movie made.

The first night that he was gone, he called me late at night. He had had a long day and was tired, so we talked for just a little while. The next day at lunch I heard that Paul Newman had died, so I called him in the afternoon to let him know. We talked briefly because he planned to call me later that night after we watched the presidential debates. That evening, I sat with my notepad and pen, taking notes on the debate. John McCain was a tough opponent and his incessant, "He just doesn't get it," tactic rattled me. I felt sorry for Obama who looked like he was trying to keep his head above water. Elliot was elated on the phone afterwards sure that his candidate had won the debate, but the TV newscasters called it differently: they declared Obama the winner. The presidential race was so close at this point that it was really a toss-up, depending on who you talked to. Time would tell who the real winner was.

Elliot came back from Orlando with enough money to spare after paying for his hotel room, meals, and gas to take me to a movie and out to dinner at a Mexican restaurant. He was excited that he had the money to treat me since I had paid for the dinner theater. I suspected that he spent what was left of his money on our night out. We went to a little Mexican restaurant where we sat sipping Sangrias and snacking on tortilla chips and salsa while we waited for our dinners to be served. Not used to drinking much alcohol lately, I sipped my Sangria gingerly finding that the strong drink made my head woozy, but I liked the fruity flavor and the little pieces of minced fruit in the drink. We feasted on tortillas and rice and beans, while he told me about his trip to Orlando, and I told him what I had liked best about his screenplay.

We finished our dinner just in time to make it to the next showing of the movie. Like two young lovers, we held hands in the car and kissed at the stop lights. At the movies, Elliot put his arm around me as I leaned up against his shoulder, feeling relaxed and content, thrilled to have someone to take me out on the town for the night. I knew he couldn't afford to do this often, but his insistence on taking me out meant a lot to me. He was generous with his money when he had some, but for now, he was just making ends meet with a little bit left over. That didn't leave a lot for me, but I had his companionship and that was worth more to me than money.

Elliot was sure that something would break eventually on his projects. He had big dreams of getting his movie made and buying and selling real estate, but he didn't want to hold down a regular job while he worked on his bigger projects. Years of working menial jobs had worn him down to a point that he refused to conform to society's demands. He was willing to take on sporadic work and live a frugal life while trying to make connections to get financing for his projects.

My evenings became totally centered on Elliot. We ate dinner at seven o'clock and then cleaned up the dishes and rested until we began saying the rosary at half past nine. I stopped going to ESL classes on Tuesday evenings. The cutbacks at the library due to the bad economy had resulted in a change of staff. I missed the camaraderie of the original staff, so I stopped going to class, instead staying home to say prayers with Elliot. I also found myself going to the beach less and less, preferring to cook dinner and spend time with him. Patrice commented one day that I never went to the beach anymore. I told her that it was because of Elliot. I was tired of doing things by myself and wanted more than anything to fill the role of a faithful partner.

Elliot no longer talked of helping Patrice to finance the hostel, but she was eager to finance his movie with business partners in Tobago. Elliot informed me that one of her business partner's, Raul, was flying in from Tobago to bring a letter of intent stating that they would put up the majority of the cost of production. Elliot would be required to contribute his share of capital. He drove Patrice to the Miami airport to meet with Raul and bring back the letter of intent. This was a big breakthrough for him in getting his movie financed. When they got back to the hostel, they called me into the office to sign my name as a witness on the letter of intent. Elliot thanked Patrice profusely. Patrice wasn't too excited yet, saying that Elliot needed to go through the rest of the steps to get his share of the capital.

Elliot tried everything he could think of to get the money he needed: he sent e-mails to private investors, met with an advisor at the Small Business Administration, and set-up appointments with bankers or talked to them over the phone. But the banks were leery of lending money for a movie to a novice filmmaker, and the timing of the whole affair couldn't have been worse: money had completely dried up from the credit crunch. I'll have to say that I admired Elliot's gall. He would walk into a bank and tell the banker that he needed a million dollars like he was asking for a glass of water to quench his thirst. Of course they wanted his previous tax returns and banking statements which were painfully lacking in income. Elliot was a poor man, but a man with a dream.

Through talking with him, I discovered that it wasn't so much the movie that he wanted to make, but the money it would generate to fund his Blessed Mother's Brigade, an organization he had formed while he was in Virginia of which he was the International Executive Director. He created Blessed Mother's Brigade as an endeavor to pay homage to Mother Mary by having the rosary prayed continuously throughout the day around the world. I was surprised to hear him say at dinner one evening that he would probably hire someone else to produce and direct the movie because of the amount of work involved. I wondered if Patrice was aware of that. Up until that time he had always talked of either producing or directing it. Now he wanted to pass it off to someone else.

I never discussed Elliot and I's private conversations with Patrice and vice versa. I had a loyalty to Elliot and a loyalty to Patrice, and as long as everything was going smoothly, I could handle the balancing act. But had I dared to compare notes with Patrice at this stage in the game, I often wonder how different the outcome of our lives might have been; especially mine. Through all of this wheeling and dealing with movies and financing the hostel, I don't know who was more delusional: Elliot, Patrice, or myself.

Eager for another evening out, I made reservations for Elliot and I to go to a Polynesian restaurant for dinner and a show. Again, I paid for the tickets. Elliot liked going out as much as I did, but he didn't like that I was paying so often. I didn't realize how much it disturbed him until later that week when I came into the room after to work to shower and take a nap with him. He was already in bed and stirred when I came in the door.

"Lu, come over here and sit down for a moment." He patted his hand on the bed next to where he was lying.

I went over to sit next to him, my arm resting on his shoulder. He sounded so serious that I wondered what he wanted to tell me. I looked anxiously at him, waiting for what he had to say.

"Baby, let's stay home this weekend. We can have dinner here and watch a movie. I don't like it that you are spending so much money to go out to eat."

I leaned over and kissed his cheek. "Honey, I have to tell you something. When I was up at college for all those years, I never went out. I stayed home and studied all week long. I didn't date. I just went to class and studied and worked. Then when I moved down here the first time, I usually went out by myself because I didn't find anyone I wanted to date. I don't mind paying when we go out. I'm just happy to have you to go out with."

"But, baby, I don't feel right about this. How I wish you could have known me when I was younger, and I had a good job and money."

"Please don't let this bother you," I begged him. I wrapped my arms around him and hugged him to me. "We'll stay home this weekend."

I liked that Elliot called me 'baby' as a term of endearment until one day when I heard him address Patrice in the same way. Then I heard him use it when speaking with a female guest. I began to think of it as something left over from his Hollywood days, used as a casual and impersonal term.

We did end up going out that weekend, but it was Elliot's

idea. He had done a few extra driving jobs so he asked me to go to the lounge at the Seagull Inn for a Piña Colada which was our favorite drink. He set our date for ten o'clock Friday night.

We walk through the gate of the hostel and start down the sidewalk towards the hotel. He pushes me to the inside of the sidewalk so that he is on the outside nearest the passing cars. I am touched by his gallant action. I slip my arm through his as we stroll a few blocks down past the tall condo buildings and then across the street to the hotel. The night air is warm and there is only a faint breeze. The only sounds are from the passing cars.

The bar is empty as we take a seat near the window. The waiter takes our order and serves our drinks. Elliot takes out a twenty dollar bill and holds it up in front of him, fingering it slowly as if kissing the last of his money goodbye. He suggests that we sit outside on the veranda, so we get up and walk outside. The veranda is deserted at this late in the evening. We find a place to sit in a row of rocking chairs along the railing overlooking the ocean. A full moon lights up the night sky, illuminating a wide swath of silky water below us. The surf breaks gently on the shore as a breeze coming in from the ocean stirs the air around us. Sea oats sway in the soft breeze at the foot of the railing. The palm trees on each side of the veranda stand guard like sentinels. We sit while sipping our drinks in awe of the beauty around us.

"Lu, I think that we were meant to be together. I was in New York City before I came here and had planned to stay there, but then the job I got fell through, so I decided to come down here to be near my sister in Miami."

"I think so, too. I was planning on going to St. Thomas in the Virgin Islands. I even bought my airline ticket, but then I decided to come back here instead."

"What made you change your mind?"

"I was afraid I might not be able to find work in St. Thomas. I figured my chances at finding employment would be better here," I said wistfully. Glancing over at him, I continued, "Also, there is something else that happened. I've never told you this before, but my daughter, Laura, knew that I was going to meet you. She told me that there was a man who was going to come into my life soon who was from another country, or had been born in another country, and that he had darker skin."

"How did she know that?"

"She has a psychic ability. I have it, too." I hesitate for a moment wondering if I should confide in him further. Not everyone is receptive to psychic ability. Deciding to take a chance, I continue, "I have to tell you what happened when my father died."

Curious to hear my story, he turns his attention away from the ocean to look at me.

"My father was in the nursing home. He had fallen down and broken his hip. He wasn't doing very well. At night, I used to lie in my bed, and through telepathy, I would tell him that I loved him. I did this every night for at least a week. Then one morning, I was driving up the interstate to go to a seminar in a nearby city when all of a sudden a powerful force took hold of me. I felt my father crying out to me saying, "Don't let them do this to me." I had no idea what he was talking about. He told me to get my mother, have her call a priest, and for us to come to the nursing home. I was shaking and crying so badly that I was afraid that I would wreck my car. I drove to the doctor's office where my mother worked and went inside to tell her what happened. She hesitated and gave me an odd look at first, but then sensing my distress, she got out the phone book to call Father Bill. When we got to the nursing home, we found out that they had been trying to call her because they thought my father had had a stroke. Father Bill came over that afternoon and gave him his last rites. The doctor thought that he would last a week or so. He died that night. We were all there."

"That is an unusual story."

"Yes, it is. I shall never forget it."

The bartender shuts the lights off in the lounge and locks the door behind us. We sit a while longer in silence lost in our thoughts, gazing out over the moonlit sea.

Elliot fidgets in his chair. "Are you ready to go, baby?"

"Yes. Thank you for the drink. This is nice. We must do it again sometime."

"We will."

Election Day arrived and I had set the alarm for six o'clock in the morning so that we could be at the polls early. A heavy turnout was expected so we wanted to get in line early so that I could get back to work on time. When the alarm went off, I reached over and shut it off and turned on my bedside light. The lamp illuminated the corner wall and something crawling up the wall caught my attention. It was a bed bug. I quickly picked up my flip-flop and smashed it, leaving a smudge on the wall. I shuddered at the thought that it had probably been in bed with us and was on its way back to its nest when I turned on the light. We quickly dressed and went down to vote at the church.

Despite a heavy, early voter turnout the weeks before the election, the line was already wrapped around the front and the side of the church when we arrived. Excitement and suspense filled the air. Everyone was in a good spirits as we stood talking to the people in line around us. A woman next to me asked who I was voting for, but I declined to say. This area was middle to upper class residents, who were mostly conservatives. I was the 'odd man out' and preferred to keep my politics to myself. We stood in line for an hour and a half before it was our turn to vote.

Driving to the grocery store that afternoon, the city was alive with civic enthusiasm. A man waving a sign that read, 'Vote for Barack Obama,' stood in the median strip of a busy highway as people passed by honking their horns. In another part of the city, a man with a sign for John McCain stirred up passing motorists. There was an excitement and sense of togetherness that comes from strangers sharing something important.

That night, Elliot had a driving job, so I sat in our room alone, waiting for the election results. The election was too close to call, so I was prepared for a late night of waiting for all the results to come in. In the early evening, when I thought they were going to project the results of another state, to my surprise, Wolf Blitzer from CNN declared Barack Obama as the president-elect. Momentarily stunned, I stared blankly at the screen not yet quite believing what I had heard. When the words sank in, I leapt from my chair and jumped up and down with glee, tears streaming down my face. We had just elected our first African-American president.

Chapter 11

Confinement

    A romantic blend of soft instrumental music flowing from the stereo and the fragrant scent of orchids from the burning candle on the dining room table permeated the air in our little room, as I set the table for dinner. I carefully positioned two glass tumblers filled with ginger beer above our place settings in preparation for our nightly toast. The light from the lamp mounted on the wall beside the table cast a soft, intimate glow over the dining area. I glanced around the room with a sense of satisfaction.
    Elliot was in the kitchen draining the spaghetti. I went to help him and together we brought the sauce and spaghetti to our room and placed them on the table. I took the French bread out of the wrapper and sliced a few good-sized pieces from one end.
    We sat down and joined hands, and with our heads bowed, Elliot said the blessing. The nightly ritual was concluded with our toast. "Here's to you, baby!" he said with a grin on his face, as we clinked our glasses together.
    Hungry from not eating all day, Elliot ate in silence while I prattled on about my day. He wiped up the remaining sauce from his plate with his French bread as I finished filling him in about the guest who dripped some concoction all over the floor after I had mopped it.
    My tale completed, I watched as he picked up his napkin and

wiped off his mouth.

He gazed upon me with eyes full of love and tenderness. "Lu, I just want to thank you for everything you've done for me; for making a home and taking me out to dinners, for your total love for me. I think that God sent you to me. Your love for me is like God's love for me."

I listened in silence, taken by surprise at these sudden accolades.

"Honey, you're welcome," I said as I got up from my chair and walked over to give him a kiss, then rested my head on his shoulder. Elliot once told me that I loved deeply, and I did, from the bottom of my heart. I felt secure in the love that we had for each other, knowing that it was fortified by our love for God.

Wednesday morning I sat at my desk sifting through my paperwork. As I worked, guests started to come into the office to check-out. They had discarded their sheets and towels in the laundry baskets outside the door and now stood impatiently waiting to turn in their keys for their key deposits. I quickly counted the cash drawer and refunded their key deposits so that they could go on their way. A few of the guests lingered wanting information on the bus service, or were waiting for a taxi. In high spirits, they chatted amongst themselves discussing the next stop on their itineraries. I would have liked to spend more time talking with them, but I needed to get my paperwork done.

It was going to be a busy day. Patrice had left a note with the available rooms, and I began to assign the guests their rooms, jotting down a room number beside each of their names. Thankfully all the guests were due in before midnight. Occasionally, a guest would request a late check-in after midnight. I dreaded the thought of having to work until one or two o'clock in the morning as Patrice had done a few times in the past. The office was closed between midnight and ten o'clock in the morning. If a guest arrived during that time, they had to wait in the lounge areas, sleeping in hard plastic chairs with their luggage piled around them until the office opened in the morning.

Lola started cleaning on Wednesdays, so that I could work in the office all day. When she arrived for work a few minutes before ten o'clock, I handed her the list of rooms to clean along with a note from Patrice to change the foil on the burners on the stoves and clean out the refrigerators. Lola left to get started on her cleaning, and I turned my attention back to the room assignments.

My paperwork completed, I tucked the cordless phone in my fanny pack and went to get started on the laundry. Two overflowing laundry baskets stuffed with sheets and towels were waiting outside the office door for me. I gripped the handle of one of the baskets and wheeled it to the laundry room. From the look of things, I knew I would be doing laundry until ten or eleven o'clock that night.

With the first load of laundry in the washer, I returned to the office to sort through the day's mail and check the online reservations. When the office door swung open, I looked up to find Patrice standing in the doorway not yet quite awake. It was unusual for her to be up this early on her day off.

"Lu, is Elliot up yet?" she asked with a yawn.

"Yes, I was just in my room to get some fruit, and he was sitting in the recliner, saying his prayers."

"Do you think he could drive me to the store now?"

"I would think so. Just go knock on the door and ask him."

A short time later, Elliot was sitting outside Patrice's room waiting for her. I went over and sat in his lap to keep him company while he waited. We were in a carefree, happy mood as we sat talking beneath a clear, blue sky. Patrice finally came out and I gave Elliot a kiss as he left to take her to the store. I went back to work on the laundry between taking calls for reservations.

All was quiet in the hostel at lunchtime, so I decided to eat my lunch in my room and watch the news on my TV. As soon as I got back to the office, I realized I had forgotten to take the phone with me. I could have kicked myself. Having to take the phone with me every time I stepped out of the office was a nuisance, but it was important that I did in case someone called to make a reservation. I glanced nervously at the message display, hoping that no one had called while I was at lunch. Relieved that there weren't any messages, I grabbed the phone and went back to the laundry room to start another load of laundry. The phone didn't get any reception in the back of the hostel, but at least I had it with me in case someone tried to call when I was walking back and forth to the laundry room.

On my way back to the office loaded down with an armful of towels, I ran into Patrice in the courtyard as she was frantically searching for me with an anxious look on her face. Elliot followed close behind on her heels.

"Luuuuu, where have you been? I've been trying to call you on the office phone and your cell phone. I didn't get an answer on either one!"

I couldn't understand why she was so upset. "I have the phone right here," I said holding it up for her to see from underneath the towels. "I didn't hear it ring." I hesitated for a moment. "Oh, you must have tried to call while I was at lunch. I forgot to take the office phone with me, and my cell phone wasn't turned on."

Backing down, she said, "I was trying to call you to see if you wanted anything for lunch from the Cuban restaurant."

"Oh, that was nice of you, but I already ate my lunch."

Patrice went into her room, and I returned to the office a bit rattled by her distraught manner. When I hadn't answered the phone or been in sight when she came back to the hostel, she must have thought that I took off somewhere and was shirking my duties. I sensed an element of distrust in her demeanor, as if a past employee had taken advantage of her. I would have to be more careful about making sure I had the phone with me at all times. I didn't want a repeat of what had just happened.

At four o'clock when I went to lie down during my break, Elliot took Patrice to the casino. I slept soundly for a few hours, and feeling refreshed, I got up to get ready for my evening shift. Before I had a chance to walk out my door, the door bell beckoned me to the gate. I glanced at my watch. It was just a few minutes before six o'clock.

Three young Asian men were patiently waiting for me. Happy to have arrived at their destination, they were all smiles as I checked them in and got them situated in their rooms. There wasn't much else to do except answer the phone and wait for the other guests to arrive, so I went to my room to eat dinner. It never failed that right after I took a bite of food, the phone would ring. I chewed frantically and swallowed my salad by the fourth ring. A tourist was inquiring about availability, and since I didn't have the reservation book in my room, I bolted to the office to get it. Since I didn't expect Elliot back until after midnight, I decided to work out of my room. I gathered up the phone and reservation book and went back to my room and opened the blinds so that I could keep an eye on the office.

I liked that I could work out of my room. Although I was on duty, I could do my laundry, clean, watch TV, or surf the internet on my laptop computer. With the cooler weather, I would leave my door open for easy access to the office. Guests would stop by to talk about their day's events or ask for information. The pleasure I felt from having the room all to myself that evening quickly dissipated when I looked out the window to see Elliot and Patrice coming through the gate shortly after nine o'clock. Elliot came straight back to our room and, with remote in hand, sat down in the recliner and started flipping through the channels.

"Honey, you're back early," I said with a hint of dismay.

"Yes, Patrice didn't want to stay late at the casino. I think she is trying not to spend so much money there."

I was glad to hear that, since we didn't have money for cleaning supplies at times. Going out to the casino seemed to be the only thing that Patrice cared to do on her time off, but she was spending money she couldn't afford to lose.

Piqued by the intrusion on my solitude, I glanced over at Elliot not bothering to disguise the tinge of resentment I felt.

Elliot was ready to relax for the evening, but I still had three hours of work to go. As much as I loved Elliot, I didn't want to spend every waking hour with him. His Wednesday excursions with Patrice gave me a chance to have my own space for awhile.

Living in one room was very confining for two people. We had nowhere to go to get away from each other except to the bathroom. I often wished that we had a separate bedroom with a TV in it and a door between the rooms that we could shut when we wanted some privacy. At the present time, we had no choice but to make do with the one room. I worked on my laptop a little while longer, then packed up my things and went back to the office to work.

The next day after I finished cleaning, I stopped by the office to drop off my supply list. As soon as I set foot in the office, I could tell by the look on Patrice's face that she wasn't in a very good mood.

"Ramon has been gone for a few days and hasn't paid his rent. I need you to collect all his belongings and bring them to the office. He can't get them back until he pays his back rent," she said in a dour tone.

"Okay. I can do that now." I wondered what happened to Ramon, but it didn't seem like a good time to discuss this with Patrice since she wasn't in the best of humor. As I turned to go out the door, I remembered there was something I wanted to tell her. "By the way, that guy you check in yesterday, Harold. He's kind of strange."

"Oh, I thought so, too. I thought maybe it was just me."

"He acts like he is out of it; like he is on drugs. I tried talking to him last night, but he gave me the creeps."

Patrice was an astute observer of people. I was surprised that she had second guessed herself. When working around people all the time, you learn how to size people up relatively quickly. Sometimes you can be wrong, but first impressions are usually pretty accurate. Harold was gone a few days later, chucked out like a bad apple. If one of us thought someone was strange or acting oddly, we might let them stay for a day or two to see how they fit in. But if we were both in agreement, the next time they came in to pay their rent, we would tell them that we were full and didn't have room for them.

I left the office and went to the supply closet in search of a few plastic trash bags for Ramon's belongings. This was the first time that I had to bag a guest's belongings and I wasn't looking forward to doing so. Slowly I climbed up the steps to his room and knocked on the door. Ramon roomed with Stuart, Tim, and Bryan. Thankfully there wasn't anyone there. Ramon's bed was on the far side of the room. I walked over and stopped a few feet from his bed. Everything was just as he had left it. A colorful Mexican blanket covered the foot of his neatly made bed. His white chef's jacket hung over the back of a chair beside his bed, his folded work pants and a brown leather belt rested on the seat. On the floor beside his bed were two brown paper bags filled to the top with jeans, shirts, underclothes, and socks. His tennis shoes and leather work boots were tucked under the edge of the bed. I gathered everything up and stuffed it into the trash bags. As I pulled the sheets off his bed, I noticed a coffee cup, ashtray, cigarette lighter, and a few packages of condoms on the window sill beside his bed. I swaddled the items in a tee-shirt and carefully placed them in the bag. I tied the top of the bags and lugged them down the steps to the office and set them down beside each other in a corner. My job completed, I stepped back and sadly gazed down at the paltry sum of Ramon's worldly possessions. My mind conjured up an image of his smiling face as he proudly handed me some cookies that he had made at the restaurant where he worked. I was worried about him and hoped he was all right.

A week later, Ramon was back as if nothing had ever happened. I went into the office one morning and Patrice told me that he had paid his rent and was back in his room. Nothing was ever said about where he had been. I was happy and relieved that he had returned, but it wouldn't be the only time that Ramon disappeared.

Since Lola started cleaning again on Wednesdays, Patrice decided to schedule her to come in on Fridays, so that I could have a day off. It was such a luxury to have a day to myself after working seven days a week for the past few months.

Now that I had a day off, Elliot decided he no longer wanted to work on Sundays. He informed Patrice that she would have to find someone else to drive her on Sundays, and that he didn't want any driving jobs from the guests either. Sundays were supposed to be a day of rest, and he wanted to devote the day to going to church and praying.

At church one Sunday, I noticed an older woman wearing an ivory mantilla, a traditional lace head covering. I had worn one in grade school back when women were required to cover their heads in the Catholic Church. Many years ago, decades actually, the church changed their policy and I had not worn one since. I pointed the woman out to Elliot after mass and told him that I wanted to start wearing one again. Since he was a traditionalist, he wholeheartedly agreed.

As we walked through the parking lot after mass, I barely noticed a homeless man sitting idly on the curb near our car until Elliot unwrapped my arm from his and walked over to him. I stood back and watched him as he took out his wallet and handed the man a few dollars. I was touched by Elliot's gesture. That he didn't have much money, but could still find it in his heart to give something, touched me deeply. If I had been by myself, I would have walked right by the man without much thought. I still hadn't learned to give unselfishly.

The first part of November, Ramon and Mitch, a quiet spoken French Canadian who was going through a divorce, approached me about making plans for a Thanksgiving Day dinner. Stuart and Nathan soon joined in. I was somewhat bemused at this role reversal; usually women were the ones to start planning holiday dinners. After some thought, I realized that the men were yearning for a sense of family and tradition. It seems that the desire to be part of a family is so inherent that individuals are drawn to form family units, even in the absence of blood ties. We each had our place in this pseudo family unit of which I was so happy to be a part of. I told them that I would discuss it with Patrice and let them know.

One sunny afternoon as I walked through the courtyard on my way to the beach, I looked up to see Patrice and José carrying a mattress out of a dorm room.

Walking over to them, I asked, "Patrice, what are you doing with the mattress?"

I couldn't help but notice the brooding look on her face as I followed them out the back door where they heaved the mattress up against the wall. She wiped her forehead off with the back of her arm.

"We have bed bugs in that room again," she said as she started back towards the office. "This is just too hard. Maybe I should just turn this place into all long-term rentals with just two beds in a room. That way there wouldn't be people coming and going all the time. It would be less work and less problems with bed bugs."

I walked along beside her, trying to match her long strides. "But you enjoy working with all the guests we get here. Wouldn't you miss them?" I asked.

"Yes, I suppose I would." She turned the key in the door and walked in the office with me right behind her.

Curious, I asked, "Patrice, how did you end up here at the hostel?"

She gave a little laugh at the thought. "I got off the bus at the Greyhound station in Fort Lauderdale. Someone had stolen my wallet at a stop along the way, so I only had a little bit of money on me and no identification. When I got off the bus, it was the middle of the night, so I slept in the bus station. I was afraid to go outside on the streets that late at night. On their bulletin board, I noticed an advertisement for renting a bed in this hostel. I didn't know what they meant by renting a bed;

I had never heard of a hostel before. So I came here the next day and checked it out. I started staying here while waiting for my sister to send me some money. Then when the cleaning lady suddenly quit, I started doing the cleaning in exchange for my rent. Just like what happened with you," she said with a chuckle as she motioned with her hand in my direction. "When the owner wanted to sell the place, I told my Uncle Carlos about it and he bought it. That's when I started working in the office, running the place for him. I've been here for a couple of years now . . ." her voice trailed off with an air of disbelief at her good fortune.

"Wow. That's quite a story. It's like fate brought you here."

A smile spread across her face. "Yes, I guess so. I love it here."

"So do I. I really like meeting people from all over the world and you never know what will happen next. Oh, that reminds me. The guys are asking about Thanksgiving dinner."

"Already? That's three weeks away."

"I know, but they are excited about planning a dinner, so I thought I better mention it to you."

She stopped to think for a moment and, then, having made up her mind, she said with firm conviction, "I will provide the turkey and ham. Everyone else can bring a covered dish. Maybe you could type up a sign-up sheet."

"That's a good idea. I'll get one typed up tomorrow. I'll spread the word around so they can start thinking about what they are going to bring."

That evening, I filled Elliot in about our plans for Thanksgiving dinner. When I mentioned a covered dish, his face lit up. Excitedly, he offered to make his peanut butter fudge that he used to make for family gatherings. His face beamed as he recited the ingredients and the step-by-step instructions on how to make his fudge. As I listened, again I was amazed at the tenacious desire to belong to some type of family. His enthusiasm was infectious and I soon found myself thinking about what I should bring. As I pondered my options, I was distracted by tufts of frizzy, gray hair bushing out from under the sides of the cap that he wore on his head.

"Honey, you need a haircut," I said earnestly. "You know, I used to work as a hair stylist and I still have my scissors. Let me know when you want me to cut your hair."

He ripped the cap off his head in one swift stroke. "How about right now?"

His exuberant response made me giggle. He wasn't wasting any time in taking me up on my offer. "Okay. Let me go get a sheet to put around you." I ran back to the laundry room cabinet and removed a couple of queen-sized sheets that I had stored there and grabbed the broom and dust pan.

I set a chair in the middle of the floor and turned on some soft, flowing music on the stereo. Suddenly, our little room was transformed into a barbershop. Elliot sat down and I draped the ample folds of cotton sheeting around his bulky frame, securing it snuggly around his neck. I hadn't cut hair for awhile, so I was a little nervous that I might mess it up. I took a deep breath and started to cut his thick, wavy hair. Little tufts of hair, like miniature tumbleweeds, scattered across the floor, as I cut away the bushy growth. To cut the very front, I straddled his legs and sat down on his lap facing him.

"I don't usually do this, but since you are my boyfriend I can get away with this," I said teasingly.

"Did men ever ask you out when you cut their hair?"

With a little sigh, I said, "No. No one ever asked me out."

"Well, they didn't see what I see."

"Oh, and what do you see?"

"That you are loving and kind."

"Yes, to the right person - you." I leaned forward and planted a kiss on his lips.

I finished his haircut and walked around him in a circle, scrutinizing my work. It had turned out better than I expected. He went to look at his hair in the bathroom mirror while I swept the hair up off the floor and discarded it in the trash.

"How does it look?" I peeked into the bathroom to find him smoothing back his hair with the palm of his hand.

"It looks good. Thank you."

I gathered up the sheets, broom, and dust pan and went to the laundry room to put them away. When I walked through the TV room, Stuart was passed out in a chair, sprawled out like a rag doll, with the TV blaring. It was only a few minutes after eight o'clock. I had seen Stuart like this a couple of times in the past few weeks. He would drink all day, and then pass out in the early evening. I turned my head away, finding it painful to see him like this. Eventually, he would wake up and go up to his room to sleep it off.

As I walked back to the room, the light from the full moon caught my attention which gave me an idea. When I went inside, Elliot was sitting in the recliner watching TV.

"Hey, honey, guess what? There's a full moon tonight. Do you want to go to the Seagull Inn for a Piña Colada?"

"I don't really have the extra money for that right now."

"Well, we're in luck, because I found a twenty dollar bill this morning when I was sweeping the parking lot. Come on. I'll treat." I was practically jumping up and down at the thought. I loved going to the ocean to look at the moon, especially with Elliot.

"Are you sure you're okay with this? I don't like it when you have to pay," he protested.

"I'm not paying. Whoever who lost their twenty dollars is. Come on, get up!" I went over and tugged at his arm, a playful attempt to pull him out of the chair.

He slowly rose and put his cap on his head. We turned out the lights and I slipped my arm through his for the short walk to the Seagull Inn.

"Honey, this can be the start of a new tradition for us. Every month during the full moon, we will go to the Seagull Inn for a Piña Colada," I said with a spring in my step.

Elliot quietly looked over at me and smiled.

Thanksgiving Day morning was calm and quiet as I went around the hostel hanging up decorations of pilgrims and cornucopias that I had made on the computer. I also posted open invitations to let all the guests know that dinner would be served at six o'clock. We had a few guests come in the day before, and I wanted to make sure everyone knew they were invited, even if they couldn't bring something. Elliot and I watched the Macy's Thanksgiving Day parade on the TV in our room. Every so often, I would get up and go out to the kitchens to check on the progress of dinner preparations. Ramon had the turkey stuffed and in the oven before lunchtime, and Mitch baked the ham. Evelyn was whipping up a casserole dish of sweet potatoes with brown sugar and marshmallows. I spent the afternoon in the kitchen, peeling ten pounds of potatoes which I cooked in two separate pots for mashed potatoes.

In the middle of the afternoon, the men started to set up the dining area. They had to be resourceful since we didn't have a lot of furnishings to work with. Ramon decided that we should eat at a makeshift banquet table on the upstairs terrace. With Ramon in charge, the men collected all the tables from various parts of the hostel and lined them up, one after another, to form a long banquet table. Ramon had brought linen tablecloths and napkins home from work. He and Mitch draped the table cloths over the tables and then used two coffee cans filled with flowers for centerpieces. Evelyn folded the linen napkins into triangular shapes and placed them on a round table by the door leading out onto the terrace.

We decided to set the food on tables in the upstairs kitchen. Again, in the spirit of resourcefulness, I made up two buffet tables by placing large, rectangular pieces of plywood on top of smaller round plastic tables and used queen-sized flat sheets for tablecloths.

Ramon pulled the golden brown turkey from the oven, and after letting it sit for awhile, he removed the stuffing and carved it while Mitch sliced the ham. One by one, we placed our covered dishes on the buffet tables until the unsupported edges began to bend slightly from the weight. Luckily, nothing slid off the tables. A sumptuous feast of turkey, ham, stuffing, mashed potatoes, candied sweet potatoes, various salads and vegetable trays, green bean casserole, cranberries, croissants, and gravy was spread out before us.

Stuart brought pumpkin pies which he placed beside Elliot's fudge on a smaller table that had been set up for desserts. Elliot had made his peanut butter fudge the day before, and I had cut it up into squares and arranged them on a dish, keeping some in our room for us to eat later.

With the food in place, we all gathered in the upstairs kitchen and formed a large circle, holding hands as Elliot said the blessing. Then everyone waited patiently in line for their turn to fill their plates. Evelyn stood in the doorway, handing each guest a linen napkin as they went out onto the terrace to sit down. When everyone was seated, we passed the wine bottles to fill our glasses then raised them in a toast to all the guests, American and international, who came together in the spirit of fellowship to make our Thanksgiving dinner possible. Then ravenous from the tantalizing aromas we had endured for hours, the conversation subsided into the clamorous sounds of indulgent feasting, punctuated by sporadic grunts of approval, as we dined al fresco on a warm, starry night, caressed by fresh, warm, ocean breezes.

The motley band of guests gathered around our makeshift banquet table ranged from young adults to senior citizens from America, Canada, Europe, Central and South America, Asia, and the Caribbean. Stephan, an older gentleman from Amsterdam, was not familiar with the meaning behind our Thanksgiving holiday. We Americans obligingly filled him in on how the first Thanksgiving was celebrated between the pilgrims and the Indians.

As I scanned the faces of my dinner companions, I couldn't think of any other place on earth I'd rather be at that moment.

I was filled with a deep sense of gratitude at the privilege of celebrating Thanksgiving with this hodgepodge of people from all over the world, some of whom I'd know for a few months, some just a few days.

My thoughts drifted to my family back in Ohio. I had called them earlier in the afternoon and my mother had put me on speaker phone so that I could wish everyone a 'Happy Thanksgiving.' By this time of evening, my mother, daughters, sister, and other adult family members would be sitting at the kitchen table talking and laughing, picking at leftovers, while the great-grandchildren romped through the house and played games. My Uncle John, brothers, and son-in-laws would be glued to the TV set, watching a football game. The scene was so familiar after celebrating Thanksgiving dinner at my mother's house for so many years that I felt like I was there in spirit. I missed them, but I wanted to be here for now. I wondered if that made me a bad person, or at least a bad daughter, mother, grandmother, sister, aunt . . .

My reminiscent thoughts were interrupted when Nathan passed by and offered us a beer which Elliot accepted. I was drinking a glass of wine, so I declined his offer.

"Honey, I didn't know you liked beer. We'll have to go out for a beer sometime," I suggested. I was vaguely aware of a disapproving glance from Patrice. I knew that she didn't like alcohol, but since it was a holiday and I was off duty, I didn't think anything of having a glass of wine or making plans to go out for a beer sometime. It wouldn't be long before I would come to find out what she thought about a staff member drinking alcohol.

I got up to get a piece of pumpkin pie and wished Tony a 'Happy Thanksgiving,' as he slipped a few pieces of Elliot's peanut butter fudge onto his napkin.

Tony looked over at me with an indulgent grin, "Isn't this great? It sure beats staying in a hotel room all by yourself!"

"Yes, I'm glad you found us, Tony."

Tony was a French-Canadian in his late fifties, fit and tan with pale blue eyes and curly salt and pepper hair. He was retired from a Canadian airline and flew in on standby to Fort Lauderdale a couple of times a year. He had paid for a couple of weeks stay, but after a few days, he asked me what his chances were of getting a refund. Since he had never stayed in a hostel before, he had some reservations about sharing his room with three other men. Younger people took to the concept of sharing their room much more readily than did some of the older guests who never had this type of experience before. When I checked with Patrice, she refused to give him a refund. After about a week, he decided that since all he did in his room was sleep, it wasn't such a bad arrangement after all for the price. He came to appreciate the communal environment that the hostel offered.

I did have a bone to pick with Tony, though, but I didn't say anything to him about it. When I had told him about the sign-up sheet for the covered dishes, he said that he couldn't bring anything because he didn't have a car to go to the store. I took umbrage at his refusal to contribute, since there was a grocery store only a few miles down the street and many of the guests walked there or took the bus. Besides that, unlike a few of the cash strapped guests, he could well afford to do so.

As much as I loved pumpkin pie, I ate it only once a year at Thanksgiving, savoring each delectable bite. I thought I would burst from eating so much good food. Most of the guests had finished eating and sat around the table talking and laughing. Gradually, everyone took their dishes to the kitchen, and after scraping them off into the trash can, stacked them on the counter. A few of the guests who couldn't afford to bring a covered dish had offered to wash the dishes and take out the garbage. Gradually everyone rose from the table and pitched into help tear down the tables and put everything back in its rightful place.

Friday morning, I had to spray again for bed bugs. Elliot had a bite on his neck and I had one on my finger and chest. Elliot helped me set the box springs and mattress against the wall, and after giving the room a good dose of spray, I went to take out the trash. I was mortified to find Lola and José washing some of the discarded mattresses with clorox cleaner to bring them back inside to use. Clorox cleaner would not get rid of any bed bug eggs that were left in the mattresses. The mattresses were of good quality, and I knew Patrice couldn't afford to buy new ones. But I cringed at the thought of using those mattresses again. It was best not to worry about such things since there was little I could do about it.

Later in the afternoon, I spent a few hours at the beach and then returned to take a shower. I walked out of the bathroom wrapped in a towel and found Elliot sitting quietly in the recliner with a troubled look on his face. The TV was off, and he was staring at the closed blinds on the window across the room.

"Hi, honey. I didn't know you were here."

He patted his lap. "Come sit down here for a minute."

I climbed into his lap and placed my arm around the back of his neck.

"We must pray for Patrice. She is having financial difficulties," he said.

"I know. I can't even get the cleaning supplies that I need."

"It's even more than that. She tells me that she is paying me to take her to the store, but then she will try to sneak in a few other stops without paying anything extra. I wouldn't mind if the stops were along the way, but they're not."

"I know. She has done the same thing to me, adding more duties and having me fill in for her on afternoons when she leaves early."

"I don't think what she is doing is right. If she keeps it up, I will have to say something to her about it. I have to pay for gas and my time is worth money."

"I'm sure if you talk to her about it, she will understand."

The next day, Patrice told Elliot she didn't need him to drive her that day. She left on her break with her backpack slung over her shoulder, heading in the direction of the bus stop. I had a gut-wrenching feeling that trouble was brewing, and in the days that followed, my suspicions were confirmed. Elliot's daily driving trips with Patrice became less and less frequent, and as a result, his income dwindled. He was still getting some driving jobs from the other guests, but he had relied on his pay from driving Patrice as the bulk of his income. He had to start saving the money he made from driving the other guests to pay his rent. His minimal contributions for grocery shopping came to an abrupt halt, and he started to rely on me to provide his food. Since I couldn't fit all of our food in our small refrigerator in our room, I had been storing a good bit of it in the full-sized office refrigerator. I started to keep more and more of my food in the office refrigerator as Elliot dipped into my supply of eggs, orange juice, and milk. One morning, knowing that I kept extra eggs in the office refrigerator, he came right out and asked me for some. Although it was difficult to do, I told him that I needed them for baking. He apologized sincerely for asking. I had generously cooked dinners for the both of us, but now took to cooking a dinner on Sundays only and went back to eating my salad in the evening.

    I began to look at Elliot in a different light. On the outside I put on a cheerful, nonchalant front, but a tiny seed of suspicion took root inside of me that he might be taking advantage of my generosity. When he sat in the recliner reading or saying his prayers, I would walk by and smile and talk to him as if nothing was wrong, but I eyed him warily, wondering what he was really up to. One evening as I set the table for dinner, his words came back to me haunt me, "It looks like you are playing house." Was that all this was? Were we pretending to have a normal relationship when all the while we both knew that this was just a sham that could fall apart at any moment? I was teetering on the edge of denial hoping that by some miracle I would be proven wrong. Whenever I tried to discuss the situation with him, he became defensive, telling me not to worry about his financial situation; that he would handle it. Unexpressed doubts and concerns gnawed at me, enflaming an already explosive situation. My thoughts drifted back to all the mornings he had slept in late and the long afternoon naps when he could have been out looking for a regular job.

As much as I wanted to be with Elliot, his refusal to look for a steady job put a strain on our relationship. I walked in one afternoon to find him viewing a website on my laptop for typing jobs that could be done from home. Instead of looking for a real job, he was looking for alternative ways to make money. Slowly, I felt resentment begin to build. One afternoon when I came in for lunch he said, "I feel so bad when I see you working so hard." His comment struck me as odd. I was beginning to think that he had an aversion to putting in a good day's work.

In an attempt to find part-time work, he decided to apply for a job as an extra at a local movie agency. He got up early in the morning when I was leaving for work and pulled his navy blue pin-striped suit out of the closet and hung it on the back of the door while he went to take a shower. When I stepped back in to check on him, he was buttoning his suit jacket over a snow white shirt and burgundy silk tie, which complimented his dark complexion. I was taken with how handsome he looked. Happy that he was finally looking for work, I wished him luck and kissed him goodbye, not expecting to see him for a few hours. Half an hour later, he returned.

"Honey, you're back already?"

He shrugged his broad shoulders. "Well, they wanted a professional head shot to apply, and since I'm not working, I don't have the money for that."

I looked at him incredulously. "You are a filmmaker, and you didn't know that you needed a head shot to apply for work as an extra?"

I felt my temper rising. All of the resentment and worry that had been building over the past few weeks came to a head. "I just don't know if this is going to work out between us," I snapped.

His voice rising, he said, "What? You don't want me to live

here anymore?!"

"You know, maybe that would be for the best," I replied, my voice cracking with emotion. I opened my mouth to say something more, but no sound came out. In an instant, I realized that the louver windows below the picture window were cracked wide open. I had opened them earlier to let in the fresh ocean breeze. The windows opened up into the courtyard where guests were sure to hear our heated argument.

I had struck a nerve and Elliot, who was either unaware of the open windows or too angry to care, went off. "You are breaking up with me because I don't have a job? What about love? How can you say you love me and then do this? I thought we had something special!"

I don't know why I didn't think to say something to Elliot about the windows. I just froze up. I turned away from him and went into the bathroom where I stood shaking in front of the vanity. His words about love and having something special cut me like a knife. I immediately began to regret my short temper. I had a tendency to fly off the handle and say things that I didn't always mean when I was angry. But it was too late to take back my angry words. The damage had been done.

Elliot walked out the door and slammed it shut.

In an effort to distract myself from our quarrel, I gathered up the trash and took it out back to the dumpster. Patrice was waiting for me in the courtyard when I returned.

"Lu, come to the office. I need to talk to you."

Half-heartedly, I said, "Yes, what's up?"

"We'll talk in the office," she said in a serious tone.

I already knew what she wanted to talk about. My suspicions that our heated argument had been overheard were confirmed. There wasn't much privacy in the hostel.

I shut the office door and walked over to the counter. Patrice leaned up against the wall at the end of the counter.

"Lu, I know this is not my business, but I heard Elliot getting upset with you. My concern is that this might spill over into the hostel."

"Patrice, you don't have to worry about that. It won't. I knew everyone would hear our argument since the windows were open."

"Well, I didn't hear you, just him."

"That's because I stopped talking when I realized that the windows were open. Anyways, I am upset with Elliot because he doesn't seem to want to find a full-time job. I have been generous to him and have been helping him out with food, but I'm just really frustrated with him. Besides that, I have no time to myself. Since he hasn't been driving as much, he is always in our room."

"Perhaps it would have been better if you had stayed in separate rooms and just gotten together for your special times," she suggested gently.

"You're probably right. I think it would be better if he moved back into his dorm room," I said.

"Well, I don't have a bed for him there tonight. It will have to be tomorrow. You don't think there will be a problem with tension between the two of you, if you are both here in separate rooms?"

"No. I don't think so."

"This is not a good time for him to leave here. We have business to take care of with his movie. This is in confidence so don't say anything; this movie deal is a sure thing."

I gave her a quizzical look. I knew there was no way that Elliot could ever come up with his share of the financing. As angry as I was with Elliot, I couldn't betray his trust in me and confide in Patrice as to his futile efforts at securing working capital. I had no idea how much she really knew, or what he had led her to believe. Again, I felt pulled between two separate worlds, unable to reconcile one with the other. All I could do was try to ease the situation by conducting myself in an agreeable manner.

"Oh. I'm sure we can work this out," I said.

Sarah opened the office door and stepped inside. "Patrice, I was trying to warm up my lunch in the microwave, and Elliot came over and got really upset with me and told me to get out of the way."

I turned to face Sarah. "I'm so sorry, Sarah. Elliot is upset with me. We had a little argument and he is just blowing off steam."

"Well, I just couldn't understand why he was getting upset with me, so I came to talk to Patrice about it."

Patrice walked over and placed her arm on Sarah's shoulder. "I will talk to him about it."

Sarah nodded her head and walked back out the door.

"I think I will have Elliot take me for a drive so that I can get him to cool down a bit," Patrice said.

"That sounds like a good idea." I left the office and went back to my room. It was my day off, so I had the whole afternoon to myself. I went for a long walk and returned a few hours later to take a nap. Lying on my back in my bed, I looked around the room. It was strange to have the whole room to myself. Tormented by fears of loneliness, I asked myself: Is this what you really want? To be all by yourself again? The long years of loneliness since my last marriage had taken their toll. It wasn't easy to find love in this world. Perhaps it was best to try to work things out. I felt love in my heart for him, even though I was suspicious of his motives. His words echoed in my head, "I thought we had something special." I tried to take a nap, but couldn't sleep. Instead I tossed and turned while weighing the pros and cons of our relationship on an imaginary scale, trying to determine if I had done the right thing in asking him to move out. My head dwelled on the negative aspects of our relationship, while my heart professed my love for him. After hours of painful soul-searching, I finally gave into my heart. I knew I had to make up with Elliot and set things right.

I was still lying in bed when Elliot came in the door at six o'clock.

"Can we talk?" I said hopefully.

"Not now. Maybe later." He went to the dresser and picked up his car keys and then left the room.

I spent a restless evening trying to control my overwhelming urge to speak with him as soon as possible to resolve the situation. I went to the kitchen to get some ice from the refrigerator and walked by Elliot and Stuart watching TV together. Neither one of them said a word to me. A flicker of uneasiness passed over me, wondering if Stuart had also overheard our argument. When I walked back out into the courtyard, the light from the full moon perched in the sky above the condos across the street caught my attention. My heart ached when I thought about the past two full moons when we sipped Piña Coladas on the veranda of the Seagull Inn. We had been so happy and in love. So much had changed in that short period of time that it left my head reeling.

Not wanting to be around the other guests, I hid in my room for the rest of the evening. Desperate for someone to confide in, I called my cousin Gene. She listened patiently and true to her usual, infinite wisdom, she simply said, "He can only be who he is." Exhausted from the day's events, I hung up the phone and watched TV. I finally turned the light out at eleven o'clock and laid in bed wide awake. My ears perked up at the sound of a key in the door.

Elliot sat down in the recliner to say his prayers. I listened in silence to his low murmurs of Our Father's and Hail Mary's, biding my time until he was finished so that we could finally talk. When I heard him put his rosary away, I sat up in bed. The room was dark except for the yellowish glow from the outside lights peering between the slits in the window blinds.

"Honey, don't you know how worried I am about you? What is going to happen when your money runs out?" I lamented.

Elliot heaved a great sigh. "How do you think I feel? I have a multimillion dollar movie deal in the works, and I can't get the working capital that I need because I don't have any assets. I am doing the best I can under the circumstances. You need to let me do what it is I need to do."

"I worry about you because I love you. If I didn't love you, I wouldn't care what happened to you."

"It didn't sound like you loved me by the way you talked to me earlier today."

"I know and I'm sorry. I tend to lose my temper and say things I shouldn't."

"Yes, you do. I always think about what I'm going to say before I say it. And I always try not to say things in anger. You hurt people when you talk like that, and you can't mend it by just saying you're sorry."

"Yes, I need to work on that. I've been praying about it. But you won't talk to me about things, and they build up inside of me until I get upset and lose my temper."

"It is better to talk things over in a calm and pleasant manner, like we are doing now," he said quietly.

"Honey, it's been a long and trying day. Please just come to bed now and let's get some sleep. I just want to hold you."

Elliot undressed and crawled into bed, lying on his back. "You have to kiss me to make up with me," he said.

I leaned over and firmly planted a kiss on his lips.

The next morning, as soon as Patrice opened the office, I went in to tell her that Elliot and I had made up, and that he wouldn't be moving back to his dorm room after all. I smoothed things over with her the best I could then immersed myself in my cleaning in an effort to put the whole episode behind me and get back to normal. Although, normal was really anything but normal and more like a constant dysfunctional state.

The calm waters only lasted a few days before the next storm came to pass. But this time I had nothing to do with what happened.

Elliot was unusually preoccupied at dinner. I raised my glass waiting for him to say the toast, as he picked up his fork to eat.

"Honey, what about our toast?"

He gave me a confused look, and then realizing what I was talking about, he picked up his glass of ginger beer to complete the toast.

"Honey, is everything okay? You seem preoccupied tonight."

"Well, I didn't want to say anything, but I will tell you. Today Patrice told me she would pay me to drive that couple from Germany to the mall. When we got back, he gave me a twenty dollar tip. When I went to get my money from Patrice, she said that the guests had already paid me. I told her that the money he gave me was a tip. She paid me, but she was upset."

"Oh, I can't imagine why she would do such a thing. That doesn't sound like Patrice. She has always been honest with me."

"I told her that she could check back with the guests, so that they could tell her that it was a tip and not a payment for services."

"Well, hopefully she will do that. I don't know why she wouldn't. I'm sure things will be set right once she speaks with them," I said encouragingly.

Talking about the situation seemed to ease Elliot's distress. I didn't give the incident any further thought sure that everything would be set straight once Patrice spoke with the German couple; just like I had set things straight a few days earlier after our fight.

Chapter 12

Alternate Reality

We had built our lives and staked our livelihoods on seemingly inextricable bonds with Patrice that in cold, hard reality were tenuous ties based upon her whims. Blissfully unaware of the fateful turn of events about to take place, I swept the terrace in the bright sunshine and cool morning air until I heard Patrice calling me down to the office. I set my broom aside and went to the office.

"Lu, I need to talk to you about a personal matter."

"Oh, what's going on?" I asked in a concerned tone.

Standing across the counter from me, she looked me straight in the eye and said, "It's about Elliot. I'm concerned about you and don't want to see you get hurt." She took a deep breath and continued, "Elliot may not be who he says he is. He isn't doing what he is supposed to do for this movie deal." She stood with arms crossed, waiting for my reply.

For a moment, an uncertain stillness pervaded the room while my mind frantically searched for a suitable response.

I finally spoke, "Well, thank you for your concern. I know he has been working on getting financing, but he doesn't tell me all the specifics. Anyways, it's not like we are getting married. I have been married three times, and I don't ever plan on doing that again." Inwardly I winced at my ability to lie so effortlessly and convincingly.

"Three times! I can't even get married once. But Madeline and I are engaged." Patrice held her ring finger up, displaying a slim silver band on her left hand.

"It's not something I'm proud of. As for Elliot, it's just nice to have someone to share things with," I felt a tinge of despair at my inability to confide in Patrice.

"Also, I wanted to tell you that last week when I said that this movie deal was a sure thing, I meant that on my part, not his," she said.

"Okay."

As I turned to leave, Patrice eyed me seriously. "Remember, I'm telling you this in confidence."

"Patrice, I never disclose anything to Elliot about what you say to me. Anyways, thanks again for your concern."

I walked out the office door, not quite sure what had just transpired. Again, I felt constrained by my inability to fully discuss my personal life with Patrice without betraying Elliot's trust in me. Also, I felt suspicious of Patrice's motives. Did she really have my best interests at heart, or was this just a ploy to justify her decision to no longer use Elliot as her driver? I didn't know what to believe.

I wanted to discuss the situation regarding the German tourists with her, but out of fear of offending her, I could not. Or perhaps it was more out of fear of finding out the truth. If she were to tell me that the German couple had paid Elliot, then I would have to believe he was lying to me. Or perhaps she was. There was no way for me to get to the truth without causing a major rift in my relationship with either Elliot or her. If I sided with Patrice, then Elliot would have to go. And if I sided with Elliot, then I would have to leave with him. I had to remain neutral and keep the peace at all costs. I had to just let it go and hope for the best.

Elliot and I were in love and planned to make a life together. He hadn't asked me yet to marry him, but he had hinted to me that when he was financially secure, he would like to make our relationship permanent. I wasn't being completely honest with Patrice about my feelings for Elliot. I felt a need to downplay our relationship, as if by doing so I was somehow siding with her. There was a small part of me that perhaps knew that what she said was true, but I didn't want to admit it to myself which would have jeopardized the make believe world that Elliot and I existed in. It was a world that I had created in order to fill a need, and I wasn't about to let it go no matter how fabricated it really was. My inability to be completely upfront with Patrice about my feelings for Elliot mired an already complicated situation.

The first part of December brought a flock of university students arriving from South America who were staying at the hostel while working at internships during their summer break. Patrice had her hands full making their room assignments for a month's stay. Much to her chagrin, after a few days, they would find other accommodations and ask for a refund. She refunded a few of their rents and then decided there would be no more refunds. Guests who checked out early often left vacant beds which couldn't always be sold at the last minute, resulting in a drop in revenue.

Maria and Maria Lucia were two students from Argentina who looked like sisters, but were actually best friends. They were thin, willowy creatures with long, shiny dark hair and smooth dark skin. They roomed together with two other female students, and when I went to clean their room, I had to sweep around bags of food, clothes, and shoes piled on the floor. They paled around together everywhere with Santiago, a lanky young Argentinean with dark, curly hair, who followed them around like a love-sick puppy dog. I would often see the three of them together laughing and talking in the upstairs kitchen with one of the girls usually sitting in his lap, his long arms wrapped loosely around her slender waist.

Patrice was anxiously counting the days before Madeline's arrival. Wanting to look her best, she went on a diet to lose weight. She even bought a treadmill to exercise on, which eventually ended up in one of the TV lounges for the guests to use.

In mid-December, Patrice started her two week vacation while I filled in for her in the office every day from ten o'clock in the morning until midnight, with a two hour break from four until six o'clock. Patrice offered to work on Christmas Eve and Christmas, and New Year's Eve and New Year's Day. I was happy to give Patrice a much needed vacation. She and Madeline had planned to go to Key West for a weekend, but due to financial constraints, decided against it. They planned to stay at the hostel and take a few day trips instead.

Since I was used to working all day in the office on Wednesdays, I easily slid into my new routine. I liked running the hostel by myself. Granted, Patrice was always close by in case I needed her, but I was largely left on my own. For once, I felt that I was working in a position that made full use of my skills and abilities. I couldn't believe how far I had come in such a short time. When I first arrived at the hostel six months before, I never imagined one day I would be running it. I marveled at the thought that if you dared to be adventurous, wondrous things could indeed happen.

Shortly after the mailman dropped off the mail, Patrice stopped in the office and flipped through the mail, as I sat at the desk sorting through my paperwork.

"Good morning, Patrice. I'm surprised to see you up so early," I said.

"I couldn't sleep this morning."

"Oh, you're probably excited about seeing Madeline. What time is she due in today?"

"Not until this evening about eight o'clock," she replied matter-of-factly. Averting her gaze away from me, she slipped a piece of mail into the top drawer of the desk. "I need you to tell Elliot that his rent is going up the first of January. I can't continue to give him the monthly rate on a weekly basis. I'm giving him a couple of weeks' notice."

Doing my best to keep my voice steady and calm, I replied,

"Okay. I'll tell him."

After Patrice left the office, I briefly considered calling Elliot, but decided against it. Since I knew he was going to be upset, it would be better to tell him in person. He had left earlier that morning to take a few guests to the airport. I pushed my thoughts aside and finished my paperwork.

By lunchtime, Elliot had still not returned. I ate my lunch in my room alone with my thoughts. I was eagerly anticipating the Christmas holiday which was just a few weeks away. For the past few years, I had spent Christmas alone and I hadn't even bothered to decorate. This year, I had someone to share it with and I planned to buy a little, artificial Christmas tree and some decorations. With my heart filled with joy, I studied the large picture window in my room, envisioning how I would hang a string of icicle lights and garland across them.

Mid-afternoon, Elliot returned from his errands and waved at me through the office window on his way to our room as I was folding laundry. I decided to wait until my break to talk to him about Patrice so that I wouldn't be interrupted by my duties. I continued watching out the window hoping to catch a few of the long-term guests returning from work so that I could give them their mail. I had a package for Nathan from his family in Wisconsin. A few minutes later, I saw Nathan pass in front of the window. I grabbed his package, along with his mail, and ran out after him.

"Nathan, I have some mail for you!"

"Oh, thank you, Lu," he said as he turned around and walked over to me.

Nathan stared down at the package and started to laugh.

"What's so funny?" I asked.

"I put my return address in the wrong place! This package was supposed to go to my mother in Wisconsin!"

"What? You're kidding me!" I looked down at the package in Nathan's hands. There scrawled in bold letters was Nathan's name and address for the hostel in the 'send to' space with his mother's name and address plainly printed in the 'return address' space. Nathan had sent himself a package. I burst out in laughter. Nathan's antics again had the effect of reducing me to a giggling school girl. Leave it to Nathan to do something like that.

Nathan clutched his package in his arms, and still laughing, started to walk away when he suddenly stopped and turned back around. "Hey, Lu. Is Patrice here? I need to find out what time she wants me to take her to the airport."

His words stung me.

"I haven't seen her for awhile. I think she's in her room. You can try knocking on her door," I replied as nonchalantly as possible.

"I'll take this to my room first," he said holding up his package.

This was more bad news. Patrice had recruited Nathan to take her to the airport to pickup Madeline. She had completely stopped using Elliot as her driver. Not only that, from what I could tell, they were no longer speaking to each other. I quickly walked to my room to talk to Elliot. When I opened my door, I found him sprawled out on the bed fast asleep. My news would have to wait until dinner.

Elliot was still asleep during my break. I laid down beside him and tried to get some sleep. I needed to get some rest. I had to work a week straight before I would get a day off on Christmas Eve. After a restless nap, I got up and made my salad for dinner. My movement about the room prompted him to get out of bed for dinner. He heated up some leftover spaghetti and we sat down to eat. We each took a few bites before I gathered up enough courage to relay the bad news.

"Honey, I need to talk to you," I said, measuring my words carefully. "Patrice stopped in the office today and said that you need to start paying the weekly rental rate the first of the year."

Agitated, Elliot squirmed in his chair and set his fork down. "I have to leave here ASAP." There was a curtness in his voice that alarmed me.

"What? What do you mean you have to leave here?"

"Patrice knows I'm hurting financially, and yet, she is asking me to pay higher rent. This doesn't make sense. She also has promised to finance my movie deal, but won't even front the working capital that I need to get my share of the financing. What does that say about what she really thinks of me?"

"Can't you find another job here?" I pleaded.

"I have been looking for a job. I can't find anything. I better leave here before I end up cussing her out."

"Honey, that will only make the situation worse. Anyways, where will you go?"

"I don't know. I have to think about this."

"You know, Nathan is taking Patrice to the airport to pick up Madeline. I was talking to him this . . ." The office phone rang, interrupting me mid-sentence. Annoyed at the intrusion, I plucked the phone off the table to take the call. Arriving guests were stuck in Hallandale twenty miles south and needed a ride to the hostel.

Quickly, I asked Elliot, "Honey, can you pick up some guests in Hallandale?"

I jotted down the guests' location and description and handed the information to Elliot as he got ready to run out the door without finishing his dinner, eager to make some extra cash. I finished my salad in silence, choking back tears. I felt numb. Everything was beginning to fall apart. I still kept hoping for a miracle that somehow this would all work out. Or was this just a bad dream and I would wake up and realize it wasn't for real. I cleaned up my dishes and went back to work in the office. It was going to be a long night.

Elliot returned an hour later, and I checked in the guests that he had picked up. I spent the rest of the evening in the office to avoid discussing the situation further with Elliot, until we could do so without the constant interruptions from running the hostel. Shortly after ten o'clock, Patrice returned from the airport with Madeline, and they went directly into her room.

At midnight, exhausted, I climbed into bed beside Elliot and snuggled up against him, consumed with thoughts of him leaving. It broke my heart, and I was overwhelmed with sadness. I wrapped my arms around him and tried to choke back my tears. Elliot leaned over and kissed me.

"Honey, I don't want you to leave," I whispered.

"Things will work out. We must have faith in God. He will get us through this."

"But, I don't want us to live apart. What kind of relationship is that? Sometimes you have to fight for what you have. You have to swallow your pride and make the best of the situation. I have done this a number of times with Patrice; for the sake of keeping the peace. Maybe it would be better if I looked for another job, and we moved into an apartment so we could get away from here."

Elliot rolled over on his back and stared up at the ceiling. "I have thought about going back up north."

"Up north? Where?"

"To Lexington, Virginia. I've been thinking about going back there for a few weeks now. This would just be a separation. We would get back together sometime in the future when things are better and I'm working."

"Would we, really? I think that we will drift apart and I will never see you again if you go there," I replied caustically.

I was devastated to hear that he had thought about returning to Virginia weeks earlier. He had never said a word to me about it. I surrendered completely to the tears welling up inside me, sobbing uncontrollably. I felt so sad that our relationship had come to this. All my hopes and dreams shattered in an instant.

Elliot reached over and stroked my face. "I wouldn't be here right now, if it wasn't for you."

The next morning, Madeline stopped by the office to introduce herself. Her fair complexion was in stark contrast to Patrice's dark skin. She was quite tall, with cropped, light brown hair and a long face. She was friendly and pleasant, and we chatted briefly about her flight and late arrival the night before.

A lone Christmas tree ornament hung on a tree near the center of the courtyard. The tree was about fourteen feet high; its narrow trunk endowed with long, spindly branches each bearing a handful of green leaves. At closer inspection, I smiled at the sight of a plastic crab ornament with a red stocking cap on its head. Tradition was again making itself known in the hostel. Lacking a traditional Christmas tree, one of the guests had decided to find a suitable replacement. As I stood looking at the solitary ornament, I suddenly had an idea to make this our official Christmas tree. The guests could place ornaments on the tree, and I would buy some lights and garland. I felt my mood lighten as I was filled with thoughts of the upcoming holidays.

Sunday morning, Elliot and I got up early so that we could go to church before I started working for the day. I pinned my black lace mantilla on the top of my head as we went off to mass. After church, we stopped at the store so that I could do some shopping for Christmas decorations. I piled garland, lights, tree ornaments, and a small artificial Christmas tree for our room in my cart. Giving the Christmas decoration aisle one last sweep to see if anything else caught my eye, I caught a glimpse of a fiber optic angel encased in a smashed box sitting forlornly on the top shelf. I reached up and lifted the box from the shelf. The angel was undamaged and clothed in a red, shimmery gown adorned with golden ribbons. I looked at the angel's sweet, angelic face and my heart went out to her. I felt like I had unearthed a rare treasure. I carefully set the dented box in my cart. She was my most precious find of the day.

Elliot made a brunch for us, cooking sausage and eggs. Our mood was light. We had endured some rough patches over the past few weeks, but we were still here together, enjoying our brunch and anticipating our Christmas holiday.

That afternoon, I worked out of my room so that I could decorate for Christmas. I put Christmas music on the stereo and went about decorating the Christmas tree. Elliot helped me string icicle lights across the top of the picture window and then we added a strand of red garland on which I hung large, shiny bulbs of gold, green, and red. I covered a little end table with a sheet of cotton sprinkled with gold glitter and placed the Christmas tree in the center. I gently set down a small, white nativity set that Elliot had given me on one side of the tree and the angel on the other side. Excitedly, I plugged in the lights to the tree, the angel, and the window and then stood back for a few minutes to admire the decorations.

Walking out back to discard my trash, I found Maggie, a long-term guest who worked on yachts, deftly dabbing hair color onto Evelyn's roots as she sat smoking a cigarette, her shoulders draped with the cleaning towels they had asked me for earlier. Exchanging a short greeting with them, I smiled at the thought that you never knew what you might see at the hostel.

For dinner I made a batch of manicotti and took a plateful over for Patrice and Madeline. Elliot and I sat eating our dinner surrounded by Christmas decorations and listening to Christmas music. I had found a little piece of happiness in my day getting ready for Christmas and cooking a nice dinner. Elliot had shared my lighthearted mood earlier in the day, but now there was a sudden change in his tone as he started in on financing for his movie.

"Baby, I have a new plan to get money for my movie."

"Oh?" I replied dubiously while wondering what he was up to next.

"Yes, I plan to ask Patrice to guarantee the money that she is putting up for the movie. I want it in writing."

"I thought that was what the letter of intent was for?"

"Yes, well, it is. She could get into a lot of trouble for saying that she is going to finance my movie and then pulling out of it. I can sue her. I have a good mind to find a lawyer and file a lawsuit."

All of my Christmas cheer suddenly evaporated. I stared at him in disbelief, dumbfounded as to why he would want to sue Patrice when she had tried so hard to help him. A ghostly shadow of myself rose from my seat at the table and floated out the door in search of Patrice to tell her that Elliot was talking about suing her. My ghostly musing didn't stop there. Patrice and I returned to my room, grabbed Elliot by each of his arms and escorted him out of the hostel for good. Maybe that is what I should have done, but something stopped me. Some inner need kept me hostage to Elliot's nonsensical rants.

Back in reality, I shook my head in disgust. I sat in silence nibbling at my manicotti like it was a plate of sawdust. That Elliot was talking such utter nonsense, and that I didn't act on it, made me sick to my stomach. Elliot's desperation was becoming evident. He was acting like a cornered animal, lashing out at this perceived injustice in retaliation. He was blowing off steam, but his tone had an alarming ring to it.

Eddie was two days behind on his rent. He was a tall, gaunt middle-aged man with leathery skin from working outside on boats all day and smoking too many cigarettes. His eyes were his most arresting feature; sparkling blue like the Caribbean Sea on a sunny day. He was a heavy drinker, and unfortunately, his rent money often went for booze. I had to track him down a number of times to get his rent money. Patrice had instructed me earlier in the day to make sure that he paid his rent or he would have to leave. He had promised to bring it in the day before at noon, but had never showed up. I watched for him all day, but never saw him. The next afternoon, he sat in the courtyard talking to Patrice. Finally, I had a chance to nab him about his rent. I gave my best performance in front of Patrice, conducting myself in a firm and businesslike manner. He was full of excuses, as usual, and promised to bring it the next day. Later that evening, Patrice approached me and told me not to talk to guests in the courtyard about their rent. Then she stuck up for Eddie, saying that he hadn't gotten paid yet and that, from now on, she would take care of collecting his rent. I looked at her in disbelief. She was the one who had goaded me into going after him for his rent money. Even though Patrice usually took a hard stance with alcoholics, at times they would bring out her soft side, and she would become protective of them, even mother-like.

I shrugged my shoulders happy to be relieved of the duty of hunting down Eddie for his rent money. This had gotten to be a weekly occurrence and I was tired of it. I often had to go into his room to inquire about his rent money where I usually would find him lying in his bed asleep or at least pretending to be asleep. One night after I closed up shop at midnight and returned from locking up the laundry room out back, I saw him leaving the hostel smoking a cigarette like he didn't have a care in the world. He had a way of sweet talking us to buy extra time with no intention of following through on his promises to pay his rent. He seemed to be under the impression that unlike everyone else, he shouldn't have to pay to stay here.

With high season in full swing, I kept a close watch on the guests going in and out of the hostel. When I checked them in, I tried to memorize their names and faces. With so many guests coming and going, it was a difficult to remember all of them. The combination lock to the gate had broken, and since there was only a latch keeping the gate closed, anyone could walk in off the street to use our facility.

One day as I walked into the courtyard, I caught a young man whom I had never seen before, walking up the steps to the computer room. When I asked him if he was a guest, he shook his head 'no' and said he just wanted to use the computer. I promptly asked him to leave. Another time, a young woman from Canada stopped in the office to ask where she could find a computer to use. When I suggested the local library, she tried to argue her way into using our computer. I patiently explained to her that our computer was for guests only at which she took offense. I offered to make a reservation for her to stay with us for a day or two, which she declined in a huffish manner. Finally, after seeing that I wasn't budging on the matter, she left.

Greta stopped by in the afternoon and I didn't have any

almonds for her. I gave her some sunflower seeds and dried French bread, but she sat looking at me expectantly, refusing to touch any of it. I think that I spoiled her. She finally gave up and left.

The washer was still not working right. Patrice had pulled the drainage hose out of the back of the washer to make sure that it was draining correctly, which it was. She was trying everything she could think of to fix it. She even let Eddie try his hand at it which resulted in him dismantling it to the point where we could no longer use it. He didn't even bother putting it back together, leaving the pieces strewn about the laundry room floor.

Patrice and Madeline had to go to the laundromat to wash sheets and towels. They pulled the plastic bags loaded with laundry right past Elliot who was watching TV in the lounge. I couldn't help but notice that neither one of them said a word to him as they walked by directly in front of him. I watched them tug the bags out to the waiting taxi while thinking back to all the times when Elliot had gone to do the laundry and had been Patrice's driver.

The coup de grâce in Elliot and Patrice's relationship was the dispute involving payment from the German tourists. But it was a silent blow that only made itself known by Patrice's actions over a period of time. Patrice gradually replaced Elliot as her driver by enlisting the other long-term guests to drive her. As far as I could tell, she was also no longer speaking to him. She never said a word to me about the incident and I never asked. The tension between them was unbearable. An uncomfortable silence pervaded the room when they were both in it. None of the long-term guests who were aware of the situation said a word about Elliot's sudden ousting, at least not to me. I'm sure there was gossip going on, but it was when I was out of earshot. I couldn't help but wonder what they thought about Elliot; and me.

I suspected that the only reason she let Elliot continue to stay at the hostel was because of me. I continued to talk to Patrice as if nothing was wrong. Then I would spend time with Elliot, acting like there wasn't anything going on between him and Patrice. I had dug a hole and put my head in it, preferring to be oblivious to the whole situation. My whole world revolved around Elliot and Patrice. That the two of them were not getting along was a threat to my well-being and lifestyle that I didn't want to admit. Somehow it was easier to just play along with things, hoping that it would all right itself in time. I was trying to bury a ticking time-bomb that was just waiting for the opportune time to go off.

As a form of avoidance behavior, I immersed myself in my work. Early one afternoon, I received a call from two young ladies who had reservations and were due to arrive by Greyhound bus. One of them had called to confirm their reservations, and when I asked the time of arrival, she said it wouldn't be until after midnight because the bus was running late. I explained to her that the office would be closed at that time. She became very upset and started to give me a hard time. I held the phone away from my ear while a loud, incredulously irate voice bemoaned, "You're going to leave two young girls in the middle of the night on the streets of Fort Lauderdale with our suitcases!"

Trying to sound sympathetic while not losing my patience, I explained that they could stay inside the bus station until we opened in the morning. I was not being cold hearted, but realistic. I was working long days, and I valued my sleep. At an impasse, we both hung up, hoping that things would work out and they would arrive before the office closed. Luck was with us that night. The girls called shortly after eleven o'clock and Elliot drove to the bus station to pick them up, returning at a quarter till twelve.

Another afternoon, I looked up from my desk to find an Adonis staring back at me. A tall, sinewy young man with a goatee, a head full of beautiful golden curls, and big blue eyes stared back at me from across the counter. Chris was from Calgary, Canada and as I checked him in I found out that he just arrived from a mission with the Hands On Disaster Relief Organization in

Haiti. After digging mud out of houses for two months eating only rice and beans, he wanted to know the nearest place to get a cheeseburger.

One evening, a guest approached me and complained that there was a terrible stench coming from another guest in the TV lounge. As we spoke, I glanced briefly at a young man ensconced on the futon watching TV, oblivious to his offending odor. After a short discussion, we suspected that the odor was coming from his shoes. This was a delicate situation that had to be handled with the utmost tact. I gathered up my courage and walked into the TV room to talk to the offending party. The young man was polite and friendly, and agreed to take his shoes off outside where I promptly sprayed them with air freshener.

A few days before Christmas, after a long period of no reports of theft, I received two complaints about beer missing out of the refrigerators. It was difficult to pinpoint the perpetrator since the incident occurred during the middle of the night when most of the guests, including myself, were asleep. Evidently, someone was imbibing in the holiday spirit. I suggested to the guests that it was best to either drink all of their beer at night, or take the remaining supply into their room with them to store.

Two vivacious young ladies with sleek, blonde, shoulder-length hair and manicured fingernails burst into the office early one evening to check-in. They were travelling while on winter break from college. Leaning across the counter flashing their gold rings and bracelets, they looked at me intently and asked if we had bed bugs. They had just left a hostel in Miami Beach where they had been bitten by bed bugs. In my most convincing voice, I told them that we did not, since we took regular precautions and sprayed for them. It wasn't quite a lie; the room I assigned them to did not have bed bugs.

Ramon received his Christmas bonus from work and stopped by the office to pay his rent. He patiently waited for me to complete his paperwork before he confided in me about an incident that had occurred the night before. He had gone to bed early since he needed to get up at 5:00 a.m. to get ready for work. Bryan got home from work around midnight and had come into the room and started to make noise, which woke him up. Ramon asked Bryan to keep the noise down and Bryan responded by cussing him out. Their altercation moved from their room to outside their room, and then ended up in the parking lot with Bryan chasing Ramon around the parked cars. Ramon managed to get away from Bryan and spent a good part of the night trying to sleep in the TV lounge afraid to go back to his room.

I suppressed a smile at the thought of Bryan's lanky extremities flailing about, his shoulder length hair swishing back and forth during the pursuit in the parking lot. Somehow the whole thing seemed absurd, but Ramon was almost in tears, so I kept my amusement to myself. In an effort to accommodate Ramon, I offered to move him to another room, but he refused. His room was home to him and he didn't want to move. Later when I saw Patrice, I filled her in on the incident. Concerned that there would be another occurrence, she told me to move Ramon to another room until she could talk to Bryan.

Later that evening, I told Ramon he needed to move to a different room. He instantly became defensive and irate that he had to be the one to move when it was Bryan who had been the aggressor. I explained to him Patrice's concern about a further altercation. He assured me there wouldn't be one and pleaded with me to leave him in his room. Sensing his despair, I relented.

The next day I found out from Patrice that she had talked to Bryan who claimed that Ramon had made inappropriate sexual advances to him on several occasions and the disagreement from the previous night had set him off. Bryan didn't want to move to another room either, so they were both told to work things out and get along; which to their credit, they did. A few days later I found Ramon in the laundry room doing Bryan's laundry!

Elliot was keeping to himself a lot. He was busy working on a collection of prayers for his book. At dinner we didn't talk much. He seemed preoccupied, and I was constantly getting interrupted by guests ringing at the gate or calling on the phone. With so much tension between him and Patrice, I felt it best to keep to myself as much as possible and concentrate on work. I stayed out of our room as much as possible, working in the office until midnight. Getting back to our room after I closed up shop, I was relieved to find Elliot in bed fast asleep. I was too distraught to want to discuss the situation, preferring to just embrace the oblivion of sleep.

    With Christmas a day away, I got up early the next morning to find the best Christmas present of all: a new washer compliments of Carlos! I walked out back to find Carlos tearing away the cardboard to reveal a gleaming white washing machine sparkling in the winter sun. I was so happy that I wanted to run up and hug, first, Carlos and, then, the washing machine. Finally, after all those months of coaxing and chiding the old washing machine into submission, we had a brand new much needed replacement. It was like a dream come true. Carlos promptly hooked up the new washer and I spent the day catching up on laundry.

Chapter 13

Glad Tidings!

After a week of working twelve hour days, I woke up on Christmas Eve morning filled with a sense of joyful liberation. I had two delectable days off for Christmas and I planned to do some Christmas shopping. I had already sent gifts to my family back home, but still needed to buy gifts for Patrice and Elliot. I sprang out of bed with the zestful determination of a woman on a mission, eager to get started on my day.

The streets and stores were crowded with last minute shoppers. My first stop was at the mall to pick up a gift set of Aramis cologne and after shave, Elliot's favorite scent. I also found a boxed Aramis soap-on-a-rope which added a nice touch to his gift. My next stop was Las Olas Boulevard where I bought a box of Belgium chocolates for Patrice. I then made my way to the grocery store to pick up a leg of lamb for dinner and a few bottles of red wine.

Driving back to the hostel buoyed by my holiday purchases, I jubilantly sang along with Christmas music, as I gazed at the slender palm trees bathed in streams of sunshine that playfully pranced on the surface of the sea as I drove down Ocean Boulevard. It had been a long time since I had someone to share Christmas with, and even though things were not quite the way I would have liked them to be, I was celebrating Christmas in

Florida with the man I loved in the place I loved working. Except for the little nagging voice in the back of my head, all was right with the world.

I arrived back at the hostel before noon. While unloading my car, I noticed Patrice peering out the window at me from behind the office counter. Anxious to give her my gift, I picked up the golden gift bag bearing her chocolates and went to the office. As I burst through the door, she turned in her chair to face me. With a smile on my face, I slid the gift bag across the counter by its handles until it plunged over the opposite side, swaying slightly as it dangled from the edge of the counter in front of her. My Christmas offering was met with a silent, dumbfounded look.

"This is for you," I insisted. "Merry Christmas!"

"Oh . . . aren't you coming to the Christmas dinner tomorrow night?" she stammered.

"Well, yes, but I wanted to give you your gift now."

"Okay, thank you, but I thought you'd wait until tomorrow."

"I have to go start my leg of lamb that I'm making for dinner tonight," I said happily as I shrugged off Patrice's odd behavior and went back out the door humming a Christmas carol.

I could hardly contain my joy at having someone to cook dinner for on Christmas Eve. It had been over seven years since I had done so. I sipped red wine while I basted the lamb in garlic and butter, roasted the sweet potatoes, and cooked the peas. As we sat down to dinner, soft Christmas music filled the room as Elliot and I savored the succulent lamb and toasted our first Christmas together with a glass of wine while surrounded by festive decorations. We were in our own cozy little world, caught up in the joy of having found each other, and sharing our first Christmas together.

The wine flowed freely, and after we polished off the first bottle, I uncorked the second. We had plans to go to midnight mass, but that seemed like a long way off. It was only early evening and the wine had the effect of giving me a warm glow inside and out. Buoyed by wine and cheerful conversation,

I suggested that we take a drive to see the Christmas lights on Las Olas Boulevard. Elliot was good-natured and seeing my excitement, he agreed to go. After taking in the beautiful Christmas decorations on Las Olas, Elliot suggested that we stop by Patrice's favorite casino for a drink. I had always wanted to go there, so off we went. I had dropped Patrice off there a number of times, but had never been inside. Finally, I would get to see it, too.

The bright lights of the casino against the dark sky beckoned to us as we pulled up and parked our car. After walking around for awhile, we found a good spot to have a beer and watch people go by. Despite the alluring facade of the outside of the casino, I found the interior to be cold and artificial with its profusion of glaring, flashing lights and the constant pinging of slot machines manned by human automatons dropping coins into slots and pulling at levers, hoping to get lucky. It wasn't my idea of a good time. I didn't like gambling and considered it mostly a waste of money. I didn't even bother playing a slot machine. By the smile on Elliot's face, I could tell that he enjoyed the hustle and bustle of the place.

By the time we finished our beers, it was going on eleven-thirty. So much for midnight mass, I thought to myself. But deep down inside, after my first sip of wine earlier that evening, I knew I never intended to go to midnight mass. One glass of wine always led to another and then to some bottles of beer. It helped me relax and let go and that was all I wanted at the moment.

On the way home, we drove in silence except for the sounds of Christmas carols drifting from the radio. We passed by a large church where cars and people streamed into the parking lot on their way to midnight mass.

Elliot glanced over at them wistfully out of the corner of his eye. "They're going to midnight mass," he said with a hint of sadness and regret.

I nodded in silence, his disappointment tugged at my conscious and my heart.

Elliot had an airport run early on Christmas morning. I heard him get out of bed as I rolled over and went back to sleep. When he returned, I woke up to see him tearing open the Christmas gift I got him. I couldn't believe that he was opening my Christmas gift, and I wasn't even out of bed yet. When I had placed his gifts under the tree a few days earlier, I had visions of us sharing a special Christmas morning, opening our gifts together. I thought it rude of him to open his gifts without me. I knew how much he missed his favorite cologne, Aramis, and I was looking forward to seeing the look on his face when he opened his gifts.

My eyes now wide open, I finally decided to speak, "Do you like your Christmas presents?"

He pulled the cap off the cologne and took a long whiff from the top of the bottle, "Yes! Thank you. It has been a long time since I've had some of this." He held the box of scented soap in his other hand. "This is nice, too," he said. "I can't wait to try it."

I slipped out of bed and walked over to him as he wrapped his arms around me and gently kissed my lips. "Thank you for being so nice to me."

"You're welcome, hon. Of course I'm nice to you because I love you. I want to make you happy."

"Oh, you do." He whispered in my ear and tightened his hold on me.

I wiggled out of his arms and made my way to the bathroom. "We better start getting ready for mass! It is already after ten o'clock!"

Upon entrance to our church for high mass, we were greeted with the heavenly voices of the choir and a resplendent view of the altar adorned with clusters of red poinsettias nestled at the foot of a row of verdant fir trees wrapped in golden ribbons and bright, twinkling lights. Elliot commented on the beauty of the mass and decided that attending mass on Christmas morning wasn't so bad after all. I felt exonerated from my behavior of the night before, and my guilty conscious was given a reprieve.

We left the church, arm in arm, and went home to eat our Christmas brunch of sausage, egg, and cheese omelets which Elliot prepared for us. As we sat at our table nibbling on our food, I suddenly jumped up and went to retrieve my Christmas presents from Elliot. There were some small packages wrapped in brown paper with a card tapped to the outside. I thoughtfully opened the envelope and slipped the card out. It was the same religious Christmas card that he had sent out to others; hardly a card that you would give a girlfriend. I hoped that my disappointment didn't show on my face. I set the card aside and carefully pulled the tape off the wrapping revealing a leather-bound book of *Footprints*. Beneath it was another book about heaven that someone had written after having a Near Death Experience.

Looking up to meet his gaze, I whispered, "Thank you, hon. I will treasure these always."

"I'm sorry I didn't get you a nicer card, but I couldn't find one that I liked."

Biting my lip, I replied, "That's okay." But inside a little voice said, "I know he doesn't have much money, but he could have at least bought me a nice Christmas card!" My thoughts churned on further as I thought, "What does this really say about his feelings for me?"

In an effort to smooth over an uncomfortable moment, I groped around for something more to say. Suddenly a shadowy memory crystallized in my mind of a Christmas present my youngest daughter, Elizabeth, had given me many years ago.

"You know, I once told my youngest daughter, Elizabeth, 'that the best gifts come from your heart and are made with your hands,'" I said brightly.

Elliot listened intently as I continued my story.

"One Christmas morning when she was about twelve years old, I went to pick her up at her father's house, and when she got in the car, she handed me a small strand of colorful beads that she had strung together on a piece of leather string. When she gave them to me, she said that she was sorry that she didn't have money to buy me a gift. I took the beads from her and hugged her. To me it was the most beautiful gift in the world because she had made it especially for me. I hung it on my rear view mirror in my car, where it stayed for years afterwards, as a constant reminder of the special gift of love that she had given me." I blinked back tears. I didn't want Elliot to see me crying. Elizabeth was now up north over a thousand miles away celebrating her first Christmas with her new boyfriend.

A sudden flood of memories came to mind of past Christmas Eves at my mother's house where all my family gathered for a dinner of stuffed cabbage, ham, and potato salad, and then exchanged gifts. As I closed my eyes tightly, I could see their happy, smiling faces as they sat around the table laughing and talking well into the night; the younger children dashing about the basement in eager anticipation of opening gifts. Then the ensuing ruckus as my mother handed out gifts, followed by the sounds of wrapping paper ripping apart, unveiling much anticipated Christmas gifts.

Everyone in my family got along well and holidays were a time a joy and love. A part of me felt that I should feel guilty for not being there with them, but I didn't. As much as I missed them, I was with them in spirit and that was enough for me. I knew where they were and exactly what they were doing, as they had done so many times in the past. There would be other Christmases when I would be with them. Right now, I was where I wanted to be, however selfish that made me out to be.

During the afternoon, I strung a set of lights and garland on our pseudo Christmas tree in the courtyard to complement the ornaments placed there by the guests in the past week or so. Nathan produced a long extension cord to plug the lights into and tacked the cord to the ceiling so that no one would trip over it.

While in my room putting away the boxes from the lights, I heard a loud knock at my door. I swung the door open to find

Patrice standing there with an outstretched arm holding an envelope in her hand. "Here, this is for you," she said. "Merry Christmas!"

"Thank you," I replied with a smile as I took the long, white envelope from her hand. After shutting the door, I opened the envelope. Inside was a gift certificate from a nearby beauty salon for a manicure in the amount of $32.50; the exact amount that I had spent on her box of chocolates. I wondered how she had found out the amount. She must have either called the shop or looked it up on their website. I felt it was such a slap in the face that she would find it necessary to reimburse me in this way for what I had spent on her gift. Or perhaps I was being overly sensitive and this was all just a coincidence. I knew I would never really know for sure, but my suspicion put a damper on my holiday spirit. I had a feeling that I would never use that gift certificate. I nonchalantly dropped the gift certificate on the table and went back outside with my camera to take some pictures.

For our Christmas dinner, Ramon spent the afternoon in the kitchen baking the ham and turkey. Nathan, Stuart, and Bryan along with some of the other guests transformed the courtyard into an outdoor café by filling it with all of the round plastic tables and chairs that they could find. A long, rectangular table was set up near the Christmas tree for the buffet. There was a festive spirit in the air as all of the guests scurried around getting ready for the dinner. With everything in place, I decided to take a short nap before dinner.

Awaking from my nap, I heard a light rap on our door. I quickly dressed and when I opened the door, I was surprised to find Stuart who, immediately upon seeing me, thrust a small neatly wrapped gift into my hand. Caught off guard, I stammered, "Thank you!" As he turned to leave, almost as an afterthought, I exclaimed, " . . . Merry Christmas!" I was so touched that Stuart thought to give me a gift which I never expected. I tore away the wrapping paper, exposing a small, silver pen poised in a tabletop pen holder. I hadn't gotten anything for him or any of the other guests. I knew he didn't expect anything in return. His joy was in giving and his reward was my delight in receiving.

Elliot rolled out of bed, and we decided to take a walk along the ocean while waiting for the guests to gather. Before leaving for our walk, I plugged in the strand of outside Christmas tree lights and stood back to admire our handiwork. I felt a sense of satisfaction in the knowledge that there wasn't another Christmas tree in the whole world quite like ours. Our Christmas tree was a reflection of the unique surroundings and individuals who had come together from many distant places at this particular point in time to share in the celebration of the birth of Jesus. I felt so fortunate to be a part of this celebration. I thought of all the families who gathered in their same homes in the same city, year after year, and felt sorry for them that they should miss out on such adventure. Somehow their lives seemed so predictable and uneventful. I thanked my lucky stars for where I was at this moment in time.

By the time we returned from our walk, many of the seats at the tables were already filled. Ramon grabbed Elliot on our way in and asked him to do the honor of carving the turkey. As if on cue, the guests began to form a line when Mitch and Elliot started carving the ham and turkey, respectively. Again, all the guests had pitched in and contributed their own special dishes to the feast. Due to the lack of time and energy, my offering consisted of a box of store bought Christmas cookies. We filled our plates and reveled in the camaraderie of our newfound family. Many of the same guests who had shared Thanksgiving dinner were still present for Christmas dinner with the addition of some new guests. Patrice had invited some of the South American university students who had left to live in apartments to come for dinner. Maria and Maria Lucia turned up looking tanned and beautiful as ever with red and white Santa caps on their heads. Stuart paraded them around the courtyard with one on each arm.

The tables filled quickly, and by the time Elliot finished

carving the turkey, we were left with no place to sit. We fixed our plates and went to sit in the TV room with Kathy and her teenage daughter, Samantha, from Pennsylvania. They had arrived only a few days before to spend Christmas break at the hostel. Kathy was enamored by the kinship among the many, diverse guests and by the size of the sumptuous Christmas dinner that everyone so generously contributed to.

Patrice and Madeline sat at a table with a few of the regular guests across the courtyard from us. Not a word of Christmas cheer was exchanged between Elliot and Patrice. Madeline also kept her distance from him, but did return his greeting earlier when we came back from our walk.

Trying to keep the peace, I finished my dinner and walked around to mix with the guests and take some pictures. I took special care to take some pictures of Patrice and Madeline to give to them afterwards as a keepsake. Patrice was enjoying herself immensely, and every time I went to take her picture, she was scooping a fork full of food into her mouth. Evidently, her cares about her weight were far behind her now that Madeline was here.

I had hopes that Patrice's Christmas cheer would spill over onto her feelings about Elliot so that they could start their relationship anew by letting bygones be bygones. That did not seem like such a huge thing to hope for. Could a twenty dollar tip really cause so much animosity between them? It didn't make sense to me. I shook my head in an effort to dispel such gloomy thoughts and made an effort to immerse myself in the laughter and cavorting of the moment. This was Christmas and I was going to enjoy myself and let tomorrow take care of itself.

Later that evening, Elliot called his step-daughter, Tameka. I overhead him say that "we went for a walk earlier in the evening." Quick to catch on to the word 'we' she prodded him into telling her about me. To my knowledge, this was the first time that he had ever mentioned me to anyone in his family. He had sisters who lived in nearby Miami whom I had never met.

He was not close to his family and did not talk to them often. I was used to my weekly calls to my family back home and found it odd that he didn't make an effort to keep more in touch with them. Although he got along well with his daughter, it was a cause of concern to me that there was a lot of bad blood between him and some of his family members. But for now, I was happy that he at least told his daughter about me.

Christmas night I clung to Elliot in bed, our arms tightly wrapped around each other. At that moment our lives were not perfect, but at least we had each other. Somehow I had to hold on to the thought that things would work out, and we would always be together. For the first time in so many years, I finally had someone to share my life with. Drifting off to sleep, I wouldn't believe it could be any other way.

Friday morning the day after Christmas it was business as usual. My two days off for Christmas were over and it was back to working ten o'clock in the morning to midnight. I sat in the office sorting through the morning mail when Freddy from the pest control company came through the door. I reached for my keys expecting him to ask me to unlock all the doors so that he could spray the rooms. Instead he stood looking down at me from the other side of the counter.

"I stopped by to tell you that I can't spray today because your account is 90 days past due," he said matter-of-factly.

"Oh, it is?" This was the first I had heard of this. "Well, I will speak with Patrice. Maybe there was a mix up with the payment," I suggested hopefully.

Reaching over the counter he handed me a business card. "Here, call this number about your account," he said patiently.

"Okay." I dialed the number and spoke with a woman on the other end of the phone who emphatically told me that no payments had been received. I promised her I would check with Patrice and get back to her.

Freddy wished me a 'Happy Holidays' and headed out the door to his next stop.

I was aware that Patrice was having financial problems, but this was the first time that I knew of that a bill had gone unpaid. Still, it could possibly be an oversight. I would have to speak with her about it as soon as possible.

There was no sight of Patrice and Madeline when I went to lunch around noon. The hostel was unusually quiet with everyone either still recuperating from last night's party or off at the beach. By mid-afternoon the guests started stirring. On my way back from the laundry with my arms wrapped around a load of sheets, Sandra and Lisette, two guests from the Netherlands followed me into the office.

I set the sheets down on the back counter and turned to face them.

"We have a complaint," Lisette said rather shyly.

"Oh, what's wrong?" I asked.

"Well, last night after dinner we were upstairs talking and Evelyn came over to me and put her head between my boobs and said, 'I want to suck you tits!' She was horribly drunk and I just pushed her away. She just laughed and walked away. It was awful!"

Aghast, I replied, "Oh, good heavens! I'm so sorry!"

Evelyn had a way of drinking too much, but this is the first time she has ever done anything like this that I knew of. "I will speak to her about this as soon as I see her," I promised them.

The girls stood looking at me nodding their heads in unison. Sandra finally spoke up, "We would appreciate it. It's not something you'd want her doing to your other guests."

"Absolutely not!" I assured them. "I will take care of it."

They promptly left the office as I mulled about in my head how on earth I was going to approach Evelyn about such a ghastly thing. I decided it would be best to just be forthright and tell it like it was told to me. I wasn't looking forward to having such an embarrassing conversation, and I felt my face turn red at the thought of it. Evelyn was normally a friendly, innocuous young lady, but when she had too much to drink, she could be overbearing and obnoxious. Now I had two problems that I needed to speak to Patrice about. I kept wondering when she was going to make an appearance, and I anxiously looked over at her door through the office window.

Finally, on my way out the door to retrieve my next load of laundry from the dryer, Patrice pulled open her door and stepped out into the sunshine.

"Oh, there you are!" I stammered.

She smiled brightly and abruptly blurted out, "How do you like your new boss?"

"My new boss?" Shaking my head slightly, I was clueless as to what she was talking about.

"Yes, Madeline. She's your new boss."

"Oh?" I didn't quite know what to say.

"Well, yes, you know, since we are together, she is going to be my partner in running this place."

"That's nice, Patrice." I said encouragingly. This was news to me. Madeline was off at university in Denmark for the most part of the year, coming to visit Patrice for a few weeks a couple of times a year. I couldn't imagine what kind of relationship they could possibly have. They seemed happy to conduct a long distance relationship by phone and e-mail. I wondered how long a relationship could survive under such circumstances.

"Patrice, there are some things that I need to speak to you about."

She followed me into the office where I proceeded to relay the day's events to her. She assured me that she would speak with her accountant about the lapse in paying the pest control bill, and I assured her I could handle the issue with Evelyn. Madeline popped into the office to retrieve Patrice for their outing. They each swung a backpack over their shoulder and headed out through the gate, leaving me to contend with Evelyn. It wasn't long afterwards that Evelyn surfaced, pushing her bike through the courtyard. Not wasting a moment, I ran out the office door after her.

"Evelyn, wait! I need to talk to you."

Evelyn stopped pushing her bike and turned around to look at me. "Oh, hi Lu. What do you need?"

"Well, please come into the office." I motioned towards the door. Evelyn followed me in, and I closed the door behind us. I took a deep breath and looked Evelyn straight in the eye.

"Evelyn, I had a complaint about you today."

"What sort of complaint?" she inquired nervously.

"Well, Sandra and Lisette stopped by earlier to tell me that last night you put your head between Lisette's breasts and said, 'I want to suck your tits.'" I lowered my eyes to the floor as the last of the words tumbled out of my mouth.

I cleared my throat as I recovered my composure and looked up at Evelyn for her response.

Evelyn's eyes widened in horror, "Oh, I can't believe I would do that!" she exclaimed emphatically. "I wouldn't do something like that!" she insisted.

"Well, Evelyn, I can't imagine that they would make up such a thing. I know you were drinking last night and sometimes you get a little carried away with that."

"Yes, but still, I wouldn't do such a thing!" she said desperately.

Eager to end the conversation, I said, "Evelyn, just please be careful about what you say and do when you're drinking. You know that something like this is grounds for removal, and I wouldn't want to see that happen."

Evelyn started for the door still mumbling, "But, I didn't do anything like that."

A sigh of relief escaped my lips after she shut the door behind her. There was never a dull moment at the hostel.

Irritated by the day's events, my Christmas high wound down and the realities of life cast dark shadows over what was left of my Christmas spirit. Throughout the day, thoughts about Elliot's predicament poked and prodded at me. I kept trying to shut out the thoughts about his lack of a job and money, and especially my worst fear that he would up and leave me and the hostel.

The situation between Elliot and Patrice grated more and more on my nerves. Even though I tried my best not to let the tension between them affect me, I found myself getting short tempered with the guests. The long hours didn't help much either. My schedule didn't leave much time for rest and relaxation, and the heavy demands of a continuous flow of guests wore my patience thin.

One morning as I started counting the cash drawer at the start of my day, a group of guests descended on me like a cloud of locusts immediately putting me in a foul mood. Three impatient guests needed to check-out, and four eager guests wanted to check-in early. I always counted the drawer before refunding any key deposits. A bevy of eyes enveloped me as I attempted to count the cash drawer. After my fourth attempt, the amount still did not add up to the correct amount. Indignant at the intrusive stares from the crowd of guests gathered across from me, I finally asked everyone to wait outside the office until I could get everything in order. With gripes and groans, the guests filed out one by one. Every so often, I would look up from my work to see a sea of staring faces intently watching me through the office window as if their efforts would hurry me along. Finally I completed my duties and went to open the door.

"Okay. First, I will take the guests checking out who need their key deposits. You need to make sure that you put your dirty sheets and towels into the baskets out here before I can give you your refund." As I spoke, the group of outgoing guests hurried past me on their way back into the office.

"As for you early check-ins, I have your room assignments and will get to you in a moment. Thank you for your patience." I managed to plaster a slight smile on my face despite my irritated, short-tempered mood.

The guests weren't supposed to check-in until after Lola cleaned the dorm rooms, but since there were available, empty beds, I went ahead and let them into their rooms. Often guests just needed a place to drop off their belongings so that they could go to the beach or sightseeing. They didn't care if the room was clean or not. And at this point, neither did I.

In the middle of the afternoon, John, an older man on disability, appeared at the counter clutching the note in his hand that I had tapped to his door the previous day. I tried to ignore the note shaking uncontrollably in his unsteady hand. His face betrayed a sense of anxiety and I had difficulty looking him in the eye.

"John, I see you got my note. I need you to move to another room for tonight. We have a group coming in that will be staying in your room."

"Alright, I can do that," he said. He had dark circles under his eyes and his clothes were rumpled.

"Oh, also, Patrice wanted me to tell you that tonight will be your last night here," I said struggling to maintain a pleasant and upbeat tone.

"Oh, what's wrong? I thought I would get to stay!" he wailed and I thought he might start crying.

"I'm sorry, John, we have some groups arriving and we are sold out for the next week or so," I lied. I did my best to hide my true emotions as my heart wrenched from the unfairness and despair of it all. My mind wandered back to Christmas day when I had made up a plate of food and gave it to him as he watched TV in the lounge area. He wouldn't come out on his own to make a plate despite my insistence to do so. I don't think he felt welcomed by the others. John kept mostly to himself. He was quiet and didn't cause any trouble. Patrice singled him out because he was an alcoholic and anti-social. He didn't fit in with the other guests. She also had reports of beer missing from the refrigerators late at night. Whether John took the beer or not was hard to say. John slept late in the day and stayed up late at night. The sad truth was that John was being weeded out as an undesirable. This wasn't a rehabilitation home for alcoholics and wayward souls. We had a business to run and sometimes decisions had to be made in the best interest of the other guests in the hostel, no matter how hard it was to do so.

John didn't argue with me. He accepted the bad news with grace and understanding. I didn't think for a minute that he believed my story. He knew deep down that he was being asked to leave. It probably had happened to him in the past. As I watched him walk out the door, I wondered where he would go. I felt an uneasiness in my conscious that I couldn't quite dismiss. I said a little prayer for him and wished him the best. I hoped he would be able to find another place to stay without too much trouble. So many people had passed through our gates at the hostel since I had arrived there six months earlier; each with their own story. We were a stop at a crossroad on the path of their lives; some happy, some not so happy.

Elliot's weekly rent was due. I had no idea if he had the money or not. Wrapped up tightly in our own cocoons, we had stopped sharing our thoughts. Perhaps it was a way to protect each other from the reality of our situation. The rent was due before noon. I glanced nervously at my watch. It was already a quarter past twelve. Elliot had gone to mass earlier in the morning. He returned briefly to our room and left again, waving at me as he walked by the office window.

The weather was cooler now, and I grabbed my beach chair and went outside to sit in the sun. I lifted my face upwards to absorb the sun's warming rays. I took a deep breath of the cool, dry ocean air that swirled around me caressing my skin. The peaceful calm of the quiet afternoon soothed my soul. The courtyard was deserted. Patrice and Madeline were out on another one of their outings for the day, so I had the place to myself.

Despite the calmness of the day, my mind was in overdrive trying to make sense of the situation with Elliot. We lived together day-by-day without any thought of future plans. Each of us bought our own food except on the occasions when I cooked a Sunday dinner that I shared with him. We enjoyed each other's company and had some things in common, especially watching classic movies together. Our deep spiritual bond was the solid foundation on which our relationship was built. Ours wasn't a rocky relationship; we were basically happy with each other.

My biggest concern was Elliot's refusal to find a job. He said he was looking, but he didn't give any specifics. He appeared to be waiting for something, as if a job or money would magically appear. His heart was set on money coming through to finance his movie, but since he couldn't come up with his share, that didn't seem likely to happen. The country was still reeling from the fiasco on Wall Street, and the government was bailing out the banks and financial institutions to prevent further deterioration of the markets. I knew his money was sure to run out before long and then something would have to give. I wondered if he thought I should bail him out. But that wasn't going to happen. I was resentful that he had let so much time go without really looking for a job. I thought of all the times I found him asleep on the bed when I was sweating my butt off cleaning the hostel or dealing with guests. I came to the conclusion that he had had all kinds of time to look for a job, and I wasn't about to bail him out of his financial situation. I had some money saved and could easily do so, but I was adamant that I would not. It was hard for me to do this since my heart's inclination was to help him out since I really did love him. But something in me wouldn't let me do so. Perhaps it was out of fear that he was using me or taking advantage of me. I was suspicious of his intentions, wondering if he was with me because he knew I had a soft heart and had been generous to him in the past. There was an element of distrust that I harbored towards him. I wanted to believe that he loved me, but how do you ever really know for sure? I had been deeply hurt in past relationships, and now that I finally gave my heart away to someone again, I had to face the prospect that it might be happening again. I made up my mind that I wasn't going to worry about the situation and that whatever happened, happened. At least that is what I told myself. The truth was I felt drained and tired of worrying about Elliot's financial situation.

The thought that he could up and leave at any time was never far from my mind.

I kept reminding myself not to throw away a relationship just because things were not to my liking. It is easy to let a point of contention swell up out of proportion until it chokes the life out of a relationship, even a relationship with some redeeming qualities. I had gone for seven years without someone to share my life with and knew how difficult it was to find someone where there was a mutual attraction. There are so many people in the world that you would think it would be so easy to go out onto a busy street and just bump into someone who could become that special person in your life. But I knew it didn't work that way. I had walked by thousands of men in the past seven years, yet, the few that I did get to know, I wasn't interested in or not attracted to.

I also learned the hard way that even though you loved someone, that doesn't mean he is good for you. I had my share of past relationships where we ended up bringing the worst out in each other, eventually destroying our relationship. In retrospect, my whole life seemed to be a string of broken relationships where I spent years afterwards picking up the emotional pieces in an effort to put my life back together again, only to make the same mistakes over again.

That is why I went so long without someone in my life. Years of wretched loneliness with no one to share my thoughts, joys, and sorrows with except my cat. Days often went by where I didn't speak to another human being while I was holed up in my apartment, completing my studies at the university.

Absorbed in thought, I was surprised to look up and find Elliot staring down at me. "I just came back from an interesting meeting," he said. "Hopefully, they can work something out with me."

"Oh, that's good, hon," I replied as I got up from my beach chair. I had no idea what he was talking about. This was the first time he mentioned any 'meeting' to me.

He glanced over at Patrice's door. "Is Patrice here?"
"No, she and Madeline are out for the day. Why?" I inquired.
"I need to talk to her about my rent," he said nonchalantly.
"She'll be back later."
He leaned over and kissed me. "I'm going inside to read the newspaper."
"Alright. See you later."
Patrice was still gone when he returned later with money in hand to pay another week's rent. He had decided not to talk to her after all. We were safe for another week. As for his meeting mentioned earlier, I never heard another word about it.

That evening we sat down to dinner together in the early evening. I pushed a piece of lettuce around my plate absentmindedly.

"You seem preoccupied tonight. What's on your mind, baby?"
Elliot's words broke into my thoughts. "Oh, I was just thinking about John," I replied quietly.
"John?!" The rise in his tone of voice betrayed his suspicion that I was referring to my ex-husband, John.
Adamantly, I replied, "John, the guest staying here. You know . . . the older man who keeps to himself a lot. Patrice isn't letting him stay here any longer."

Elliot visibly shrank back and continued eating his dinner as I filled him in on my conversation with John earlier in the day. Despite Patrice's insistence that I not discuss matters pertaining to guests with Elliot, I found that at times I needed to unburden myself. Elliot was the only person at the hostel who I could confide in. He always listened to me patiently and with a sympathetic ear, sometimes doling out advice as he saw fit. When I finished talking, I stressed that what I told him was in confidence.

Later that evening when I passed by the TV lounge, I noticed Elliot sitting in a corner talking to John. "Maybe they misunderstood you . . ." I heard him saying to John. I stopped dead in my tracks.

I stuck my head in the lounge door. "Hi, hon! Do you have a minute?" I asked waving him over to me.

"Yes, sure," he said rising from his seat.

I walked with him towards our room and opened the door. We went inside.

"Hon, you weren't telling John what I told you earlier, were you?" I asked with a worried tone. "Remember, what I said was in confidence."

"No, I wouldn't do that," he insisted.

"Okay, I just wanted to make sure. I heard you say something to him about being misunderstood."

"No, we were just talking about . . . things."

I gave him a dubious look. "Okay. I just wanted to make sure."

The end of December was fast approaching. The long days of covering the office and the situation with Elliot were wearing me out. Bad dreams of someone trying to hurt me haunted my sleep at night. Elliot clung to me so tightly throughout the night that, at times, I couldn't breathe or move. One morning when the alarm went off at seven o'clock for mass, I told him to go on without me. I was too tired to get out of bed and needed some extra sleep.

We had a full house and trying to keep up with the office work, laundry, and guest relations was taking its toll on me. That afternoon, two university students on winter break turned up to check-in. They had called the week before to change their arrival date, and when they showed up, I discovered I had written the wrong date in the reservations book. We had a full house and there wasn't a bed to be had. As the girls stood eyeing me expectantly, I hemmed and hawed trying to come up with some solution to the situation when I remembered that we had some extra mattresses stored away. They were only too happy to sleep on the mattresses on the floor of the large women's dorm room at a reduced rate. My personal problems were distracting me from my job duties and I was beginning to make mistakes. I honestly felt that I was beginning to crack under the weight of it all.

My four o'clock break arrived and I gratefully climbed into bed for a nap after taking a couple of aspirins. Elliot joined me. No sooner had we both fell into a peaceful slumber when there was a loud knock at the door. As Elliot rolled out of bed and pulled his pants on to answer the door, I glanced over at the clock. It was only five o'clock. We had barely been sleeping for an hour, so much for my much needed nap.

I heard Nathan outside the door talking to Elliot. Before I understood what was happening, Elliot walked back into the room and snatched my hostel keys off the hook where they hung on a small cabinet and thrust them through the open door to Nathan.

"Hon, what's going on?" I said in a raspy voice. "Does Nathan need the key to the laundry room to do his laundry?" The laundry room was not usually open to guests until after six o'clock in the evening, but we made an exception for the long-term guests.

"No, baby, he just needs to get into the laundry room to change a fuse," he said as he went about sliding off his pants to get back into bed.

I instantly sat up in bed. "What?! What do you mean he needs to change a fuse?! What fuse?" I asked rather hotly. "I don't think you should have given him my keys without asking me first."

"I'm sorry. I didn't think it was a big deal. He just needs to unlock the door," he replied defensively while pulling his pants back up and clasping his belt around his waist.

I jumped out of bed, dressed quickly, and put my glasses on. I was in such a rush that I didn't even bother to put in my contacts, something I never did since I hated wearing my glasses.

As I slipped on my flip-flops, I asked, "Does Patrice know about this?"

Elliot shrugged his shoulders. "I don't know, baby."

I ran out the door to the laundry room, but the door was

locked with no sign of Nathan. Patrice was out with Madeline, and I was the sole person responsible for the hostel while she was gone. I couldn't have guests taking care of things without permission from Patrice or me. The last thing I needed was to have Patrice upset with me. I searched through the rooms on the first floor and not finding him, ran up the steps to the second floor, thinking perhaps he went to his room. At the top of the steps, I found him on a ladder in the computer room.

"Nathan! What are you doing?!" I asked exasperatedly.

"Oh, hi, Lu. We blew a fuse, so I needed to get in the laundry room to check the fuse box in there. I fixed the problem and just needed to change this light bulb," he said in his usual good-natured tone as he held the light bulb out for me to see.

"Nathan, where are my keys?" I asked impatiently.

Nathan reached into his front pocket and pulled the keys out, dropping them into my outstretched hand.

"You cannot do this without asking permission! You can't just go around here fixing things without Patrice or I's knowledge!" I insisted while glaring at him.

"Look, Lu, I was just trying to help," he said sheepishly.

"I understand that, but this could have waited! I am on my break and I was taking a nap!" I wailed. "This is not an emergency! You can't just knock on my door and take my keys to do things around here!" I spitted out emphatically. I don't know which made me madder; that he took my keys or that he woke me up from my nap.

Nathan looked at me strangely, his eyes narrowing at my tone. He had never seen me like this before. I usually projected an even temperament and was easy going or at least accommodating. That my tone was so vehement, took him by surprise.

"Alright, Lu. Sorry. I'm just about done now anyways. I just need to take this ladder back downstairs." Nathan folded up the ladder, and I followed him down the stairs. Now that Patrice was using Nathan more and more as her driver, he was assuming a broader role within the hostel. I knew he didn't mean any harm, but I felt he was over stepping his boundaries as a paying guest. Even if he was driving Patrice, that didn't give him the right to act like he owned the place. I stomped to my room and slammed the door shut, determined to post a sign on my door that I was not to be disturbed during my break unless it was an emergency.

I tried going back to sleep, but tossed and turned until it was time to return to work at six o'clock. I stepped outside my room and saw Nathan speaking to Patrice on the other side of the courtyard. I had a pretty good idea what they were talking about. I walked over towards them and stood a short distance away until they finished talking.

Patrice turned to me. "Where are your keys?" she asked sternly. As she spoke, Nathan quietly crept away.

My keys were clipped to my side belt loop as usual, and I reached down and jiggled them back and forth. "They're right here. I wanted to talk to you about what happened, but I see Nathan has already filled you in." I took a deep breath and launched into my explanation, "I was taking a nap when he knocked on my door and Elliot gave him my keys. He didn't realize . . ."

She cut me off midsentence. "I don't *ever* want Elliot to have your keys," she said emphatically.

The harshness in her tone surprised me. It seemed silly to me that Patrice was making such a big deal about Elliot taking my keys. Elliot had access to my keys every time I took them off and hung them on the hook in our room.

"Patrice, I realize that, but as I said, I was sleeping and Elliot answered the door. I have never given anyone my keys before. Anyways, Nathan had no right to knock on my door asking for my keys. It's not his place to fix things around here."

"I've spoken to Nathan about that. But just remember, no one but you should ever have your keys, especially not Elliot!" With that said, she walked off in the direction of her room.

I followed behind her on my way to the office. This was not turning out to be a very good day. I didn't mind getting chewed out if I did something wrong, and I was always the first to apologize if I did. In this case, the only wrong I could see was not being the one to answer the door. Patrice was more upset about Elliot having access to my keys than about Nathan playing maintenance man. It was quite obvious that she didn't trust Elliot.

I felt crushed as I sat at the computer typing up the 'Do Not Disturb During Break' sign to post on my door. Patrice's distrust and dislike of Elliot was growing more and more evident. She didn't discuss this openly with me, but it was plain to see by how she behaved towards him. I was caught in the middle of the two of them trying to keep the peace.

I printed out my 'Do Not Disturb' sign and tore off a few pieces of tape. Walking to my room to post the notice on my door, I saw Richard cooking spaghetti in the kitchen. Richard was a geologist from New York; a bespectacled, middle-aged man with a slight build and a quiet manner who lived with his parents in New York and worked as a guide in some caverns there.

"Hey, Lu, I'm making spaghetti for everyone for dinner. Will you have some, too?" Richard inquired across the room with a big smile on his face. He was having the time of his life. He enjoyed the camaraderie with the other guests and took special delight in the shared dinners and social interaction. He made a comment to me one day that he didn't date because he didn't have much money. I suspected that he led a rather solitary life, except for the company of his elderly parents. The hostel was the perfect place for him. It offered him companionship and eventful days. We were like one big family with all its noise, problems, joys, and conflicts.

After the day's events, I wasn't in the mood for dinner, preferring to keep to myself instead. A group of guests sat at the picnic tables in the courtyard eating Richard's spaghetti, laughing and talking. Richard was absolutely beaming from all the attention he was getting from everyone for making dinner.

Seeing his happiness was the one bright spot in my day. Elliot decided to spend the evening in the TV lounge, so that I could work out of our room and have some peace and quiet. I was grateful for the time alone. I put the office phone on the kitchen table and opened the blinds so that I could keep an eye on the office. Thankfully it was a quiet night with only a few check-ins, all arriving before nine o'clock.

The next day wasn't much better. Again, Patrice reminded me not to give my keys to Elliot. I just looked at her without saying a word. I got it the first time she told me and thought it unnecessary for her to repeat herself. My foul mood from the day before stuck with me, and I went around the hostel in a cloud of fury. I honestly felt like getting drunk or driving my car into the ocean. That I would even think such a thing was an indication of the depths of my anguish. When I tried to discuss the situation with Elliot, he started quoting scripture while I just shook my head and walked away. Except for business matters, Patrice and I were hardly speaking. There was so much tension in the air I felt that I could cut it with a knife. Something had to give and soon. Things certainly could not continue to go on like this.

I became fearful that Patrice would abruptly cut me out of her life the way she had done to Elliot. That could have dire consequences. Where would I go? The economy was still in shambles and no one was hiring anywhere. My whole life was here. If I left, I had no place else to go. The joy I had felt months earlier at my luck to be living and working here didn't seem so appealing now. It was like putting all your eggs into one basket.

My aggravated mood carried on throughout that night. Elliot slept soundly on his side of the bed, and I stuck to my own side. We usually took turns holding each other close on and off throughout the night, but this time I didn't even want to touch him. I was putting distance between us in an effort to protect myself. When I didn't know how to handle a situation, I tended to curl up in my own little shell.

Elliot handled the situation much better than I. He went about his day as usual going to mass and the library then coming home to read the paper and take a nap. He kept his emotions tightly locked up inside and didn't share much with me unless I prodded him. Then depending on his mood, he would either snap back at me with a put-down of Patrice, or try to ease the situation by quoting scripture and advising me to trust in God's plan.

Taking a break on my last day of work for the year, I laid back in my beach chair to enjoy the mid-afternoon sun. The sky was a beautiful pale blue with not a cloud in sight. A slight ocean breeze stirred the air around me. It was a pleasant day, almost 80 degrees, which was warm for this time of year. I was in a nostalgic mood reflecting back over the year that was about to come to a close. It had been an eventful year; one of the most eventful of my life. I wondered if I would still be here at this time next year. Caught up in thought, I suddenly felt a hand on my arm. I looked up to find Elliot leaning towards me.

"I sent out a few resumes this morning. We'll see what happens."

I smiled up at him. "You need a haircut, hon. How about I cut your hair this evening?"

He smiled back and nodded affirmatively. He squeezed my arm and walked off towards our room. I looked at his white, frizzy hair sticking out in tuffs from under his cap.

I sat back and tilted my face up towards the sun to get the full effect. My mind drifted back to the night before when I was surfing the internet for information on Near Death Experiences (NDE's). I had been reading the book Elliot had given me for Christmas about a man who had a NDE and I wanted to learn more about them. After reading numerous websites, I found that the one abiding theme in most NDE's was 'love;' unconditional love. Is that what this is all about? Love? And if it is, should we put love on a higher plane above such things as money, materialism, job security; all the things we normally look for in a spouse? For if you put love on a higher plane, then one must overlook or tolerate what lies beneath it for the sake of preserving that love.

They say that love conquers all. Maybe I had never really given love enough of a chance or didn't believe in it hard enough. Maybe I even had run away from it, afraid that I wasn't worthy of love. I vowed that this time would be different. I was determined to stick it out no matter what happened. It wasn't easy to find love in this world, and when found, it must be protected, nourished, and preserved at all costs.

That night in bed, barely touching Elliot because of my frustration with him, I reached over and caressed his shoulder. At the touch of my hand, he emitted a deep sigh of relief. He could feel my love. No words needed to be spoken. Even though I was upset with him, I still felt love for him in my heart. Who we choose to love does not always make sense. Or maybe it is love that chooses us. Love defies comprehension. It just exists independent of everything else and it is supreme above all else. There was no use trying to figure it out. And then I made a conscious decision: He might leave me in a day, a week, or a month because he didn't have money for his rent, but I would not be the one to walk away from our love.

Chapter 14

A New Year

The start of a new year is usually full of hopes and expectations for what the year may bring, but that wasn't to be for me. My life was in such turmoil, that I dared only to take one day at a time. The future was too uncertain. I was safe for the moment and that's all that mattered to me.

New Year's Eve arrived and I made a special trip to the grocery store to buy pork and sauerkraut for our dinner the next day. Elliot was waiting for me when I arrived back at the hostel in the early afternoon. It was such a beautiful day that we decided to take the water taxi to Las Olas Boulevard to get an ice cream cone. We invited Richard to tag along with us. The water taxi pickup was within walking distance of the hostel, so we took off walking. Arriving at the pier, we discovered that we had just missed the last taxi. It would be another half an hour before the next pickup. To my surprise, since he had been so eager to go with us, Richard decided he didn't want to wait that long and went back to the hostel. Elliot and I walked over towards the ocean and sat on a bench, passing the time.

We returned a half hour later to the pier in time for the next pick-up. I had been on the water taxi a number of times, but Elliot hadn't. It was a great way to see Fort Lauderdale's many waterways. The tour guide on board related in a lively manner the history of the area along with the previous and current occupants of the many mansions and yachts lining the intercoastal waterway and the New River. We passed by the port where large cruise ships were docked while preparing for their next voyage. Every so often, the water taxi stopped to pick up or drop off passengers. Elliot and I leaned against each other while enjoying the rocking motion of the boat as we made our way over the water. We stepped off the water taxi in the downtown area and walked over to Las Olas Boulevard for an ice cream cone. Afterwards, we spent some time wandering through the shops and art galleries. It was a beautiful, relaxing afternoon.

By the time we reboarded the water taxi, it was already dusk. All along the way back, the lights from Christmas displays awed and delighted us. Passing a condo facing the water, through a glass patio door I noticed an elderly woman slowly making her way to her couch, probably to watch TV for the night. It looked like she lived alone and I felt sorry for her. I squeezed Elliot's hand because I was so happy I had someone to share my life with. I knew what it was like to be all alone on the holidays.

Patrice and Madeline treated the guests to a cookout on New Year's Eve. We got back just in time for dinner. Patrice was filling a platter with barbecued chicken from the grill when we walked in through the gate. On the picnic table there was an assortment of side dishes and desserts. Elliot and I filled our plates and then decided to eat in our room. There was only a small gathering of guests for dinner since many of them had already left to go out to celebrate New Year's Eve. We thought it best not to mingle in such close quarters with Patrice and Madeline.

After dinner, Elliot said he had a headache, so he took a few aspirins and went to bed asking me to join him. It was early evening and the last thing I wanted to do was to go to bed! I wanted to have a few drinks and talk. I poured myself a glass of wine and went to call my cousin, Gene. We talked for awhile until she had to leave to go to a party with her fiancé, Vern. Undeterred, I finished my wine and switched to beer. Madeline was sitting in the courtyard with a few other guests, so I went to talk to them. Drinking beer had an inhibiting effect on me after a few drinks. I wanted to talk, sing, and dance. But most of all, I didn't want to stop drinking. I had had problems in the past with alcohol and had quit drinking for ten years. Here I was again tipping the bottle. I told myself it was a holiday and I had the right to party a little bit. But I knew better than that: an alcoholic can always justify a reason for drinking.

Having a few drinks gave me the courage I needed to finally talk to Madeline. I never quite knew what to say to her. She was quiet and reserved, and I found myself being the same way in her company. I was surprised to see her drinking a beer since I knew how much Patrice despised drinking. But Patrice was nowhere in sight. Not sure what to talk about, I asked Madeline about university. She was majoring in French and English and would graduate that coming summer. We were finally loosening up with each other when Patrice came out of her room. A group of guests were going with her and Madeline to the beach. They asked me to go along, but I declined. I had other plans. I wanted to listen to music and sing. More than anything, I wanted to listen to loud music. Life was so restricting at the hostel. When I listened to music in my room, I was always careful not to turn it up too loud. I ran to my room and tiptoed in so as not to wake Elliot. I grabbed my CD's and a few extra beers and went to my car. After starting the car up, I popped a CD into the CD player and turned up the volume. I sat in the parking lot with the car running and the music on full blast all the while singing my heart out and taking a few sips of beer in between. The only time I ever had to leave was when I had to run back to my room to go to the bathroom. Patrice and her entourage came back from their walk on the beach. She knocked on my window and I reached over and turned down the music with one hand and rolled the window down with the other. "I feel sorry for you in the morning!" she shouted. I just laughed and waved her on. I didn't know what she meant at first. Then I figured she must have meant she felt sorry that I was going to have a hangover in the morning. Never the matter, I was having a grand old time.

I stayed in my car until well after midnight. Elliot was still asleep at midnight, so we didn't even share our first New Year's kiss. I finally tired of my music and went back to my room to find Elliot sitting in the recliner reading the paper. He must have been worried about me. I was still in the mood to party, so I put on some music and began to dance. Elliot watched me dance and then he got into the action by teaching me some Caribbean dance steps; every once in a while, I stopped to take a swig of beer. I never even thought to offer Elliot a beer. He usually didn't drink, but it never even occurred to me that he might have liked a beer. Finally exhausted, we went to bed at 3:00 a.m. As Patrice suspected, I didn't feel so well the next day, but I sure had a good time singing and dancing the night before.

I slept in on New Year's Day, but did manage to get up and go to an early afternoon mass with Elliot. We lounged around in the afternoon watching TV and dozing. I got up to make pork and sauerkraut with mashed potatoes for dinner. Dinner was late that evening, we didn't eat until eight o'clock. During dinner, Elliot started talking about when he lived in Lexington, Virginia. He was oddly reminiscent about the ten years he spent living there. I didn't quite grasp the significance of his musings. When we climbed into bed that night, I fell asleep while Elliot was still talking about it.

The holidays were over and it was time to get back to work. I still had another week to work in the office for Patrice until Madeline returned to Denmark. Carlos had filled in for me while I was off the past few days. When I returned to the office, I was shocked to find out that he had only done what was absolutely necessary. None of the laundry had been washed, and the paperwork from guest arrivals and departures was scattered all over the office desk and counter. In an ill humor from the disarray, I went about putting things back in order. I spent the whole day catching up on laundry and paperwork. That night

I finished up after midnight. I took a bubble bath and climbed into bed exhausted. I looked over at Elliot who was lying on his side facing me with his hand on the side of his head like he was holding it. His eyes were closed, but I could tell by his breathing that he was not asleep. Something didn't seem right.

A few minutes later he spoke, "We have to talk."

"About what?"

Elliot swallowed hard. "My money has run out and I have to leave here. I only have about thirty dollars left and half a tank of gas."

Incredulously, I replied, "Leave? Where will you go?" I laid on my back looking up at the ceiling in the darkness and the silence of the night.

"I'm not sure yet. I'm waiting for a few people to call me back to see if I can stay with them. I could go to Miami, I have some family there." He quickly added, "I could come to see you once a week. I'll call you every night."

Fighting back tears, I moaned, "I knew this was going to happen! This is why I got so upset with you last month and wanted to break up with you!"

"Look, baby, I have to get away from this situation. I just can't seem to make it work here."

Although I knew this was coming, I was still stunned. I honestly can't remember anything else about that night except that I cried a lot and slept very little. All I could think of was that he was leaving me the next day. Before Elliot drifted off to sleep, he mumbled, "I had fun dancing with you on New Year's Eve." My heart was broken.

The next morning, Elliot announced at breakfast that he needed to talk to Patrice because his rent was due, and he didn't have the money to pay her. I sat at the table trying to force myself to swallow my cereal. Despite my best attempts to stop them, tears spilled from my red, swollen eyes. Elliot went on repeating the same things about having to get away from here as he had said the night before. Things that I wanted to say; I did not. I wanted to scream at him that if he had only gotten a regular job months ago, this wouldn't be happening. Instead, he had lounged around and slept the days away. I kept silent, got dressed, and went to work. Purposely, I avoided going into our room so that I wouldn't have to talk to him.

Later in the morning, I heard Patrice tell him that she couldn't talk to him until after she ate her breakfast and took a shower. I couldn't help but think that she was putting him off. An hour later, Patrice came into the office and told me she needed the office for a few minutes to talk to Elliot. To bide my time, I went out back and sat in the sun and smoked a cigarette, my fate hanging in the balance. A short while later, Elliot came out to get me and asked me to come to our room to talk. I followed him to our room in heavy silence.

We sat across from each other at the kitchen table, face-to-face, possibly for the last time. I really had no idea if I would ever see him again. I almost felt like he was a stranger to me, like he was just another long-term guest that I happened to share a room with for the last four months, and now it was time for him to go on his way just like so many other guests had come and gone. I expected him to pack his bags and leave at any moment. By now, I was completely cried out. He had told Patrice that he had to leave because he didn't have money for the rent. But there was more to the story than I realized.

"I owe Patrice some money," Elliot said matter-of-factly.

"You mean for the rent?" I inquired.

"No, she helped me out with rent for my office when I was trying to get some financing for her. I offered to leave my car with her as payment, but she doesn't want it. She said I could just pay her back when I get the money."

"Oh," was all I could manage to say at this point. How much more was there about this man that I didn't know about, I wondered. I didn't like that he had kept things from me.

"Would you have some money that I could borrow?" he asked forthrightly. "I'll pay you back as soon as I can. I'll leave my digital camera with you as collateral," he offered.

My mind whirled in a dizzy spin that left me reeling. He had borrowed money from Patrice, and, now, he wanted to borrow from me. Deep inside of me, something screamed, 'NO!'

"I'm sorry, but I don't have any money to lend you," I said crisply. "I spent a lot of money on Christmas presents for my family, and I'm low on cash right now," I lied. My defense mechanism had kicked in, and I put up a forceful wall between us. I was determined I would not help him in anyway. Perhaps he had been taking advantage of me all along. I didn't have a lot of money, but I was making a decent income and I didn't have to pay for rent. So much for my high-minded thoughts from just a few days earlier of how important it was to fight for love and that love conquers all. That was an ideal, something not conducive to the cold, hard realities of life.

"Okay. I understand," he said quietly.

"If you need money, then take your camera to a pawn shop." I said with a sharp edge in my voice. I wanted to get this over with. "When are you leaving?" I asked assuming it would be sometime that day.

"Patrice said I could stay one more night and pay her later," he said.

I clenched my teeth. How could I bare another night of this? After over a month of this tension and not knowing, I just wanted him to leave right now so that I could move on with my life. I had had enough of the whole situation. Whatever feelings I had had for him seemed to be no longer there. I wanted him out of my room and out of my life.

Elliot went upstairs to work on the computer, while I went back to the office where Patrice was covering for me. Madeline was sitting on a stool outside the office and Patrice stood beside her with her arm wrapped around Madeline's shoulders. I crossed the courtyard to join them.

Looking at Patrice, I said, "So we were both duped by Elliot!"

"What?" Patrice looked at me inquisitively.

"I mean that we were both taken advantage of by him. He told me how he had borrowed money from you and wanted to leave his car."

Patrice dismissed my comment with a wave of her hand. "Madeline and I thought perhaps you thought we should let Elliot stay in your room for free."

"Absolutely not!" I said emphatically. "He needs to get a job and work like everyone else to pay his rent. It's okay to have projects that you are trying to finance, but you still have to support yourself in the meantime." I continued letting off steam. "You should have told him to get his sorry ass out of here today!"

"I thought you would want him to stay another night," Patrice replied.

"No! It would have been better if he had left today."

"Lu, you look so tired. You really should try to get some rest during your break."

"I know. I hardly slept last night." I went into the office and shut the door firmly behind me. I needed some peace and quiet. I had to work until midnight and it wasn't even lunchtime yet. I kept my distance from Elliot for the rest of the day. I had enough of being upset and crying. I had work to do and it was difficult speaking to guests in such an emotional state.

There was an internal battle raging inside of me between my head and my heart. When I spoke to Patrice about Elliot, it was coming from my head and I sided with her against him. I knew he was to blame for his predicament. I had also been distrustful of him and felt he was taking advantage of my generosity. I wanted to love him, but my intellect insisted that I could do so only if he met certain conditions of how he should act. But my heart was a worthy opponent; it fought mightily for love. I had fallen in love with him at first sight, unconditionally. My mind had no say so in the matter. And how could this even be? You would think that a person operates as an undivided whole, but that's not really the case. Now my mind was fighting to protect me from the possibility of getting hurt, but my heart refused to listen. I didn't know which one to heed. But when I was with Elliot, I listened to my heart.

That evening I stayed in the office and ate a bowl of cereal for dinner. I closed up shop at midnight and went back to my room, took a bath, and went to bed hoping that Elliot would be fast asleep so that I could finally get a good night's sleep.

I laid back on my pillow thankful for a chance to get some rest. Elliot wasn't asleep; he had been waiting for me to come to bed. He rolled over on his side to face me then took my hand in his, raised it to his lips, and kissed it as he had done so many times in the past.

"I've decided to go back to Virginia. I have friends there, good friends, who will help me."

I bit my lip and refused to speak. I could feel the tears start to well up inside me again. I was determined not to cry.

He continued, "Look, baby, I'm not leaving you, this only a separation."

Flatly, I replied, "I hope you find what you are looking for."

"What if you had to leave? Say that one of your daughters was sick. I would understand."

"You will probably just find someone else," I quipped.

"I don't want anyone else. I want you." Elliot rolled on his back looking up at the ceiling, he said, "You are being unreasonable."

"What?!"

He repeated, "You are being unreasonable."

For a brief moment, I had an overwhelming urge to laugh; to grab him and roll around the bed with him like this was all a big joke. Determinedly squaring my jaw, I resisted the urge and kept a stiff upper lip.

From his side of the bed, in a small voice he said, "Aren't you going to kiss me goodnight like you do every night?"

"I don't want to kiss you." I said defiantly. I knew that if I dared kiss him or touched him, I would be up all night crying and the truth of the matter was I had another ten hour day to work the next day. I had to get some sleep . . . but I was also punishing him.

"You are breaking your promise," he retorted.

"What promise?"

"That we would never go to bed mad at each other," he reminded me.

"I'm not mad," I said. Just angry, I said to myself. "I have this feeling that we will never see each other again."

"Do all your feelings come true?" he asked.

"Sometimes."

The banter between us, though serious, had inklings of deeper feelings that weren't so easily dismissed; of a bond that was forged and not so easily broken by words, deeds, or impending distance.

Elliot soon fell into a peaceful slumber while I was in-store for a fitful night of sleep. Sometime during the very early hours of the morning I laid awake thinking. In spite of the ill feelings I felt towards Elliot for what I perceived as him getting us into this predicament, there was a flicker of a warm, glowing spot in my heart for him that grew in size as the night wore on. During my waking hours, I had effectively suppressed my true feelings, but now in the raw, dead of night there was a burning flame of love for him that I could not squelch. I knew what I wanted to do. It seemed so natural to me, like it was the right thing to do. I decided to give Elliot a hundred dollars to take with him. I etched in my mind forever the moments of our last night together, as I drifted off into a fitful slumber.

I woke early in the morning and rolled over on my side to face Elliot. He was sleeping on his side facing me, and I reached out and rested my hand on the side of his face. He reached over and drew me towards him, hugging me tightly. I buried my face in his chest, muffling the sounds of my sobs in his white, cotton undershirt.

"Baby, listen, you must keep a positive attitude. Things will work out for us," he assured me. "You tend to see a glass that is half-filled as being half-empty, where I see it as half-full.

You need to focus on the positive of every situation." He gently shook me. "Let's go to mass."

Weeping uncontrollably, I replied, "I can't go to mass like this!"

"This may be the last time we can go to mass together for a long time. We must go and offer up our sufferings to God and give glory to him," he said insistently.

"Alright, fine, I will go to mass." I rolled out of bed and made a dash for the bathroom to take a shower and get ready for church.

While Elliot took his shower, I removed the lock from my locker where I stored my money and took hundred dollar bill out of an envelope and laid it on the table. When he came out to get dressed, I picked the money up and handed it to him. "Here, this is for you. It is a gift, not a loan."

He glanced down as I slipped the money into his hand, his face softening at the realization of what I had given him.

He looked directly at me, his eyes full of gratefulness. "Thank you," he said humbly.

We finished getting ready for Sunday mass just as we had so many times in the past, only this time it would be our last. We didn't sit in our usual pew towards the front of the church, preferring instead to sit in the very back where we would be less conspicuous. As hard as I tried, I could not stop crying. As I knelt in the pew, my tears streamed down my cheeks and dripped onto the wooden pew in front of me, where luckily no one was sitting. A few times, I caught Elliot reaching up to quickly wipe a few tears away from his eyes.

We returned home to eat our breakfast.

There is silence in our room except for the clatter of dishes as I set the table. Elliot is in the kitchen preparing our breakfast of bacon and eggs. Glancing up at the closed blinds, I decide to leave them that way for the sake of privacy. I feel an overwhelming urge to talk to Elliot about our relationship. We have to work things out before he leaves, or there is a chance we may never see each other again. I will not let that happen.

Elliot returns from the kitchen carrying a frying pan and scoops out a hardy portion of bacon and eggs for each of us. Sitting down at the table across from each other, we join hands for our prayers and begin eating in silence, lost in our thoughts. After chewing my food thoughtfully for a long while, I finally break the silence.

"Hon, we have to talk about this," I say boldly. "I want to be with you. I don't want a long-distance relationship. I want someone I can cook for . . . someone I can hold in my arms each day," I declare fervently. I eagerly wait to hear Elliot's response.

"This is just a separation," he replies firmly. "We will get back together."

"I won't do this for more than six months," I warn.

"I don't like ultimatums," he retorts.

"This is not an ultimatum," I insist. "I just don't want to be apart from you for long. I will move to Lexington. We can live there together."

Elliot's eyes dart up at me in surprise. "I thought you liked it here?"

"I do for the most part. I like the warm weather, but I don't like the crime. I find it intimidating."

Buoyed by my offer to move to Lexington, Elliot finds new resolve. "We must do something about our situation. We must get married. We have to talk to a priest."

"Is this a marriage proposal?" I manage to give him a slight smile, my first in many days.

Blushing, he responds, "No, you will know when I propose."

Our breakfast finished, Elliot gets up and starts packing as I clean off the table while a new wave of fresh tears freely flows. I lean down and slide the milk into the refrigerator while trying to suppress my sobs. Elliot walks up behind me and slips his arms around me. He whispers in my ear, "I am not leaving you."

"It sure feels like you are leaving me." I say choking back tears. "I don't want you to go."

"I have to."

I turn around and embrace him. From somewhere deep inside of me a low, rumbling moan rises from the depths of my being, making its way to the surface of my parted lips, resonating in a loud wail.

Startled, Elliot asks, "What's . . . what's wrong?!"

Clinging to him, I groan, "I am so sad!"

He rocks me back and forth in his arms in a soothing manner, trying to console me.

Still sobbing, I say, "I will come up to Virginia in a couple of months."

Elliot looks at me in surprise.

"I will save my money for a few months. Hopefully, you will have a job by then, and I will have some savings to live on," I say assuredly, my tears subsiding.

I leave Elliot to finish packing and go to open the office. Patrice comes out to greet me, but her words put salt on fresh wounds.

"Lu, make sure Elliot takes everything with him. I don't want him leaving anything behind."

"He isn't," I assure her. I walk away and busy myself cleaning up the courtyard. Elliot brings his bags out of the room, and I help him load up his car. The last bag is in place and he walks off to bid goodbye to a few of the guests who are in the lounge. He shakes hands with Nathan, Stuart, and Mitch, and asks them to tell Bryan and Ramon goodbye for him. Patrice has made herself scarce. While he's saying his final goodbyes, I throw together a care package of bottled water, colas, crackers, and chocolate for the road. There is nothing left to do, except to say our final goodbye.

Before leaving our room for the final time, Elliot hands me his favorite Hawaiian bath towel.

"Here, keep my towel. You can wrap yourself in it and remember me." I clutch the towel to my heart and then set it down on the bed.

We walk to his car, wrapping our arms around each other on our way through the courtyard. A final kiss and then he climbs into his car, ready for his long journey. Everything seems so surreal, like I'm watching this happen to someone else, not me. I stand directly in front of his car as he backs out, so that I am the last person he sees. I want this last vision of me to haunt him, so that he will not forget me. I watch as his car speeds down the road, turns a corner, and is out of sight.

Walking back to my room, I can't believe he is gone, and I still have a whole day of work ahead of me. Fortunately, this is a quiet Sunday with no check-outs. Lola is coming in later to clean the rooms, so I have some free time. Nobody talks to me or looks at me. The long-term guests respectfully give me the space I need to sort out my feelings. I wonder what they must be thinking. Do they know that Elliot couldn't pay his rent? Or maybe they think Patrice asked him to leave. No one says a word to me about Elliot.

In my room, I start cleaning out the things that Elliot left behind; stacks of newspapers and magazines and some canned food. I dump the newspapers in the recycling bin and stack the cans of food in the cupboards for the other guests to use. Sadly, I momentarily look around my room and realize there is scant evidence that Elliot had ever been here. The only indication is his green towel hanging on the bathroom towel rack and a few shirts he left behind in the half empty closet. Taking the towel from the rack, I wrap my arms around it and bury my face in the green terry cloth, wiping away fresh tears. To touch something that was his helps soothe my inconsolable heart.

I knew he had to leave. The thought occurs to me that I could have just paid his rent, but that would only solve the problem temporarily. Things between him and Patrice were too far gone. He had to go . . .

Chapter 15

Purgatory

Blinking back the sun's rays peeping through the cracks in the window blinds, I rolled over on my side and slid my hand tenderly across the top of the empty pillow lying next to me. I had spent a restless night tossing and turning in bed like a vessel adrift on a stormy sea. I wasn't used to sleeping alone anymore. The scent of his body was still fresh on the sheets as if he had just slipped out of bed to go to the bathroom and would return at any moment. Cold, hard reality quickly set in as I realized I might not ever share my bed with him again. Glancing at my watch, I wondered where he was at that very moment.

The previous night after waiting for his phone call for what seemed like an interminable amount of time, I had called him shortly before ten o'clock. He had driven as far as Georgia, and in order to conserve cash, he decided to sleep in his car at a truck stop there. By now he would be on his way to Lexington to meet up with his 'friend.' He was evasive about this 'friend' who he was counting on to help him out. He had been gone from there for five years. I wondered if his friend even still lived there. It was the dead of winter, and without any savings, he was going to a small town in the mountains, during hard economic times where there was sure to be high unemployment. Where did he expect to find a job? I came from the north and knew what January was like after the holidays. There seemed a dim prospect for making a living there.

Monday morning, Patrice and I started our new schedule since Madeline had flown back to Denmark the previous night; the same day that Elliot had left. A few weeks back, we had sat in the office drawing up our new schedule. I would work mostly days from 10:00 a.m. to 4:00 p.m. and Patrice would cover nights. I would cover the office all day on Wednesdays so that Patrice could have a day off, and she would do the same for me on Sundays. Lola returned to cleaning full-time, much to my relief.

Mid-morning, while sifting through the day's reservations, Patrice made an appearance in the office. I was surprised to see her so early.

"How is your heart?" she asked sincerely.

"Sad," I replied, hoping she didn't notice my red, puffy eyes from crying myself to sleep the night before.

"You parted friends?"

"Yes, he needs to get his life in order and decide what he is going to do," I murmured without a hint of deception. I was doing it again. I was purposely misleading Patrice about my true feelings for Elliot and she was buying it wholeheartedly. I marveled at my ability to so easily deceive her.

"It is difficult to have a long-distance relationship," she remarked.

"I know. I don't know how you and Madeline do it."

"We spend a lot of time talking on the phone," Patrice admitted.

In Elliot's absence, I came to see how much our lives revolved around each other. We were all that each other had and with him gone, I felt so alone in the world. I had no social network to fall back on for emotional support. There was no one there I could even confide in.

Everywhere I went in the hostel, there were painful memories of Elliot. I expected to find him sitting in the computer room or watching TV in the lounge, as he had done so many times in the past. When someone walked in through the gate, I half-heartedly looked up expecting it to be him returning from an airport run or from the library. I would wrap myself in the shirts he left behind, so that I would feel close to him.

Laura called a few days later to see how we were doing. Embarrassed by Elliot's lack of money to pay his rent, I was hesitant to tell my family of his departure. I vowed not to say anything to her, but there was something in my voice that gave me away.

"Mom, is everything all right?" Laura queried suspiciously.

"Oh, yes, fine, just a little tired from the holidays and filling in for Patrice's vacation," I said convincingly, or so I thought.

"Are you sure? Your voice doesn't sound right," she replied, unconvinced. Laura's sixth sense had kicked in and she wasn't giving up easily.

After a few more futile attempts at covering up what happened, I finally gave in and told her. Laura, as usual, took it all in stride, and we joked about how I could listen to the book on CD that she had sent me for Christmas on my trip north to Virginia. It felt good to finally have someone to confide in. Feeling braver about discussing the situation with my family, after I hung talking to my daughter, I called my cousin, Gene, who was not quite as understanding. After filling her in on the details, she bluntly quipped, "There is no way he can love you and leave you like that!" Her mind was made up and it would be a long time before she would see things otherwise. She was one of my staunchest supporters, and in her eyes, I had been wronged. Elliot was on her blacklist.

Perhaps deep down I felt there might be some truth to what Gene had said, but I held out hope that she was wrong. I couldn't believe that our time together in the last six months was all for nothing; that it was all a lie. Regrets clouded my mind, and I began to see that we didn't really communicate. We lived in the same room and slept in the same bed, but at times we were worlds apart. He didn't confide in me about his financial problems, and he became defensive if I tried to discuss the matter with him. I was angry that he let things go until they led to his abrupt departure. Perhaps it would have been easier to just have paid his rent. At least we would still have been together. But that didn't seem right either and would only have fostered resentment. Perhaps we had both been on our own for too long and were no longer used to confiding in another person. I expected Elliot to work and pay for his share of the bills, but that wasn't what our relationship was about. More than anything, I missed our spiritual relationship: going to church together and praying the rosary, holding hands across the table when he said grace before meals and the thanksgiving prayer afterwards. Sharing simple things like eating dinner, or watching a movie together took on added significance. It was the simple, every day things in life that we shared that were important. Money didn't bring happiness; love did.

In the evenings, I took long walks along the ocean. I couldn't believe that my life, as I had known it, had come to such an abrupt end in a matter of days. I felt disconnected and disoriented. The place that had been such a source of joy and happiness had totally lost its luster and in its place was pain and anguish. I was a bitter woman, seething with the injustice of it all. I was absolutely inconsolable at having the man in my life ripped away from me after seven long and lonely years by myself. I wasn't used to being the one left behind; I was always the one who had left the men in my life.

It wasn't only the separation from Elliot that was eating away at me. I had given up everything to go back to college for my bachelor's degree: my family, my car, my life. And where had it really gotten me, except for a diploma with my name on it? I seemed to be drifting from one thing to another without any sure direction in my life, cut off from my family: A sort of self-imposed exile for my past bad behavior.

The first week, Elliot called every night. After a few nights sleeping in the Catholic Church there, he had finally hooked up with his 'friend,' who was able to provide him with a place to stay. It was only at my insistence that Elliot finally gave a name to this 'friend' who turned out to be a woman he knew from church by the name of Lenore. He was quick to point out that they were just friends and nothing more. That he even made such a statement didn't do much to curb my suspicions. She put him up in a small bedroom in the house that her parents had lived in. Both were deceased, and she was renting the house out to another couple. Elliot was allowed to live there temporarily without paying rent until he could find a job. The couple wasn't too happy about having their space invaded by an outsider, but that didn't deter Elliot from staying there. When talking to him on the phone, he seemed so far away.

The minutes on Elliot's prepaid phone were getting low, so we decided to talk once a week on Sunday evenings for fifteen minutes. He went to the library almost every day to use the computer, so we took to e-mailing each other. I wrote long, amorous love letters professing my love for him and my plans for our future together. Elliot's e-mails were short, and he often wrote that "Absence makes the heart grow fonder." He didn't seem that bothered by the distance between us.

Grudgingly, my life settled into a routine as I got used to being on my own again. Every morning before work, I went to mass and prayed with all my heart that we would be reunited. I felt sure that God had brought us together for a reason. The rest of my days were filled with work and the occasional trip to the beach. With the cooler weather, I went to the beach to sit in the sun and read, but spent most of the time looking out over the vast expanse of ocean, wondering what my future held.

January was the height of high season, and the hostel was full on a regular basis with a steady flow of guests coming and going. I picked up a few driving jobs to make some extra money, but soon dropped the idea when I found myself getting up at five o'clock in the morning to take guests to the airport. There was enough work at the hostel to keep me busy.

Ramon had disappeared again. It was now the middle of January, and no one had seen or heard from him since the holidays. The last time I saw him, he was cooking a shrimp dinner one evening for Evelyn and Maggie. When I passed through the kitchen, he had asked me if I had seen 'the girls,' vexed that they had disappeared right when he was ready to serve dinner. I laughed to myself at his apparent distress. He sounded like a mother hen.

Ramon appeared a few weeks later, as suddenly as he had disappeared. He stopped by the office to tell me that he had been in the hospital with pneumonia. Despite his darker complexion, there was a paleness and unsteadiness about him that concerned me. He confided in me that his chest x-rays had revealed a spot on his lung. His doctor had advised him to quit smoking immediately. I could tell that he was rattled by the news, and he promptly had followed his doctor's advice. Ramon's kind eyes betrayed a hint of concern that his many years of smoking had finally caught up with him. I wondered when and how he had gotten sick, but I was hesitant to ask him. I didn't want to pry into his business.

About the same time, Tim had also disappeared from the hostel unexpectedly. He stopped paying his rent, and he had left all of his belongings in his room. No one seemed to know where he was. Patrice was on a rampage to get rid of Tim's belongings. She prompted me to leave a message for him at work that he needed to pay his back rent in order to collect his belongings or she was going to call the police. I didn't like making this call, but it was my job. I was glad that Tim worked midnights, so that I didn't have to talk to him directly. He had been staying at the hostel since before I had arrived there seven months earlier. It didn't seem like Tim to up and leave without paying for his rent without a good reason.

Weeks later, I found out from Patrice that Tim had stopped by to pay his rent and pick up his belongings one day when I was off duty. She was happy to have collected her back rent, and didn't bother to say what had happened to him; and I didn't ask. I never saw him again.

I noticed that Patrice was becoming friendlier with Lola. Patrice had mentioned to me that Lola had invited her and Madeline over for dinner during the holidays. Now Patrice took to inviting Lola over for lunch after she was done cleaning the hostel. At times, Lola would sit at the outdoor picnic table waiting for Patrice to bring out lunch, slyly looking at me out of the corner of her eye, contented in her new-found favoritism. On days they didn't eat lunch together, Patrice would send Lola off toting a bag of goodies when she left for home. Sometimes after Lola finished working, they would take the bus to go shopping together. I felt like an outsider when I saw them together. I couldn't go shopping with them because I was working, but it did hurt my feelings that they never even asked me to join them for lunch. The days when Patrice had courted me by giving me fruit or buying my lunch were over. Lola had taken my place. I wondered how long it would be before I would be cut out completely. I had plans to leave, but I felt a sense of urgency in doing so.

The constant flow of guests and their attendant needs and demands helped keep my mind focused, but I no longer enjoyed the ever changing guard of guests who marched through the hostel. In my emotional state, I found myself growing ever more short-tempered with them. Late one afternoon, a group of college students from New Jersey pulled into the parking lot right when my shift was ending at four o'clock. They had called me for directions a few minutes earlier, and I had told them that I was getting ready to close the office, and they would have to wait until six o'clock to check-in. Just as I was getting ready to leave the office, they appeared at the door. A slim, boyish young man led the way with three young ladies trailing behind him. They were excited that they had made it in before I left for the day. I, on the other hand, was not pleased at all. It was a few minutes before four o'clock and now I would have to stay over to check them all in. I felt it was such an intrusion on my time. I quickly had them fill out their paper work while I grabbed their sheets and towels out of the cupboard. They had made reservations for two nights, but when they went to pay me, they said they only had enough cash for one night. I took what money they had, satisfied with their promise to stop by later to pay Patrice the balance after they went to an ATM. Glad to get rid of them, I quickly showed them to their room, and gritting my teeth, gave them an even quicker orientation. Happy to have arrived after a long drive, they ignored my obvious displeasure and threw their bags in their room so that they could head to the beach.

The next morning they appeared at the counter to check-out, asking for their key deposits.

"You made reservations for two nights," I reminded them. "If you don't pay I will have to charge your credit card," I said to the young man who seemed to be the one in charge.

"Just try to collect the balance on my credit card and see what happens!" He said with a smirk. "After all, you've been so welcoming to us," he said sarcastically. "We are college students! Look at the kind of clientele that you have here!" he spewed. "Besides that, you advertise free wi-fi, but it doesn't work!"

His uppity attitude rubbed me the wrong way. I jumped to my feet flinging my pointer finger towards the door. "Just get the hell out of here!" I screamed. "Get your stuff and get out!" My voice quivered with rage. My adrenaline was pumping blood through my body and I shook from head to toe.

His last statement was an obvious putdown of some of the long-term guests. The night before, I had seen him talking to Ramon and Mitch. He sized them up to be down on their luck transients. Despite the presence of other international students in the hostel, he seemed ill at ease with the regular long-term guests. The hostel was a cheap place to stay and the guests could be exposed to all kinds of different people. It wasn't for everyone.

He struck me as a lawyer's son who had the best of everything growing up. Staying in a $20 something a night hostel would not be his cup of tea. The hostel was not an upscale resort.

They disappeared momentarily as they went to remove their bags from their room. The young man returned, hauling his bags with his female entourage following close behind.

"Don't ever come back here!" I shouted after them.

The young man turned around and thrust his middle finger in the air. "Fuck you!"

Still shaking from the altercation, I went to calm myself in the office. I didn't even bother to try to run the balance through on their credit card. I was just glad to be rid of them. At least I thought that was the last I would see of them. They had the audacity to return later that day and ring the hostel door bell. One of the female followers thought she had left her sunglasses in the room. Since they hadn't bothered to strip their beds, I had gone in after they left to do so. I hadn't seen any sunglasses. They wanted to go to check for themselves, but I instructed them to remain at the gate while I went and looked under the beds. There were no sunglasses in sight. When I went out to tell them, I had the sneaking suspicion that they didn't really believe me. They probably thought that I kept the sunglasses to spite them.

The free wireless was a concern. It actually hadn't been working for over a week or so. When I asked Patrice about it, she would tell me she was taking care of it. I began to wonder if she hadn't paid the bill. I had no way of finding out what was really happening, so every time someone asked me about it, I told them they needed to speak with Patrice. Eventually, she switched to a different wireless carrier and the problem was solved. She didn't confide in me about such matters. Our relationship had deteriorated to the point that we only spoke about the guests on a need to know basis. She didn't confide in me about business or personal matters. I was no longer sure exactly where I stood with her and there was a growing fear that she would get rid of me as she had done to Elliot.

Hostel by the Sea

A few days later, a young couple from Key West arrived to check-in. They looked to be in their mid to late twenties. The man was clean cut with short, well-groomed hair and dressed in a natty sports shirt and khaki shorts. His girlfriend wore a blue and white striped top with white Capri pants which set off her golden tan. She sported a full head of dirty blond, shoulder length dread locks which seemed out of place with their dress. They had reserved a private room for a week's stay. I checked them in, and after issuing their sheets and towels, I escorted them to their room. Five minutes later, the young man showed up at the counter.

"Excuse me, but the lock on our door seems rather flimsy."

"Oh, is it loose?" I inquired.

"No, it's just not very sturdy and there isn't a dead bolt lock," he replied patiently.

Smiling, I said, "Well, you don't have to worry. I've never had a complaint about anyone breaking into a room here and stealing anything. Everyone enters through the front gate, and Patrice and I monitor who's on site. The only complaints we usually get here are for beer or food stolen from the community refrigerators."

"Do you have any rooms with a back entrance?" He asked as he glanced out the window scoping out the other rooms facing the courtyard.

My eyebrows shot up. I was beginning to get suspicious. "Back entrance? No, I'm sorry, we don't," I replied firmly.

My mind immediately turned to drugs. Could it be possible that he was planning to sell drugs from his room?

Noticing my uneasiness, he turned to face me and said, "It's just that we have some expensive camera equipment in our car. We were going to put it in our room, but maybe it would be better to leave it there."

"Yes, if that would make you feel more secure, perhaps it would be better. Just make sure you lock your car doors." I watched him as he walked out the door to go back to his room.

I made a mental note to discuss this with Patrice. Something didn't seem quite right with his story. I didn't have to worry for long. After alerting Patrice about my suspicions, they asked her for a refund the next day, and she obligingly gave it to them. Obviously they had found accommodations more suitable to their liking.

Wednesdays were my long day, so that Patrice could have a day off. I really didn't mind the long hours. I didn't start work until ten in the morning, and I had my two hour break from four to six to take a nap. I often spent the evening splitting the time between the office, sitting in the courtyard, and working out of my room. The time passed quickly, and before it seemed possible, it was midnight.

One Wednesday evening, a young man named Todd, from North Carolina, showed up at the gate looking for a place to stay for a few months while working construction in the area. I looked him over from head to toe, quickly sizing him up. He came across as quietly sincere, and he definitely looked like a construction worker in his white tee-shirt, jeans, and well-worn work boots. I opened the gate thinking he would be a good replacement for Tim in the long-term dorm with Stuart, Ramon, and Bryan. I took him to the office where he paid for a week's stay with the intention of paying on a weekly basis. After showing him to his room, I returned to the office to complete my paperwork when I noticed a slight odor of what I thought smelled like manure. The smell began to permeate the room and build in intensity to an overwhelming, suffocating odor. I found myself breathing through my mouth. I quickly ran to the door and opened it, swaying it back and forth in an effort to air out the room. Todd had been the only other person in the office besides me. I had noticed that he had a slight body odor, but that wouldn't be unusual after working construction all day. It didn't make sense that the odor would become so strong after he left the room.

Not long after checking Todd in, Ramon came looking for

me to complain about Todd's foul body odor. He wanted me to ask Todd to take a shower. We climbed the steps to Ramon's dorm room and stepped inside to find that Todd had decided to take a shower on his own. In an effort to get away from the manure smell that now permeated their room, Stuart and Bryan had vacated the room. Ramon pointed to Todd's boots.

"Maybe you could spray his boots with air freshener," he suggested.

"Ramon, I'm so sorry," I said in a contrite tone. "I didn't realize he had such a bad body odor or I would have never let him stay here!"

"That's okay, Lu. You didn't know."

Ramon; he was always so sweet, kind, and understanding. My heart went out to him. I ran down to the supply closet to retrieve a can of air freshener. By the time I made my way back to Ramon's room, Todd was out of the shower and stood at the foot of his bed with a blue towel wrapped around his waist.

"Todd, I need to take your boots outside and spray them down. I'm getting complaints about an odor coming from your stuff," I said unapologetically. "You also need to wash your clothes. There is a washer and dryer out back. Let me know if you need change."

Todd sheepishly nodded his head. I took his boots, and while holding my breath, I gave them a good dose of lilac air freshener and set them back inside near Todd's bed.

On my way downstairs, I looked around for Stuart and Bryan who I found watching TV in the lounge. After apologizing profusely, I went to spray the office down with air freshener. After Todd managed to clean himself and his belongings up, he lasted a few weeks in with the guys. But one day without any warning, I noticed he was no longer there. More than likely weeded out by Patrice. She was close with the guys in Todd's room, and if he didn't fit in with them, he wouldn't last long.

The long-term guys, the ones who had stayed the longest, got along well and were compatible not only with each other, but also with Patrice. They were a tight knit group who were somewhat exclusive. It was difficult to get into their group, but not impossible; with enough time and patience and the right stuff it could be done. After a brief period of time, they had incorporated Mitch as the newest member of their group. They mixed well with the other guests, but like a nuclear family, at the end of the day, it boiled down to only them.

With high season in full swing a group of long-term women guests started to form. Evelyn had been there the longest along with Maggie who came and went. Maggie cleaned yachts at the port, so her schedule varied. She would often leave for a week to drive to Jacksonville to visit her young son. Unlike Evelyn, Maggie didn't smoke or drink. She was cute and petite and I thought for sure it wouldn't be long before some nice young man would snatch her up. For the time being, though, this was her life and she made the best of it.

Nadia from Bulgaria had been staying at the hostel for about a month. She was a lively young lady with dark, wavy hair that framed her heart shaped face and her dark, brown eyes sparkled when she laughed. But I noticed she did not laugh very often, most of the time she seemed serious and reserved. She left the hostel at various times of the day and night, but no one seemed to know where she went or if she had a job. She always paid her rent on time and got along well with Evelyn and Maggie, so she became part of the long-term women's group.

Everything was going well with them until Ceyda from New Hampshire showed back up to stay for a month over high season. Patrice had put Ceyda in the large women's dorm with Evelyn, Maggie, and Nadia. Everything went well, at first, but after about a week, a rift developed between Ceyda, who was older and more set in her ways, and the younger girls. Ceyda started to pick on the girls about leaving their clothes lying about the room. She also went to bed in the wee morning hours and liked to sleep in late. She complained to the girls about the noise they made when she was trying to sleep in.

One morning, Ceyda stopped by the office to complain that Nadia was leaving her dirty dishes in the sink of the upstairs kitchen. I promised her I would speak to Nadia about it. Since she was older and more mature, Ceyda took it upon herself to act like she was the house mother to the other guests, especially the female guests. She didn't mean any harm, but some of the guests found her obnoxious.

When I saw Nadia going into her dorm room, I ran up the stairs and knocked on her door before entering. She was changing her clothes, when I stepped inside.

"Nadia, I need to talk to you for a moment."

Nadia finished pulling her shirt over her head and wiggled her arms through the sleeves. Looking over at me from behind her bed, she said, "Yes, what about?" Nadia spoke perfect English with only a hint of an accent.

"I've had a complaint that you are not doing your dishes." I said matter-of-factly.

"That's not true. I do my dishes! Who said such a thing?" she asked with her voice rising.

"Nadia, I can't tell you who said it, but they said you've done it more than once. A number of guests have complained about this to me," I lied so that she wouldn't blame just one person.

"I know who it is – it's that snoopy Ceyda! She's always putting her nose in our business and telling us that we need to clean the room and be quiet!" Nadia's face was turning red.

"Nadia, I can't say who it is, but you do have to respect the other guests here." I said firmly.

Nadia started pacing back and forth across the dorm room floor. "I've had enough!" she shrieked while holding her head in her hands. "I'm sick and tired of all of this!" And she suddenly began crying.

I was trying desperately to keep control of the situation. To me, it seemed that Nadia was overacting. I wondered if there wasn't something more going on here that I wasn't aware of.

"Nadia, if you don't want to follow the rules here, then you have the option of leaving. You don't have to stay here!" I said rather unsympathetically.

"Why should I leave? I haven't done anything wrong!" she cried. "I want to speak to Patrice about this!"

"Patrice is not on duty, I am. You need to discuss this with me, not her." I said with my voice rising.

Before I could stop her, she lunged for the door and ran down the steps to Patrice's room. I ran after her hoping to stop her before she got there.

Nadia ran up to Patrice's door and pounded loudly on the door while sobbing. I crossed my fingers and prayed that Patrice wasn't in her room.

The door slowly opened as Patrice's head emerged through the crack in the doorway, her eyes barely open. "What's going on?!" she asked blinking her eyes in the bright sunlight.

Nadia continued her rant. "Lu said I have to leave if I don't follow the rules! I didn't do anything wrong! It is all Ceyda's fault. She is always picking on me and the other girls!"

Speechless, Patrice looked over at me.

"Patrice, I had a few complaints that she wasn't doing her dishes and all I did was ask her to please do her dishes," I said apologetically. "I really don't understand what all this drama is about. I didn't say she had to leave."

"Yes, you did!" Nadia cried.

"Nadia, all I said was that if you don't follow the rules that you would have to leave!" I said in exasperation.

Patrice looked back and forth between Nadia and me. When she looked back in my direction, I whispered, "She is making a big deal out of nothing."

Patrice looked over at Nadia, "Get your things and leave if you can't follow the rules! Lu will give you a refund for the rest of your stay."

"Fine, I will leave!" Nadia shrieked as she stomped off in the direction of her room.

"Lu, give her a refund and make sure she doesn't leave

anything behind." With that said, Patrice disappeared back behind the closed door.

I went to the office to wait for Nadia. She had thrown her things together and dropped them on the ground outside the office before she came in. I handed the refund to her without saying a word. Nadia gathered up her things and set them down outside the gate. She sat there for awhile and I thought she was waiting for someone to pick her up. The next time I peeked over the top of the gate, her small stack of belongings draped under a frayed pink and white blanket were still there, but she was gone. Patrice noticed them later in the day and instructed me to make sure Nadia removed her things off our property. Thankfully, I never had the chance to. The next time I looked out, they were gone.

Bewildered by what had happened with Nadia, later that evening when I saw Patrice, I commented on how distraught Nadia had been when I tried to talk to her. Patrice shrugged her shoulders and said, "She has some problems. She was brought her to spend time with men."

Prostitution? I thought to myself. I was shocked. Patrice didn't go into details, and I really didn't want to know any. For days afterwards, I wondered what happened to Nadia and if she was alright. She was so young and all alone. I kept seeing her pink and white blanket covering her pitifully small stack of belongings. I wished I would have handled things differently. I blamed myself in part for Nadia's departure. I was convinced that in my current state of mind that I came across harsher to her than was necessary.

Igor from Russia stared at me intently from across the counter after arriving from the airport one sunny afternoon. He was tall with a friendly face and he spoke in halting English. He had made his reservation through Hostel.com for a few nights stay.

"Are your rooms okay?" he asked.

"Well, yes, they are," I answered assuredly while pulling his reservation out of the file folder.

Leaning over the counter looking right at me, he said, "Look me in the eye and tell me they are good."

What an odd request I thought to myself. I stopped shuffling through my reservations and made myself look over at him, straight in the eye. "Yes, we clean our rooms every day and we have them sprayed for bugs," I said while thoughts of rampageous bed bugs flooded my mind. But there was some truth to what I had said: There weren't any bed bugs in the dorm room he was assigned to, at least not to my knowledge. My response satisfied him and he opened his wallet to pull out some crisp dollar bills to pay for his room.

Bed bugs were an ongoing problem. Even after Elliot left, I still had to tear down the room every other week to spray for bed bugs and wash all the sheets and covers. I had bite marks on my neck, lower legs, and finger. I couldn't figure out if I was getting the bites from doing the laundry or at night while sleeping. Except for the one time on election day, I never saw any bed bugs in my room, but my overactive imagination conjured them up while I was trying to drift off to sleep. I was sure they were somewhere peering through the cracks at me, or under the sheets just waiting for their chance to pounce on their dinner. The idea of becoming a potential entrée was not a welcoming thought while drifting off to sleep. I finally had to resolve myself to the fact that if there were bed bugs in my bed, then so be it. I had to get a good night's sleep. I did my best to put the thoughts of them out of my mind. But to this day, I have bad dreams about bed bugs.

A frigid cold front out of Canada plunged south pushing cold air all the way to southern Florida sending everyone scurrying for blankets. Like many places in southern Florida, our rooms had no heat. Cold spells were far and few between and usually only lasted a few days. Most residents had electric heaters to use during cold spells, but we didn't have such a luxury for our guests. A steady stream of guests turned up at the office asking for a blanket. After handing out the last of the blankets from a large storage container, I frantically called Patrice to find out if we had any more. She sent me to look for some in the laundry room. I rummaged through the laundry room storage closet and found a few very worn but salvageable blankets that needed washed. I threw the few, pitiful blankets that I scrounged up in the washer and went back to the office where I found our two young guests from Norway, Margaret and Elsa, waiting for me outside the office door dressed in layers of clothing. Most guests didn't come prepared for cold weather. Warm and sunny weather were expected as the norm. Caught unprepared, guests would wrap themselves in multiple layers of clothing or run off to buy a jacket at the store.

I pulled my jacket tighter around me and quickened my step, eager to get back to the small electric heater tucked under my desk.

"Good morning, ladies! Are you keeping warm enough? You probably feel like you are back in Norway," I quipped. With their shoulder length blonde hair, blue eyes, and light skin they looked more like sisters than best friends. The only difference between them was Margaret's few more inches in height.

"Oh, it's much colder there now," replied Elsa with a slight laugh. "But we do need some blankets. Last night we had to keep warm by piling extra clothes on top of us to keep warm while we were sleeping."

"Oh, I'm so sorry. I don't have any blankets right now, but I do have some in the washer," I offered.

"Well, we are leaving now. Can we pick them up later?" asked Elsa.

"How about I put them on your bed for you when they are done?" I offered.

"That would be great, Lu, thanks so much!" They both smiled back at me.

"Which beds are yours?" I inquired.

Margaret finally spoke up and said, "We have the bunk beds along the wall on the right side."

"Okay, they will be waiting for you on your beds when you get back." I smiled at them as they turned to leave. "Have a good time today!"

I finished the wash after lunch, and as promised, took Margaret and Elsa's blankets up to their room. They were in the large women's dorm with eight beds. I walked over and placed them lovingly on their beds just like I would do for my own daughters. In a way, the students that came and went were like my own children. I often did for them what I would do for my own family and it gave me a warm feeling to do so. It was the first warm feeling I had in many weeks.

Later the girls returned and stopped by the office on their way in.

"Hello, again! Your blankets are on your beds!" I said with a smile.

"Thank you so much, Lu," replied Elsa in a subdued tone. "We need to talk to you about something that happened to us today."

Slightly alarmed, I looked from one to the other. "What happened?"

"We were at the library using their computers. I set my wallet down beside my computer while I was checking my e-mail. When we went to leave, it wasn't there."

"Oh, I'm so sorry to hear that," I interjected empathically.

"There was a black girl sitting beside me. She must have taken it while we were looking at the computer," said Elsa.

"You have to be very careful here," I warned them. "Never leave your purse or wallet out in the open. She probably reached over and slid it off the table when you weren't looking."

Both girls looked glum.

"Did you have much money in your wallet?" I asked. "And what about credit cards?"

"Yes, both," replied Elsa. "But just mine. Margaret still has hers."

"You can file a police report, but I doubt that will do much good," I said. "You can also try reporting it to the library, but whoever took it probably took out the money and credit cards and threw the wallet away somewhere outside the building."

"Thanks, Lu," replied a somber Elsa. "I will call my parents and ask them what I should do."

I watched as the girls dejectedly walked off in the direction of their room. The innocent bliss they possessed earlier had suddenly been marred by misfortune. Like me, they probably came from small towns with low crime rates. In big cities, vigilance was a must. I never left anything visible on my car seats. I put everything in the trunk. Thieves thought nothing of smashing your side window to whisk a purse or package out of your car. Car jackings were also a source of worry, prompting me to always drive with my car doors locked and the windows up. The local newspaper recently carried an article about thieves who were riding motorcycles through grocery store parking lots, snatching women's purses off their arms as they walked to their cars. The crime in Fort Lauderdale was masked by the lure of the sun, sea, and sand; but it was there, lurking just beneath the surface. You had to act accordingly.

That afternoon, Carlos stopped by the office and helped himself to a bottle of water from the refrigerator. "How are things going?" he asked nonchalantly. "Have you been busy?"

"Yes, things are going great." I replied. "We have been sold out almost every night for the last week."

I didn't think much about filling Carlos in on how business was going. He often stopped by to check on us when he was working in his office. I liked Carlos. He was down to earth and easy to talk to. But I would find out shortly that Carlos's inquiries weren't as innocent and friendly as they seemed.

"Good, I'm glad to hear that," he said with a smile. "Is Patrice in her room?"

"I'm not sure. I haven't seen her yet today. Try knocking on her door."

On my way to heat up my lunch, I stopped by the laundry

room to start another load. Lifting the lid of the washer, I was surprised to find the washer full of clothing. Irritated, I reached down and grabbed a handful of what turned out to be men's short, tops, and underwear. The clothing was dry to the touch and covered with powdered laundry detergent. The washer dial had mistakenly been set on spin. I pulled the clothes out of the washer and set them on top of the dryer. Someone would come along eventually to claim them. I was just stuffing the last of my load of sheets into the washer when Shaun, a timid, young British chap with curly, red hair, freckles, and a wiry frame appeared in the doorway.

"Hi, Shaun, what can I help you with?"

Shyly, Shaun inquired, "Are my clothes done?"

"These are your clothes?" I asked in an accusatory tone.

"Well, yes, I need them for tonight," he explained.

"You are suppose to ask for permission to use the washer and, besides that, it is not available for guests' use until after six o'clock," I said in a brusque manner.

"Oh, I'm sorry I didn't know," he said as he shrugged his shoulders.

"Well, there is a sign on the laundry room door. And you didn't set the dial right on the washer. These clothes are dry and have detergent on them because you set it on the spin cycle," I said while pointing to his heap of clothes on the dryer.

"Well, I'm going to the beach this afternoon and I wanted to have clean clothes to go out in tonight. This is my last night here."

"Just let them stay here and you can wash them later when you get back from the beach," I huffed unsympathetically.

Shaun turned and walked out the door. I emptied the dryer and took an armful of towels to the office to fold all the while grumbling to myself about ungrateful guests who did as they pleased. I smartly snapped the towels as I folded them to vent my frustration.

Breaking for lunch, I was relieved that it was Saturday

afternoon and my work week was almost over. I was emotionally exhausted from dealing with guests and personal issues. Alone in my room while eating my lunch my mind kept drifting back to the bewildered look on Shaun's boyish face. A tinge of guilt from my harsh words prodded at me. I walked to the kitchen and scraped off my dish and quickly washed it in the sink. Walking back to the laundry room, I emptied the sheets from the washer and then scooped up Shaun's clothes and dropped them in the washer. Later I returned to dry them, and then after neatly folding them, I placed them in a laundry basket and took them to his dorm room. No one was in sight when I carefully placed the stacks of freshly washed clothing on his bed and smiled to myself as I closed the dorm room door behind me.

Saturday night I was ready to let loose. After a short nap, I got up and went to the grocery store for groceries and picked up a bottle of wine and a six-pack of beer. I was in the mood for a party. After all my emotional turmoil I wanted to have some fun. I sipped a glass of wine as I grilled some chicken and talked to Nathan and some of the other guests in the courtyard. After dinner, I started in on the beer. I sat outside drinking for awhile and then had an urge to listen to music. I was a happy drunk; after a few beers, I liked to sing and dance, something that I rarely did when sober. I ended up in my car again with the volume turned full blast. I wasn't used to drinking and, once I started, I never wanted to stop until I had my fill which usually wasn't until the early morning hours. Climbing into bed a bit tipsy, but happy to have been released from my troubles at least for a little while, I drifted off into a peaceful slumber. I didn't make it to church the next day.

I spent the day at the beach napping and recovering from the previous night. I was looking forward to my Sunday evening call from Elliot. That night at the appointed time, I heard the upstairs phone ringing at nine o'clock. I bounded up the stairs to answer the house phone.

Breathless, I stammered into the receiver, "Hello!"

"Hi, baby."

"It's so nice to hear your voice. I miss you," I said wistfully.

"I miss you, too, baby. How are you doing?" Elliot asked.

"Somewhat better. At least I'm not crying every day. Now I just cry every other day," I said jokingly.

"Remember that absence makes the heart grow fonder," he reminded me.

"Yes, I know, but it's not an easy way to have a relationship. How are you?" I inquired in a worried tone. "Did you get settled in your room yet?"

"Yes, Lenore took the boxes out of my bedroom and painted it. I'm glad I don't have to sleep on the couch anymore."

"How are things going with your roommates?" I inquired.

A moment of silence was punctuated with a sigh, "Well, I don't see much of them now. I try to stay in my room as much as I can, so I don't disturb them. I'm only going to be staying here for a short time until I can get on my feet again and get my own place."

"Well, they're probably not used to having other people around them like we are from living in a hostel. Most people would probably be uncomfortable sharing their home with someone they didn't know. I'm sure they'll be alright once they get to know you," I said encouragingly.

We kept our call to the promised fifteen minutes and Elliot signed off by giving me a kiss through the phone. I chuckled at his attempt to show his affection in such a manner. Feeling better after hearing his voice, I went to bed happy with thoughts of soon joining him in Virginia.

Monday morning I was back at work in the office when Patrice stopped by in the late morning. I started in on my usual spiel about the day's business while she listed intently standing next to me at the front desk. My litany completed, I looked up at her waiting for her response.

Squinting her eyes slightly, she asked, "Did Carlos stop in her recently?"

"Well, yes, on Saturday morning, he stopped by with his grandson," I replied.

"Did he ask you about how business is going?"

Thinking back to our conversation, I replied, "Well, yes, he wanted to know how full we were for the weekend, so I told him we were sold out on Saturday night."

"When Carlos stops in here from now on, don't tell him anything about our business. It's not your place to tell him. He should be asking me," she informed me.

"Oh, I'm sorry. I didn't think anything of it."

Patrice started around the counter, and then stopping, she turned to face me. "Also, I don't want someone working in the office who drinks! When someone drinks alcohol, you can smell it on them, and I don't want the guests smelling alcohol on my staff!" After having her say, she promptly went out the door, leaving me behind a bit dumbfounded about both her comments.

Although she hadn't outright accused me, she had insinuated that I had been drinking, which I had done on Saturday evening, mostly in the privacy of my room. This was Monday morning, and I had taken two showers since then. Surely she couldn't smell alcohol on me two days later. I knew Patrice was sensitive about alcohol, but I chaffed at what I considered an intrusion on my privacy. What I did on my time off should not be any of her concern, as long as it didn't cause any problems within the hostel or with the guests.

I wasn't the only one on Patrice's bad side for drinking. A few days later, Patrice approached me about Evelyn. Lola had broken her foot, and Patrice had enlisted Evelyn to fill in for her. Evelyn was notorious for her large consumption of alcohol, but she managed to get up every morning to perform her housekeeping duties, while apparently reeking of alcohol. I was surprised when Patrice confided in me about Evelyn's offensive alcohol odor. Despite smoking, Patrice had a sensitive nose and Evelyn's late night binging didn't escape Patrice's early morning detection.

"Lu, Evelyn smells like alcohol every morning. I'm thinking

about finding someone else to do the cleaning," Patrice stated matter-of-factly.

"Oh, maybe she doesn't take a shower before coming to work," I offered in her defense. "Perhaps you should talk to her first, to give her a chance to clean herself up before coming to work. She might not realize that she smells like alcohol."

Patrice thought for a moment and then nodded her head in agreement. "Okay, I will say something to her."

I couldn't help but notice Evelyn a few days later jauntily sweeping the sidewalk in the courtyard, freshly showered and dressed in crisp, clean clothing. Patrice told me later that Evelyn was aghast when she approached her about her indiscretion, and after profusely apologizing, promised to clean up her act, as she obviously did. I liked Evelyn. She was friendly and easy to get along with and tried really hard to please. She had a penchant for the bottle, but that didn't make her a bad person. She did on occasion get out of hand and one night Patrice even made her go to bed and tucked her in. Patrice outwardly took a hard stance against drinking, but at times, she betrayed a glint of compassion for those who did.

Later that week, I noticed there seemed to be something wrong with our trash pickup service. Every week as always, I put the trash out on Sunday and Wednesday evenings for collection the following morning. Because of the large amount of trash generated at the hostel, we had six large-sized trash receptacles usually filled to capacity by trash pickup days. Thursday morning when I went to bring in the trash bins, I noticed the trash had not yet been collected. I checked on the trash throughout the day, but the bins sat in place just as I had left them. For the next few days, I found an extra trash bin to use, and after filling it up, I started to add more to the bins I had rolled out to the curb earlier in the week. Our trash pile was growing by leaps and bounds, and eventually, all the bins were overflowing with trash. I started to pile bags of trash against the wall in the back of the hostel where the empty trash bins were usually kept.

I mentioned this in passing to Patrice, and she waved me off with a shrug attributing it to the trash collectors not doing their duty. By the following week, I had had enough and decided to call the city myself. The woman's voice on the other end of the line informed me that our bill hadn't been paid for some time, and they had discontinued our service. After hanging up, I had a sinking feeling in the pit of my stomach. In the past few months, our services for pest control had been interrupted for nonpayment and now this. I began to wonder if that was why the wireless service had been out for a few weeks. Patrice had recently switched wireless providers, claiming the new service was a better deal, but now I wasn't so sure now.

A few days later, Patrice announced that we were going to reduce the number of trash bins to two, to reduce the cost of trash pickup. I just nodded in agreement. What could I say? I knew there was no way we could ever fit all of the trash into two bins, but this was something out of my control. I just shook my head and went about my business, wondering what was going to happen next.

On Saturday morning, Patrice stopped by the office to let me know that Nathan's mother and sister were arriving on Sunday for a week's stay in one of our private rooms. To my surprise, she then instructed me to move Nathan's roommates to another room so that Nathan and his girlfriend could have the room to themselves for the week. I didn't even know that Nathan had a girlfriend. Although I saw him on different occasions conversing with female guests, he generally hung out with his male drinking buddies.

José, Lola's husband, appeared that afternoon to help switch Patrice's futon which folded down into a full-sized bed with Nathan's single bed, so that he and his girlfriend would have a bed to share. I was touched by Patrice's thoughtfulness. Patrice had a kind heart that was especially apparent to those she was fond of.

Nathan's dorm room was on the second floor, so I pitched

in to help Patrice and José carry her futon up the steps to his room. Patrice sent me off to rummage through the laundry room cabinet in search of a set of queen-sized sheets to make up the futon. I retrieved a set of slightly musty smelling sheets from the cupboard and took them up to Nathan's room. I made a comment to Patrice about their slight odor, but she dismissed my concern and we made up his bed.

Sunday evening, I returned from my walk along the ocean to find Nathan and his family sitting around the table in the courtyard. I went over to introduce myself and welcome them to the hostel. Nathan introduced me to his mother and sister, and then to a petite young woman sitting next to him who he introduced as his girlfriend, Jenna. With a great deal of curiosity, I studied Jenna's face closely. A pair of warm, brown eyes set in a smooth, bronze complexion stared back at me. Her shiny, dark shoulder length hair was parted to one side and when she looked back down at the table, her hair slid forward like a veil, partially covering her face and hindering any further attempt at conversation. She had an elusive air about her that was in direct contrast to Nathan's friendly, outgoing manner. I had heard through the hostel grapevine that Nathan had met Jenna when she stayed briefly at the hostel a few months earlier. She was from Brazil and worked as a nurse somewhere in Las Vegas. Never one to remember names, I did have a penchant for remembering faces. As hard as I tried, I could not place her from her previous stay. I was usually aware of all the guests who passed through the hostel, even if they were there for just a night or two. I wondered how it could be that we never crossed each other's paths.

The following morning, Nathan showed up in the office with an armful of sheets. His girlfriend had complained about the smell, and he asked if I could wash them. Emitting a deep sigh, I took the sheets from Nathan. I knew I should have just washed them the day before. After Nathan left, I washed and dried his sheets and went to put them in his room. I knocked gingerly at the door, half expecting Jenna to answer. After a few minutes, there still was no answer. I stood uncertainly outside the door, clutching the freshly washed sheets in my arms afraid to use my key to open their door. Maybe Nathan and Jenna were taking a nap on the bed without sheets. But my mind didn't stop there. My vivid imagination conjured up images of Nathan and Jenna deeply caught up in the throes of passion, making mad love on their bed without sheets. I listened intently outside their door. All was quiet except for the hum of the air conditioning unit. I glanced over at the large, picture window to their room which was completely covered by a drape, concealing any hint of illicit activity on the other side of the curtain. I gently slipped the key into the lock and turned it, cracking the door open slightly. I positioned my lips near the crack in the door and with a loud burst of bravado, I shouted, "Housekeeping!" All my efforts produced no response, so with the stealth of a prowling thief, I quickly put one eye to the crack in the door and scanned what I could see of the room. A solitary lamp next to their bed illuminated a bare mattress with two pillows strewn about the bed. There was no one in sight. Relieved, I quickly walked in and laid the sheets on the bed, and just as quickly, backed out of the room and closed the door behind me.

I was happy for Nathan that he had found a girlfriend and looked forward to seeing the two of them around the hostel. But as the week wore on, the only guests I ever saw with Nathan were his mother and sister. He had taken the week off from work to show them around Fort Lauderdale and I was under the impression that Jenna was to have joined them to get to know his family better. Jenna seemed to have disappeared into thin air. It was like she never existed: a phantom guest who made a brief appearance and retreated back into obscurity. Her name was never mentioned by any of the other guests. I felt so bad for Nathan, but I never had the nerve to ask him about what happened to her. He had paid for her entire stay, and now, he was sleeping alone on his clean, queen-sized sheets.

I no longer looked forward to my evening walks along the ocean. Like a programmed machine, every evening at six o'clock, I took a stroll down the sidewalk along the ocean as I had done so many times in the past; my once lively gait reduced to a mechanical shuffle. I looked indifferently out to sea at the lights on the ships in the harbor. The steady procession of slow, rolling waves lapping the shore no longer had any appeal to me; I walked only for exercise. I no longer derived any pleasure from my surroundings; instead, I felt mocked by it; alone in a paradise without someone to share it with. A cruel turn in fate had left me with a clear ultimatum: remain in my paradise alone or move north to be with Elliot and closer to my family; a pivot point in my life; a path with a 'Y' in the road. Perhaps this was a lesson in life and love.

Back in my room after my evening walk, there was a slight tap at the door as I slipped off my walking shoes to change into my flip-flops. I hopped to the door on one foot and was greeted by an unusually smiling Patrice outside my door.

"Lu, I have proposition for you," she said exclaimed brightly.

"Oh?" I couldn't imagine what she was talking about.

"How would you like to move into Carlos's office? He is moving out soon. If you move in there, you can have a separate bedroom and living area, and I can start renting out your room again to guests as a private room."

I was completely caught off guard. From the look on her face, I knew she expected me to jump at her offer, but something held me back. Thinking quickly, I stammered, "Let me think about that and I will get back to you."

"Okay, but let me know in a few days."

I closed the door behind me and leaned up against it. Patrice had no idea that I planned to follow Elliot north as soon as I could. I was just biding my time there, while saving some money. It wouldn't be worth it to move into the other room for only a few weeks or possibly a few months. I was truly touched by Patrice's offer. She was offering me a larger living quarters when she could just as easily have claimed it for herself. Not only that, earlier in the week she had asked me to pick up a 'No Parking' sign to post in the parking lot so that I would have my own private place to park.

I was in a quandary. I didn't like be being deceptive to Patrice, but I didn't dare tell her of my plans for fear that she would boot me out of the hostel. It was essential that I waited until I had enough money saved to move to Virginia. I had no idea how long it would take to get a job there, and I would have to have money to live on to see us through until Elliot and I both could get work. It would be best to stay where I was for the time being.

The next afternoon, I checked into one of the private rooms a very pleasant middle-aged woman named, Louise, from Colorado. She was meeting up with a girlfriend who was flying in later that day from California to spend a week together. Louise wanted to check into her room early, so that she could go to the beach for awhile. I helped her with her sheets and towels, and led her to her room. When I opened the door, I noticed that the two twin beds had been pushed together by the couple who had rented the room the previous night. I motioned to the beds and offered to move them apart. Without looking at me, Louise stated matter-of-factly, "We'll have to see what Shirley thinks about that."

Slightly embarrassed, I replied, "Oh," and left her to make up her room. As I walked away, the realization settled in on me that they were lesbians. I would never have guessed it by Louise's demeanor. She looked like somebody's grandmother. I shook my head amazement, "You just never know," I mumbled to myself as I made my way back to the office.

Louise's 'friend,' Shirley, checked in later in the day, a nicely tanned middle-aged woman with short blonde hair. Although friendly, she came across as assertive. Louise was still at the beach, so I showed her to her room. They were well traveled and had stayed in hostels before. They mixed well with the other guests and were especially good with the younger guests. Shirley took a personal interest in any of us who smoked and gently pleaded with us to consider quitting. She had been a smoker at one time and was the first to expound the health benefits of not smoking. After listening to her well-intentioned lecture, I squished out a cigarette in my ashtray and told her that someday I would quit for good, which I have held true to.

The week was winding to an end and, although we e-mailed each other daily, I eagerly looked forward to Elliot's usual Sunday night call. With the passing days, I found myself more and more regretful that I didn't just pay his rent until he could find a job. Perhaps it wouldn't be too late to do so. I began to think it would be better for Elliot to just move back to Fort Lauderdale until we could save enough money to move to Virginia. He had his heart set on living in Lexington because it was in the 'safe area.' When his Sunday evening call rolled around, I decided to try to talk him into coming back.

As soon as I heard his voice that night, I was deeply concerned. He didn't sound like his usual self. His voice was flat and expressionless. He sounded depressed.

"Hon, are you okay? You don't sound very good," I asked.

His tone lifted slightly, as if trying to disguise his true feelings, "Oh, I have lots on my mind; just trying to hang in there until things turn around for me."

"Hon, I've been thinking. Why don't you just come back here and live with me until we can save some money to move to Lexington? Patrice has offered me Carlos's office to live in which would give us a lot more room. What do you think?"

He must have been feeling really down, for to my surprise, he agreed. "Do you think Patrice will let me come back?" he asked dubiously.

"You let me handle her," I replied confidently. I jumped up from my chair with excitement. "I will go down to the office and talk to Patrice and then I will call you right back."

I slammed the phone receiver back in place and ran down the steps to the office where Patrice sat working on the computer.

Breathless, I ran through the office door and up to the counter. "Patrice, I need to talk to you!"

Looking up at me, she replied, "Oh, did your check bounce?"

"Wha….what?!" I stammered. She had given me my two-week paycheck on Thursday which I had deposited in my bank the same day.

"No, not that I know off." Although caught off guard by her comment, I was determined not to let it distract me from my most pressing concern. I continued, "Anyways, I came here to talk to you about Elliot. Things are not working out well for him, and I want to know if he can come back here. You offered me Carlos's office and I thought . . ."

"That is off the table!" she snapped.

"Oh?" I stumbled to get my bearings, "Well . . . okay, but he still could come back to live in my room. I'll even pay his rent until he finds a job . . ."

She dashed my hopes quickly and decisively. "No, I don't want him back here, *ever*! I have been getting complaints about him looking at porn on the computer late at night and trying to push his religious views on others during the day."

My mouth dropped open in response to her accusations against Elliot. I couldn't believe what she was saying about him.

"Anyways," she continued. "Everyone here thinks you look much happier since he left."

"Happier?!" I felt my voice rising. "I have been miserable!"

With a hint of disgust, she continued, "Also, you both went behind my back when he moved into your room, and you were living together without my knowing it."

"We didn't go behind your back! I told you right after he started staying with me; before that, we were just being discreet."

I could see she wasn't budging on this.

As a last ditch effort, I continued, "You know, I have done a lot of work around here." For added emphasis, I said firmly, "I have done a lot for this place." I couldn't believe after everything I had done; she would turn me down on this.

Looking straight at me, she continued, "I want someone who is single to live and work here, who will devote themselves completely to this job."

"Patrice, I don't think that is right that you want me to give up my personal life! There is more to life than just working. I don't want to be by myself!"

My voice wasn't loud, but it was a few pitches higher than my normal tone. I was trying my best not to lose my cool. Finally, I was at the end of my rope, and I made an impulsive decision. I made a conscious effort to collect myself then, calmly and quietly, I said, "Patrice, I respect your wishes, but I can't stay here like this. Elliot and I want to be together. I'm giving you a one month's notice. I'll have my resignation on your desk in the morning."

"That's not necessary. You've already told me," she replied flatly.

"Okay. Have a good evening."

I walked out the office door, crushed by her refusal to let Elliot return. I slowly walked up the steps and dialed Elliot's number on the house phone. "Well, hon, things didn't go as well as I thought they would with Patrice. She doesn't want you to come back here. I gave her a one month's notice." I didn't say a word about her accusations of him watching porn and evangelizing. Elliot had always gotten along well with the other guests, and they seemed to have genuinely liked him. I couldn't imagine that anyone would say such things. I decided that some things are better left unsaid.

I now knew what I had to do, and I had a month in which to do it. Although still sorely disappointed by Patrice's refusal to let Elliot return to the hostel, I felt a burden suddenly lifted from my shoulders. My future no longer was overshadowed by the dark clouds of uncertainty. I was at my best when I had to take action.

Deep in thought on my way back to my room, out of the corner of my eye, I noticed Nathan looking tan and relaxed drinking a beer in the courtyard. Again, through the grapevine, I had heard that Nathan had been to Key West with his phantom girlfriend for the weekend. Curious to find out how his weekend went, I walked over to him. He was dressed in shorts and a bright blue, floral Hawaiian shirt. There was something different looking about him. He had a glow about him.

"Nathan, you are looking good. I hear that you and your girlfriend went to Key West for the weekend."

Nathan's face lit up with a smile, "Yeah, Lu, we spent the weekend together there before she flew back to Las Vegas. I dropped her off at the airport on my way back here."

Still looking at him somewhat perplexed, I exclaimed, "Well, I'm glad you had a good time. She must be good for you 'cause you sure do look good!"

That night, even though Patrice said it wasn't necessary, I sat in my room and typed up my resignation. I felt a certain satisfaction by doing so, as if by putting it down on paper it gave credence to a plan that had been too long in the making. Sleep came easy that night with dreams of things to come.

I didn't want any of the long-term guests to know I was leaving. I decided I wouldn't say anything until I absolutely had to. I didn't like the things that Patrice had said about Elliot and found myself looking suspiciously at them wondering which of them would say such things or, who knows, maybe Patrice had made it all up.

Patrice and I treated each other cordially afterwards. So much so that, to an outsider's view, no one would even know that we had had a disagreement, leading to my resignation. Our relationship remained as it had been. We talked of business only, being polite and courteous to each other, but going no further. Like Elliot and I when we shared our room, we were two separate people functioning in the same space, but each caught up in our own little worlds, caring little to share one with the other. The only reminder of our disagreement was the letter of resignation which I had laid on Patrice's desk, but was now stuffed in the bottom of a desk drawer.

I went about my duties while planning for my escape north. I started making lists of what I needed to pack and things I needed to do, just as I had done before arriving at the hostel so many months earlier. The endless stream of guests coming and going was my only distraction.

Wednesday evening while filling in for Patrice on her day off, a short man with a slight build who appeared to be in his sixties came into the office. Standing across the counter from him, I couldn't believe what I was seeing. He was dressed in a black, handmade suit and shirt with a matching black hat on his head. Having been raised in rural Ohio, I recognized him immediately as Amish. I couldn't imagine what he was doing here.

"Good evening, sir, can I help you?"

He took off his hat and I noticed there were beads of sweat spread across the top of his bald head. "Yes, ma'am," he said with the typical German accent of the Amish. "I just got here from Indiana and I would like to rent a room for a week."

"Alright, I have a room for you, but it is a dorm room. Have you ever stayed at a hostel before?" I asked with one eyebrow slightly raised.

"Well, no ma'am, but I hear this is a cheap place to stay."

"The weekly rate is $150 and I can put you in a room with three other men."

His movements were slow and deliberate. He set an old fashioned suitcase on the floor, and retrieved his wallet from his pocket. He took out the cash and paid in full. I grabbed his sheets and towel and took him to his room. After showing him the sparsely furnished room, he asked if there was a place to lock up his suitcase. I pointed to the small lockers where I told him he could lock up his money and credit cards provided he had his own lock. He mumbled something about keeping his suitcase in his bed with him. I left him to get acclimated to his room and went back to the office. A few hours later, I found him strolling through the courtyard carrying his suitcase.

Walking over to him, I said, "Good evening, Mr. Yoder, how are you doing? Is everything okay with your room?"

Mr. Yoder stood facing me hesitantly, his suitcase still in hand. "Well, I'm a little concerned about my room arrangements," he admitted frankly. "I'm afraid if I leave my suitcase in my room, someone may steal my clothes. My wife died a few years ago and I don't have anyone to make my clothes or cook for me anymore."

He looked so sad and all alone.

"Oh, I'm so sorry to hear about your wife," I exclaimed. "Really, Mr. Yoder, I think your clothes will be fine in your room. I've been here for awhile, and I've never had anyone complain to me that their clothes were stolen."

"Well, that may be young lady, but I'd feel better if I just hung onto them."

"Okay, well have a good evening."

At eleven o'clock on my way back from setting out the trash bins, I again ran into Mr. Yoder in the courtyard. He motioned me over to him where he stood still holding tightly onto his suitcase.

"Yes, Mr. Yoder, what can I help you with?" I asked curiously.

He leaned towards me slightly. "Do you know if there is a restaurant nearby here?"

I thought his request rather odd at such a late hour. At this time of night, most people were out partying. "There isn't much near here." I replied. "There is a restaurant over on the intercoastal waterway about eight blocks from here where you could probably get a sandwich," I suggested.

"No, I was looking for a restaurant nearby where I could meet a woman," he said confided hopefully.

Trying my best to remain as nonchalant as if he had just asked where he could get a cheeseburger, I replied, "Sir, I'm sorry, but there really isn't any place like that nearby here." Oh dear God, I thought to myself, what is this guy doing here?

He turned and walked in the direction of his room, and I went back to the office to read the news on the internet. A short while later he reappeared in the office still clinging to his suitcase. He decided that he didn't want to stay with us after all and requested a refund. Normally, we didn't give refunds easily, but it was quite apparent that this was not the right place for him. I pulled the cash out of the drawer and handed it over to him. It was a quarter to midnight. I wondered where on earth he was going at such a late hour.

A few days later while driving down Ocean Boulevard, I saw Mr. Yoder sitting in a chair in front of a hotel a short distance from the hostel. He obviously had secured a room at a hotel where he didn't have to share his room or worry about someone stealing his clothes. He idly sat in the shade of a tree, watching the traffic pass back and forth on the busy road, probably hoping that a suitable wife would somehow magically appear. I silently wished him the best.

Despite Eddie's constant maneuvering to get out of paying his rent, he was still at the hostel. Anyone else would have been booted out by Patrice long ago. I couldn't figure out what hold he had over her that she kept giving him a pass on this. He called the office one afternoon while at work to find out if I had a bed available in the women's dorm for a friend that he worked with named, Pamela. I told him that I did, and he said she would be over later that day to pay for a week's stay.

Pamela stopped by the office later that afternoon, and we talked amicably as I checked her in. She was working on yachts at the port and was happy to find a cheap place to stay. She was a nice looking woman about my age who seemed to be down on her luck. She inferred that Eddie was just a good friend, who was trying to help her out. Later that night, I saw them sitting in the courtyard drinking and holding hands. They obviously were more than just friends.

A few days later as she had done with Nathan, Patrice instructed me to move the guys in Eddie's room into a nearby dorm. Eddie and Pamela had decided that they wanted to rent his room for a week by themselves. This time we just pushed two twin beds together for them to sleep on. I was beginning to feel like we were running a bordello. Pamela went shopping and stocked up on food and booze for the two of them, and then stopped by the office to tell me that she had put all of their groceries in the upstairs refrigerator. I told her to make sure that she clearly marked the bags with her name so that no one else would take them, but I warned her that that may not deter them.

Pamela and Eddie lasted all of two days in their newly found love nest. The next thing I knew, Pamela appeared one morning in the office asking to be moved back to her old dorm room.

"I'm so embarrassed," she said hanging her head. "I really had the wool pulled over my eyes with Eddie."

"What happened?!" I exclaimed. This all seemed to be coming out of nowhere, and I was totally bowled over by it.

"Well, for one thing he stole eighty dollars out of my wallet. He said he didn't take it, but it was in my wallet last night, and it is gone this morning," she lamented. "I have just lost out about three hundred and fifty dollars on that guy. I spent money on groceries for the both of us and paid for half our room for the week."

"Don't worry, Pam, we will credit your half of the room rent to your dorm room. I'm sorry things didn't work out between the two of you." I truly felt sorry for her. She had genuinely liked Eddie and wanted a relationship with him, but he proved himself to be nothing but a scoundrel.

"Oh, by the way," she said. "I think there might be bed bugs in Eddie's room. I have these red, itchy bites all over my arms and back." She held up her arms for me to see.

I looked at her arms with dismay. "I will let Patrice know. Here is your key to the women's dorm room."

This was all getting to be too much: the constant battle with bed bugs, Patrice's struggle to pay for basic utility services, and now worrying about whether my payroll check might bounce. I felt like I was dangling from a precipice by a tenuous thread that could snap at any moment, leaving me to plummet into the depths of oblivion.

Later that day after telling Patrice about what happened between Pamela and Eddie, we went to their room to check for bed bugs and moved the beds back into their former position. Patrice's apprehension was palpable as she quickly checked the mattresses for bed begs. I know all this had to be so hard on her. She couldn't afford to hire an exterminator to fully treat the property for bed bugs, but her inability to do so was causing her to have to discard bedding and bed frames, little by little, as time went on. At the current rate, she wouldn't have any furniture in a year or so. She had already decided to gradually get rid of all the wooden bed frames thinking the bed bugs favored them instead of the metal bed frames. I wasn't so sure about that. From my research, I knew that bed bugs could hide in picture frames or even in cracks of peeled paint on the walls. I feared for what she was getting herself into with this. This made my getting out of there all the more urgent.

After the episode with Pamela, Patrice had finally had enough of Eddie. The next time he was late on his rent, she told him he had to move out. He was completely taken aback and couldn't believe that Patrice was asking him to leave. He came to me to try to get me to talk Patrice into letting him stay, but he received no sympathy from me. I had also had enough of him. I had heard from some of the long-term guests that he planned to be the 'next Elliot in my life.' I felt repulsed by him. After Elliot had left, I had asked him if he would like to go mass with me some Sunday. He always kept a bible close to his bed, and at times, we would talk about religion. My suggestion was innocent with no ulterior motive. I simply invited him to attend mass with me, just as Elliot and I had invited various guests to attend with us.

One afternoon before Eddie left, Patrice confided in me about Eddie. She admitted that she had tried to help him out in the past because she thought of him as a friend. But she was quick to point out that "Eddie sees me helping him as a *sign of weakness*, so he feels that he can take advantage of me and get away with it."

Most of the time, Patrice's insights were remarkably accurate. She read people well to the bottom of their soul. She once told me after I first arrived there, that I had 'class.' She had trusted and respected me and had opened a whole new world to me. Where had this all gone wrong?

Eddie left in a huff, squealing his tires as he peeled out of the hostel parking lot. I had confronted him because he was eating his lunch in the TV room after he had checked-out, and I told him he had to leave. He slammed his plate down and wrapped his sandwich in a paper napkin. "I can't believe after all my time staying here that I can't even eat my lunch before I leave!" he bellowed as he stormed out of the room, through the courtyard, and out the gate. That was the last I ever saw of Eddie.

Elliot and I were now busy during our Sunday weekly phone calls making plans for my arrival in Lexington. I urged him to ask Lenore if I could live with him in her parents' home. We could split the rent with the couple who lived there, which would give each of us a little break. I felt better knowing that I would have a place to go to when I got to Lexington. He promised to speak to her during the week and would let me know the following weekend. We were counting the days before we would be back together again.

My behavior at the hostel became more and more intolerant. On Wednesday nights when I worked late, I ruled with an iron fist. I insisted that quiet time at ten o'clock at night be strictly observed. Like a prison guard on patrol, I walked back and forth between the two TV rooms to remind the guests to talk quietly and keep the TV turned down. I had had my fill of the late night partiers talking and laughing to all hours of the night. Evelyn and even Ramon looked at me with distaste when I reminded them to keep the noise down. "Yes, we know!" they'd say in unison and then they'd look away in disgust.

I didn't care. I was counting the days to my departure.

Chapter 16

New Beginnings

Elliot called unexpectedly one evening to tell me that we now had a place to live. He had talked to Lenore and she had agreed to let us rent part of her parents' house until we could get a place of our own. A flow of relief rushed over me at the thought of having a place to go to. All that was left to do was to start packing and wait for my time to leave.

Every evening was spent sorting, packing, and discarding belongings that I no longer needed. I washed everything that I was taking with me and tightly sealed it in plastic trash bags. My worst fear was that I would inadvertently take bed bugs with me to my new residence. I even sprayed the outside of my suitcases with bed bug repellant before I started to pack my clothes away in them. I packed everything that I didn't need to use before I left.

I cleaned out the lockers that had served as my kitchen cupboards. The food I couldn't take with me, I put in the common kitchen areas for the other guests to use. Slowly the pile of my belongings stacked on my floor grew larger as my room reverted back to its original state from when I first moved in there.

I really struggled over what to do with the furniture I had bought. I looked lovingly at the beautiful dinette set that Elliot and I had shared so many meals at and the recliner where he often had sat to read the newspaper. I checked into shipping my furniture to Virginia, but was deterred by the fear that it may be harboring bed bugs. It wasn't worth paying to have it shipped there if it would just cause headaches further down the road. All of my lamps and furnishings would also have to be left behind. I felt sick at the thought. This was the home I had put together for Elliot and me; all to no avail. I decided to give my furniture to Patrice. I remembered how much she has admired my dinette set when I first bought it. I wanted her to have it.

Patrice was shocked when I told her that I was giving her my furniture. She insisted that she should pay me for it. I adamantly refused to accept payment. I simply told her, "Patrice, you have been really good to me and I want you to have it."

She wouldn't acquiesce. After thinking a few moments, she said, "Elliot owes me some money from a business dealing that fell through. I will take the furniture as payment. Just tell him he doesn't have to pay me anything now."

"I don't know anything about this business dealing you have with Elliot," I said. "I just wanted you to have my furniture." And I left it at that.

A few days before I was due to leave, I found out that I wasn't the only one moving. Stuart and Nathan had rented an apartment together in the building right behind the hostel. Also, Patrice decided to move into Carlos's now vacant office that she had offered to me. She had bought some furniture for her new residence and gave Nathan and Stuart some of her old furniture for their apartment. When I saw Nathan that evening, I asked him if he would like to have the area rug that I had underneath my dinette set. Patrice didn't like carpeting, so I hadn't bothered to offer it to her. Happy with my offer, Nathan showed up at my door and we rolled up the carpet, which he propped up on his shoulder and took to his room for safe keeping until he moved into his new apartment.

Lola, with her foot finally on the mend, returned to work. I told her I would be leaving in a few days, and she seemed sad to see me go. I knew I would miss her, too. I liked Lola. When I first arrived there, I used to like to listen to the Hispanic music that she tuned into on the TV while she did her cleaning. That seemed so long ago and so much had changed since then. I asked Lola to take some pictures of me in the office, and I took a few of her to remember her by.

As the time for departure drew near, I told Ceyda that I was leaving and we exchanged addresses and promised to keep in touch, but we never did. Sometimes it seems more befitting to leave our memories in the places they were made; undisturbed, and preserved for life.

My last day of work ended just like all the others. I straightened up the office and locked the door behind me at four o'clock. That night, I sat at my computer and e-mailed my new address to my family. My mother had no idea I was even moving. Only Laura and Gene knew of my plans. With the final tasks completed, I went to bed.

I woke up on Saturday morning, February 14th, Valentine's Day, ready to move on to the next phase in my life. I was greeted on my final morning by a beautiful, clear blue sky lit up with bright sunshine. The air was crisp and fresh with the scent of the sea. Repressing all emotion, I kept my mind focused on what I needed to do so that I would not forget anything.

I methodically began to pack my car. The large stack of belongings piled on the floor of my room somehow had to fit into my mid-sized car. Back and forth I walked, carting my belongings to pack in my car. When I was almost done, Stuart and Nathan appeared from around the corner of the hostel smiling from ear to ear. Standing side-by-side, Nathan held his hand up high, dangling a set of shiny, silver keys to their new apartment which reflected the light of the bright morning sun. I walked over and gave each of them a hug while choking back tears. I was really going to miss them. We had spent almost every day together for the past eight months; they had been like brothers to me. They were the last of the original crowd from when I first arrived. It seemed appropriate that we were leaving at the same time. They went off to their rooms to start moving their belongings and I went back to get my last load.

I slung my backpack over my shoulder and walked to the door. I turned around and slowly surveyed the room, gathering my thoughts as I looked around. A lot had happened in the time I had stayed there. I had spent some of the happiest days of my life in this room and in the hostel; days of pure happiness like I had never known. But now everything here seemed to be devoid of any meaning or feelings. It was time to move on. I knew I was alright with my decision; I felt it in my gut.

I stepped back outside on my final pass through the courtyard. There was a young woman sitting outside at a plastic table working on her laptop. By the look on her face, I could see that she was caught up in the novelty of it all, just as I had been so many months earlier. When I passed by her, it crossed my mind that I was once the person sitting there working on my computer. But now my time had come to an end and hers was just beginning. I put my last bag in the car and went to knock on Patrice's door. It was time to tell her goodbye. Determined not to cry, I swallowed hard to dislodge the growing lump that I felt in my throat. Patrice answered the door immediately. She must have been watching me out her window as I loaded up my car.

"I'm leaving now, Patrice," I said while stretching my arms out to her.

She stepped forward, and we gave each other a hug.

"Good luck, Lu. I hope everything works out for you up north. You know, you are always welcome to come back here to visit," she said sincerely.

"Thank you, Patrice. I wish you the best. Take care." And with that said, I turned and left. I had already said my good-byes to the other hostel guests the night before, knowing that many of them liked to sleep in late.

I started up my car which was piled high with belongings and backed out of the parking lot for the last time. As I drove down

Ocean Boulevard, I kept glancing over at the sparkling ocean, creating a lasting image in my mind. It was just a little after nine o'clock in the morning and people were already coming to the beach for the day. Gently swaying palm trees waved a sad farewell as I made my way down Sunrise Boulevard to I-95 North. The long line of traffic was backed up and I had to stop at every red light. I was tired of the crowds and the traffic and longed for the countryside in the north. Finally, I arrived at I-95 and pointing my car north, I firmly pressed my foot down on the accelerator, speeding north towards Elliot and my family. I had no regrets . . .

THE END